PROPERTY SERIES

Buying Bargains at Property Auctions

Howard Gooddie
MA. (Cantab), Dip TP., FRICS.

Buying Bargains at Property Auctions
by Howard R Gooddie

1st edition 2001
   Reprinted twice 2002
2nd edition 2003
   Reprinted twice 2003
   Reprinted 2004
3rd edition 2004
4th edition 2005
   Reprinted 2006
   Reprinted 2007
5th edition 2009

© 2001, 2003, 2004, 2005, 2006, 2007, 2009 Howard Gooddie

Lawpack Publishing Limited
76–89 Alscot Road
London SE1 3AW

www.lawpack.co.uk

Printed in Great Britain

ISBN: 978-1-906971-10-6

Exclusion of Liability and Disclaimer

Contents

About the author

Howard Gooddie was head of auctions at Longden & Cook Commercial in Manchester, before retiring from the practice in December 2000. His father and grandfather were auctioneers before him and he grew up immersed in the world of auctions. During his boyhood he was a 'lotter' and clerk at many of his father's auctions. Howard's first property sale was in 1957 when he was 25. Legend has it that his audience contained only five people, of whom three were bank officials. In 1979 Howard returned to the auction world and started running quarterly auction sales, progressing to monthly sessions four years later. The firm's auction catalogue expanded rapidly when it started selling many lots on behalf of British Rail Property Board.

Novelty has always been part of Longden & Cook Commercial sales. The firm was the first to pioneer holding auctions simultaneously in London and Manchester, show pictures electronically of the properties being offered, introduce bidding paddles to property auctions and place the full catalogue on the internet.

Howard Gooddie has conducted more than 210 composite auction sales and has offered nearly 13,000 lots, inspecting virtually all of them himself. He was a member of the auctioneering skills panel of the Royal Institution of Chartered Surveyors, and is a Master of Arts from Cambridge University with a Certificate of Proficiency in Estate Management. He also holds a Diploma in Town Planning and is a Fellow of the Royal Institution of Chartered Surveyors.

Acknowledgements

When I have read acknowledgements in other books and noted that authors invariably thanked their typists, I never realised how indebted they were. It is only whilst composing this volume that I have come to appreciate exactly how much authors have to rely on the typing skills that back them up. My most sincere thanks in putting together this offering must firstly go to Diane Mercer-Brown in Longden & Cook Commercial who had to suffer far more tribulation over the preparation of these pages than I have. She was thoroughly backed up by Pat Devlin, Olga Shaw of Longden & Cook Commercial and Liz Cummins who were concerned with the promotion and co-ordination of auctions in the first firm and in Edward Mellor later.

Debbie Patterson, Anne Fanning and David Crosby, all of Wyvern Crest Limited, and Jamie Ross of Lawpack Publishing Limited were a constant support and encouragement as each of them took their part in the progressive development of the script. Anne Quirk and Gail Woodhall provided legal assistance when I needed it on the legal details, both of them then partners in Vaudrey Osborne & Mellor, now Beachcroft Wansborough. On a separate legal point, Grahame Lake from Wolstenholmes was particularly helpful and when I turned to accountancy skills, Peter Jeffery and Ray Lomax of Tunstall & Co in Warrington provided the expertise I needed from members of that profession. In the promotional field, Jane and Peter Parfait and Jonathan Willis of *Property Auction News* provided never-ending inspiration.

Finally amongst the professionals, I must thank Rodney Schofield from Royles Surveyors in Manchester, for providing me 'at the drop of a hat' with an example of a typical structural survey.

The original concept of this work was put initially to the Property Auctioneering Skills Panel of the Royal Institution of Chartered Surveyors and my thanks must go to all members of that Panel for their support, co-operation, assistance and the contribution of some of the auctioneers' anecdotes. My thanks, therefore, to John Barnett of Sallmann Harman Healey, Richard H Auterac of Jones Lang Wootton, David J Hobbs of McDowalls, M W S Bax of Bax Standen, Gary C Murphy of Allsop & Co, A J Ridgeway of Symonds & Sampson, Benjamin Tobin of Strettons and Geoffrey van Cutsem of Savills International Property.

The world of property publishing is small and practitioners depend heavily upon the relatively few magazines for promotion and advertising and the relevant organisations have all been particularly helpful and willingly provided samples for mere acknowledgement of their copyright. My thanks particularly, therefore, to the *Estates Gazette*.

Thanks are also due to Barnard Marcus, Erdman & Lewis, Walter & Randall, HMSO, The Law Society of England & Wales, The Solicitors' Law Stationery Society Ltd and The Royal Institution of Chartered Surveyors for permission to reproduce extracts.

Without the assistance from all these people this work would not be in front of you now.

Howard R Gooddie

Author's note to fifth edition

In these 'Credit Crunch' days this edition of my book is even more relevant to buying bargains at auction. In 2009, we can surely expect even more bargains to become available as houses are repossessed, generous finance is no longer available and the commercial and development property market is in flight from the yields and expectations of recent years.

This does not mean, however, that at every auction you can throw caution to the wind. The bargains and opportunities are there in greater numbers but the safeguards and research I have recommended that you apply before you buy should not be neglected.

Howard R Gooddie
May 2009

CHAPTER 1

Auctions – the place to pick up a bargain

'The main advantage to me of buying at auction has got to be the price. Compared with the prices going through high street estate agents I paid 33 per cent less.'

Don Lee, buyer of a residential property at auction.

The UK is awash with bargains

In two recent auction sales the following properties sold for prices that would not be found in any estate agent's window:

- A tenanted shop in Manchester sold at a yield of 12 per cent.
- A vacant shop in Anglia Square, Norwich sold for £34,000.
- A flat sold in Manchester at £210,000 in 2006 resold at auction at £89,000 in 2008.

These results demonstrate that there are plenty of bargain properties out there, if you only know where to look and how to go through the auction process.

What you will learn from this guide

In the following pages you will be shown:

* how auctions work;

* where to find auctions;

* how to spot a bargain;

* the price you should bid up to;

* the costs of buying at auction;

* how to handle the legal aspects of the purchase;

* how auctioneers operate;

* the best bidding tactics;

* how to sell at auction;

* what the pitfalls are;

* how to avoid losing a lot of money.

Auctions are full of mystique, but with the help of this guide, you will be taken inside how the auction process really works. It will enable you to have a clear idea of how to approach a property auction and it gives you the opportunity to pick up a bargain, saving you thousands of pounds compared with making a purchase through conventional channels.

Auctioneer's Anecdote: Repossessions at rock-bottom prices

Many building societies use the auction room to dispose of their large portfolio of repossessed houses and flats. At the end of 2008, most auction houses were reporting successful sales of between 60 and 75 per cent of the properties they were offering, but certain auctioneers publicised that they were having virtually a 100 per cent success rate in the sales of properties they were offering for one particular leading building society. To experienced auction dealers, this meant that many bargains were available and the reserve prices were set at attractive levels. The market may well see more repossessions again from 2008 to 2010.

What types of auction are there?

Auctions fall into four categories according to their size:

- Large composite
- Medium composite
- Smaller composite
- Single lot

Table 1.1 below lists the relative sizes, the number of lots to expect, the size of the audience and where they may be held. A composite auction is one where a collection of different types of property are sold at the same auction.

	Number of Lots	Likely Audience	Likely Venue
Large composite	100+	600–900	Hotel/conference centre, theatre, meeting rooms
Medium composite	5–100	200–600	Hotel/conference centre
Small composite	2–5	10–100	Hotel, church hall, pub, restaurant, sale room
Single lot	1	10–75	Hotel, church hall, pub, restaurant

Table 1.1 Size of auctions

Large

Over the last 25 years there has been a move towards large and composite auctions, run not only in London, but also in the larger financial cities outside the capital. The auctions are generally run by one auction house although, on occasion, several firms may co-operate. These composite auctions run frequently on a regular published calendar and may contain up to 50 lots offered in just a morning or an afternoon right through to 300 or 400 lots offered over several days. The sales may be restricted to a special type of property, for example vacant possession houses, residential investments, retail investments, commercial investments, shops, factories, warehouses or land, or a blend of any or all of these types. Where there is a mixture, the different categories of property tend to be offered in consecutive lots, sometimes with intervals between the various categories.

Advantages of composite auctions

Bringing together a number of lots in a composite auction produces economies of scale for the auction house. But from the seller's point of view a composite auction frequently generates more interest, a larger audience, more extensive marketing and generally a cheaper entry cost. If you are attending an auction for the first time, the scope of the catalogue and the size of the audience may seem somewhat forbidding. But by following the steps in this book, you will be able to refine your interest down to only a few lots and will learn how to exercise your presence as a bidder at the vital moments in a crowded room.

Auctioneer's Anecdote: For any given lot, the higher the price the slower the bidding

Large composite auctions need to take place in rooms of sufficient size to cope with the expected audience which will probably exceed 300. For this reason, auction houses usually choose to use hotel or conference centres, theatres or meeting rooms which can be laid out in theatre-style seating facing a single rostrum. A public address system with sufficient amplification is normal.

Medium

The medium composite auction is a smaller version of the larger composite auction, where either the lots will be restricted to a particular category, for example repossessed vacant houses and flats on behalf of finance houses or, alternatively, a mixture of lots from a single geographical region covered by the auction house. This can be a suburb where the auctioneers specialise or a regional city such as Birmingham,

'subject to planning' –

Where a property has development or redevelopment potential but there is no actual planning consent granted for that work then a buyer will need to obtain such a consent afterwards. It may or may not be forthcoming. An intending bidder may, by discussion with the development control officer at the local planning authority, be able to resolve any doubts he may have.

Thursday 11 February at 2-30 p.m. *at The Sachas Hotel, Tib St., off Market St., Manchester.*
LONGDEN & COOK COMMERCIAL (061-236 1114)
Bristol - Rent charges 375 collections. Total income £3,987.68 p.a.   w
Manchester - Vacant Land at Moston Rd., Middleton Junc'n Area 5.30a 1,468 sq yds with Ind'l Redev. Pot. suitable for B1, B2 or B8 users   F   P   w
Reddish - Land at Wayland Rd Sth., Gtr. Man. Site 16.4a apx. with Pot for apx. 7.7a Res. Dev (subj. to planning) Part occupied at a rent of £338.32 p.a   F   P   w
Oldham - Land at Oaklands Rd., Greenfield. 2.74a. vacant Land (3,599 sq yds). PP for Res. Dev. refused F   P   9,250
Lower Darwen - Land at Fairfield Drive, Milking La., Lancs. Site with PP for 10 s-d. d-h's.   F   P   w
do Land at Milking Lane, approx. 8.5 acres with PP for 80 Res. units and pot. to increase the density F   P   w
Manchester - Bracken House, Charles St. Mostly vacant modern City Centre Office Bdg. 31,060 sq ft on 8 fls. Pt. grd flr let 25 yrs from 1988 at £7,750 p.a F   P   w
Stockport - Redhouse La., Disley, Gtr. Man. Commercial Invest. 4,160 sq yds comprising Goods Shed & Garage. Income from tenants £13,300 p.a   F   *pvt.* 125,000
Hyde - Land at Railway St., Gtr Man. Site area 1a. 3,484 sq yds. Income £15,000 p.a. 7 yrs UT. Planning prepared for Res. use with adj. 2.4a. site F   w
Huddersfield - Vacant Land at Manchester Rd., Linthwaite, West Yorks. Area 0.9a. (4,356 sq yds)   F   P   *n.o.*
Bolton - Vacant Land at Greenwoods La., Hardy Mill Rd., Harwood, Gtr. Man. Agr. or amenity land with potential. Apx. 8.5a. and adjoins existing Res. Devel. F   P   29,500
do Land at Cox Green Rd., Dimple, Egerton. Apx. 45a. Agr. Land let on yr to yr agr. ten. £50.00 p.a. F   *pvt.* 22,000

Illustration 1. Extract from Under the Hammer

Manchester, Liverpool or Edinburgh where there is a source of mixed lots available, but insufficient lots on offer at regular intervals to produce larger composite auctions.

This size of sale can still produce an audience of between 200 and 500 people depending upon the popularity of the lots being offered and the amount of marketing that has taken place. Therefore, the auctioneers will need to choose a venue similar to that necessary for large composite auctions with similar facilities.

Small

There are occasions when a smaller number of related lots are appropriate for being auctioned consecutively at the same place and at the same time. This may be a number of adjoining building plots, or retail or domestic investment properties, or land and agricultural property in a particular vicinity.

Look out for special themes

Thus the small composite auction will generally follow a theme. It may contain lots which result from the 'break-up' of an individual estate. Examples of this are:

- A large agricultural investment estate where the owners have decided that the best prices can be obtained by offering portions of the estate in small lots.

- The owners of a portfolio of residential investments in one particular suburb or of a row of shops in a particular centre may decide that they will obtain the best price by offering the properties individually.

In such cases it is logical for the auction house to bring together its marketing and advertising and produce a single brochure, one set of advertisements and run just one auction session. The number of people attending is likely to be fewer than those attending a larger auction and therefore there is no need for the auction house to organise a sale in a large venue. The auction room may well be a smaller hotel, church, village hall or similar sized building.

The single lot

If a vendor (also called the seller) chooses to offer a single lot, it is often because the auctioneer believes there will be a tremendous demand for the property.

The costs of promoting a single lot sale will be considerably higher than for a composite auction. This extra cost must be justified by the belief that the property is one for which there is a spectacular demand. The audience may only be between ten and 75 people and the auction room will need to be of a corresponding size.

What properties are offered for sale by auction?

Thatched cottages

Some rural and suburban firms of auctioneers specialise in offering for sale by auction country cottages of which the 'thatched cottage' is the prime example. These are usually sold in single lots and occasionally in small, themed sales. Even when other types of auction during the 1950s were unpopular, the 'thatched cottage' sales were still held quite frequently, as both vendors and auction houses believed that considerable competition could be engendered between would-be buyers, by offering this type of property for sale by auction. That belief was furthered by the belief amongst valuers that it was almost impossible to judge precisely what price such a property would realise. From the owner's point of view, therefore, the possibility of a crowded auction in a hotel or public room one evening with bidders fighting to buy was irresistible. Although the romantic cottage exemplifies the type of property which vendors feel are best offered for sale by auction, it should not be forgotten that other types of property that are particularly attractive, for whatever reason, may also benefit from the 'thatched cottage' syndrome, and realise a high price in the auction room as a result of exceptional competition.

Why not pick up an exceptional property?

Other properties that might benefit from exposing themselves to exceptional competition include:

- houses that are unique because of their historical associations or their exceptional position;
- building or development prospects that are in pockets of exceptional interest or demand;
- investment properties of a type that are particularly in vogue at the time;
- plots or buildings that hold the key to development or profit-making prospects;
- sites or buildings appropriate for uses that follow fashions of the time. (Over the years these have included post offices, launderettes, petrol stations, food take-aways, nursing homes, bowling alleys, multi-screen cinemas, flat development opportunities and docklands, to name a few.) Dealers and entrepreneurs who have spotted the next trend or vogue will already be combing the auction rooms for their future stock.

Properties that are almost unsaleable

The auction route has often proved more successful than the private treaty sale method in the disposal of properties that are nearly unsaleable. Presumably this is because at auctions there is an element in the audience who are able and willing to 'chance their arm', particularly if they feel that a lot is apparently a bargain.

The sale rooms have seen the successful disposal of various properties that have been:

*   derelict;

*   subject to compulsory purchase orders;

*   subject to major disrepair or fabric failure;

*   subject to local authority repair notices;

*   subject to closing orders;

*   offered with unsatisfactory legal titles;

*   sold without access;

*   sold with major fencing, paving, drainage or other similar responsibilities;

*   sold subject to easements, covenants or restrictions which prevent their satisfactory use;

*   in derelict or unpopular areas.

Auctioneer's Anecdote: Read the particulars carefully

There is a long-standing joke in the auctioneers' profession that those auctioneers who sold land on behalf of Railtrack needed long thin catalogues because of the long thin pieces of land which they had to offer. One particular piece, first offered by their Property Board, was near one of the conurbations and was three-quarters of a mile long but only several yards wide. It was disclosed in the catalogue and in the title for sale that the land had no access other than through other people's land, was being sold with no access from the railway line and the purchaser had to erect a new fence along the entire three-quarter mile length adjoining the line. These factors did not inhibit some enthusiastic bidding when the property was offered. No doubt the bidders felt that around the £1,500 mark they could 'not go wrong'. Three months later the auctioneer was approached by the successful buyer to reoffer the land because it had no access and because the fencing covenant was about to be enforced. The land sold a second time at a slightly lower price at auction. Over the next two years, the auctioneer was instructed to offer and succeeded in selling the land no fewer than five times in total and not always at steadily reducing prices. Presumably, the only parties to whom any of the transactions gave a satisfactory result were Railtrack and the auctioneers.

A London bargain. Lot 30, a one-bedroom flat in Penge which sold for £55,000.

Repossessed houses

Unfortunately for their previous owner-occupiers, this category of property continues to feature considerably in many auctioneers' catalogues in the waves of repossessions that occur from time to time. Whilst feeling for those that have been dispossessed, there is no doubt that auction houses, speculators, builders and new owner-occupiers all benefit from such situations. The losses registered by the finance houses and the insurers may only be the result of a drastic domestic property revaluation or may also have been occasioned by the surfeit of vacant houses offered in the sale rooms because of a high level of repossessions at any one time.

But there is no doubt, there are some very good value-for-money properties to be purchased at auction. 'Repossession' is not to be considered synonymous with 'bargain'. You should still thoroughly research your target property.

Investment properties

Properties that are owned for the benefit of the income they produce are frequently included in auction catalogues. Investors cover a range of buyers from large pension funds and commercial investors at one end, through to medium-sized investment companies and smaller private pension funds, right down to individual investors, looking for a satisfactory return on their money.

The range of properties includes:

- office investments;

- shop investments;

- domestic investments (single houses, blocks of flats and portfolios of houses);

- ground and chief rents;

- investments in land;

- investments in easements;

- reversionary investments (where the investor is concerned with long-term income or growth in it).

What affects the price of investment properties?

Prices paid for investments depend on many factors which include:

- security of the covenant of the payer of the rent;

- the quality and position of the property;

- the potential growth or variation of the income collectable;

- the frequency of rent reviews;

- the investor's view of the future of the money market and future interest levels;

- the investor's view of the yield that is appropriate for the type of property;

- the nature and responsibilities of the landlord;

- the nature and responsibilities of the tenant;

- other factors which could affect the future income of the property favourably or adversely.

A portfolio of lots being sold by property dealers

You should be aware that occasionally the same properties feature in different auctions at different times. A tenanted shop in Liverpool may first of all sell at an auction in that city and then some time later reappear at an auction in London. A vacant repossessed house may be sold at an auction just outside the capital and subsequently reappear in the hands of a local auctioneer in the town in which the property is situated. A portfolio of domestic investments may be offered 'en bloc' in the capital, appear in another auction in that city six months later broken up into smaller units and then perhaps 50 per cent of that portfolio will be represented in individual lots in, for example Manchester, Birmingham or Liverpool 12 months later.

Do not be totally discouraged from being interested in these dealing lots, but do watch out for them by combing auction advertisements frequently. If you see a property that interests you, approach it with care and only after thorough research.

The auction houses

The principal firms of property auctioneers are listed in Appendix 5, with a great many firms offering their services throughout the country. There is no way you can monitor all their auctions, their results and their withdrawn lots.

Select firms that cover your area

You will have to select the firms you examine acknowledging there are:

1. varieties of specialist firms who only deal with particular types of property and who are generally London-based;

2. other auction houses in the capital who cover a wider range of properties, generally in composite auctions but occasionally in specialised ones as well;

3. London-based firms who deal with property throughout the UK, sometimes only offering it in the capital but occasionally running sales in the regions;

4. auction houses based upon the larger cities and towns throughout the country who run regular composite auctions, generally specialising in properties in their area rather than specialising in particular types of property; and

5. local firms who run smaller auctions on demand.

Within these broad divisions, as you become acquainted with the auction field, you will discover that there are certain specialisations and subspecialisations which various firms have developed through design or their past history and it is only by research that you will establish which auction houses to patronise, as a buyer or as a seller.

How to choose which firms to follow

1. Visit a few local auctions of any kind.

2. Decide upon the type of property in which you are interested.

3. Decide upon the geographical area you propose to cover.

4. Research auction advertisements in the property and local press.

5. Respond to those advertisements with specific requests for specific properties in which you are interested.

6. Subscribe to the mailing lists of firms who specialise in your type of property in your area.

7. Start visiting the auctions of your chosen firms on a regular basis.

By and large you will find that the sales of the majority of the firms are conducted in a similar manner. British auction houses are relatively traditional in their manner of offering with only minor variations in style, speed of selling, presentation and marketing.

'From a purchaser's point of view, I would have said you were going to get quite a good deal at auction, particularly in this climate.'

Michael Kirby, Chartered Surveyor.

Key point

Whether you are a dreamer or a speculator, an entrepreneur or an investor, a would-be owner-occupier or a developer, an intending purchaser of many lots or only one, good luck in your hunt for bargains. Remember they will only come with thorough research and plentiful experience. Follow the advice that follows and you should not go wrong.

CHAPTER 2

How to find your bargain property

'I was living in Manchester and noticed there were a number of run-down properties in the inner city part of Manchester. They had been built as private houses and there had been problems with them simply because the people who had bought them could not pay their mortgage. They were quickly vandalised and went down in value like the rest of the property market. I negotiated a price of £12,000 for it after the auction and it only needed another £1,000 to put it into liveable condition. I was surprised they did not go for more.'

Don Lee, buyer of a residential property at auction.

First, find your bargain

Finding your bargain property can be immensely enjoyable. First, you need to know what steps to take to find your bargain and once found, how to decide what price to pay for it. The following checklist gives the key steps (from your initial search right up to going to auction) to help ensure you are successful in obtaining a bargain property.

Pre-auction checklist: For the bargain hunter

1   Find the newspapers that advertise auctions in the area that interests you. ☐

2   Go on auctioneers' mailing lists. ☐

3   Subscribe to *Property Auction News*. ☐

4   Subscribe to the *Estates Gazette*. ☐

5   Look out for For Sale boards. ☐

6   Comb the auction catalogues. ☐

7   Inspect the properties that interest you. ☐

8   Find out the guidelines and reserve price (if possible). ☐

9   Appoint your solicitor. ☐

10 Instruct your surveyor. ☐

11 Consult your builder. ☐

12 Read the conditions of sale. ☐

13 Decide on your maximum bid. ☐

14 Consider a 'dummy run'. ☐

15 Take your accountant's advice. ☐

16 Arrange the finance. ☐

17 Don't forget your other buying costs. ☐

18 Look out for pitfalls. ☐

19 Consider putting in a bid before the sale. ☐

Finding your property – the first steps

Where can I find out about auctions?

The auctioneer has a responsibility to his owner to give as much publicity about his auctions as possible. You would think, therefore, that all auctions are extensively advertised. In practice, since advertising is expensive and auctioneers' budgets are limited, auction adverts may not receive tremendous exposure. As a bargain lot hunter, you would be wise to take other steps to ensure you hear about all the properties that are being offered in the area that interests you. Appendix 5 lists the majority of auctioneers' firms in the UK who advertise their auctions regularly. But no reader should treat this list as comprehensive, particularly since some firms may stop auctioning and others are likely to enter the market.

How to get on a mailing list

Most auctioneers maintain a mailing list of potential buyers to whom they send details of forthcoming auctions. Certain firms require a nominal payment to receive details, which in most cases is worth paying. However, many firms provide this service free of charge. Since servicing a mailing list is an expensive operation, auctioneers revise their lists at frequent intervals. It is worth checking how long each auctioneer will keep you on their list. Alternatively, check at least every six months whether your name is still on their list and how long they will continue to send you details.

Narrow down your choice of firms

You will often find that auctioneers specialise in certain types of property or certain regions. By telephoning a number of auctioneers and asking if they offer properties of the type you are seeking, you will be able to narrow down the number of mailing lists you go onto. This way, it is possible to reduce the number of wasted catalogues that come through the letter box.

Where auctioneers do not maintain a mailing list, the only reliable way of finding out the date, location and type of property being offered is to ring them up at frequent intervals.

Questions to put to an auctioneer:

- Do you have a mailing list?
- Do you charge for names to go on your mailing list?
- How long will you keep me on your list?
- Will you tell me if my name is about to be removed?
- What types of property do you auction?

Where are auctions advertised?

Two major property magazines are published: the *Estates Gazette* and *Property Auction News*. Table 2.1 lists their addresses, telephone numbers and subscription charges. Each of the two property magazines has a slightly different approach to the auction world. None of the magazines focus solely on residential or commercial properties or any specific part of the market.

The major property magazines

Property Auction News has become the bestselling publication dedicated to property auctions in the UK. Thousands of readers have bought cut-price property after learning about the potential of auctions through its pages; invaluable and highly recommended.

The *Estates Gazette* provides a page every week of commentaries on sales that have taken place.

Property Auction News
Streetwise Marketing, Eden House, Genesis Park, Sheffield Road, Rotherham S60 1DX Tel: 01709 820 033 Website: www.propertyauctionnews.co.uk
Published: Monthly

Estates Gazette
1 Procter Street, London WC1V 6EU Tel: 01444 445 335 Website: www.estatesgazettegroup.com
Published: Weekly
Price: £3.95 per week
Subscription: £196 for a year's subscription

Table 2.1 The major property magazines

Cottons

CHARTERED SURVEYORS
RICS Auction Department

Forthcoming
Auction Sale

23 February 2007

To be held at:

Aston Villa Football Club

Holte Suite, Villa Park, Aston, Birmingham

70 LOTS

To include a range of Residential and Commercial
Vacant and Investment property along with
Land and Freehold Ground Rents.

*For further information on any aspect of selling, or
to register for a catalogue please contact:*

**The Auction Department
361 Hagley Road
Edgbaston, Birmingham B17 8DL
Tel 0121 247 2233
or email auctions@cottons.co.uk**

Figure 2.1 Estates Gazette advertisement

What am I bid: Oxfordshire quarry

Investors with an eye for potential will be interested in this former quarry offered by Savills later this month.

Lot 58 has a reserve price of just £1,000 and although the quarry is filled in, it is unrestored. The 55.7-acre site is located next to the MOD's Bicester Aerodrome in Oxfordshire.

The lot forms part of a 76-acre site in Stratton Audley that includes a recycling centre guided at £10,000 to £20,000, and 1.5 acres of land with a fishing lake used by a local angling club that is guided at £20,000 to £30,000.

James Cannon, Savills' commercial auctioneer, said: "This is probably the second quarry I've sold in the past 12 years – the first was a working quarry for industrial sand, a different proposition.

"This is quirky but it has advantages. It offers opportunities for landscaping. There are various issues with quarries but auction is a good way to reach an amicable price.

"I suspect it will provoke considered bidding and interest from people in the locality. We have already received many enquiries."

E-mail your bid

● What price will this lot achieve? Send your "e-bid", along with ideas for future "What am I bid?" articles, to estelle_maxwell@yahoo.co.uk. The most accurate prediction wins a £25 Thresher's voucher.

Bicester site: three separate lots

Figure 2.2 Extract from Estates Gazette

Figures 2.1 and 2.2 illustrate extracts from some of these magazines.

Apart from the specialist property press, certain newspapers are known for their auction advertisements. They often specialise in their regions or in the types of property that they cover. There is no alternative in your search for auctions to combing local and national newspapers and the internet until you have discovered which ones carry advertisements for auctions of the type of property that interests you.

Other publications also advertise and list auctions, but almost invariably they relate to the sale of chattels rather than properties. They are thus, to the property buyer, of no use.

What else will help in the search?

For Sale boards

Many estate agents, if pressed, will admit that more than half of their initial enquiries from successful purchasers come from a Sale board erected on-site. This high level of response is not as usual for auction properties but, nevertheless, most auctioneers will erect a Sale board (or at worst put up a poster) at the property being offered. If you are looking for a property in a particular area, For Sale boards can be very useful. It may be worth trawling frequently through that area to look for boards.

Whilst travelling through the district you may find that the auctioneers have also used poster sites for the erection of For Sale bills, which gives details of their auctions and a brief summary of the properties that are available. The use of such bill-posters is an old habit that seems to be dying out, so you should not rely on this source of information.

It will only be the most inefficient auctioneer – or one suffering a very limited advertising budget – who will rely only on a For Sale board. Combing the columns of local newspapers and the internet will generally be quite as effective as combing the district. You may well consider this 'armchair' approach much easier!

How to unearth a bank or building society repossession

'Years ago it wasn't the done thing to buy property at auction but now it is more the norm, especially on repossessions and investments. It's a quick way to buy a property. It gets the deal done.'

Michael Kirby, Chartered Surveyor.

Look for the clues to repossessions

Some banks and building societies are very coy about the public knowing that they have repossessed properties and take considerable steps to avoid it being known that properties included in auctions are the result of repossessions. Other societies and banks are quite open. You can look for the clues.

In the initial advertisements, the auctioneers may disclose that certain properties are being sold as a result of repossession. The advert may contain a general list of the clients for whom they are selling which will then include the names of the societies and the banks. This information may be repeated in the auction catalogue itself, either in a general statement or on the relevant lots. The catalogue may give less specific references with phrases such as 'On behalf of mortgagees in possession', 'By order of ...Building Society', 'On the instructions of an LPA Receiver' or 'On the instructions of a liquidator' or similar.

Without these clues there can be more subtle indications. The solicitor acting may have as his address that of the head office of a building society or bank. Even without that direct indication it is possible that the name of the building from which the solicitor operates is an indication of the society for which he works. It may even be possible to link up the solicitor's telephone number quoted or the one quoted for access to the property.

If all else fails, an outright enquiry at the auctioneer's office or at the co-agent's office may tell you if the lot you are considering is as a result of a repossession.

What information will an auctioneer give me?

The property details (or particulars)

You will probably be accustomed to the standard estate agents' particulars. Similar particulars are always produced by auctioneers and will invariably contain, apart from the normal property details, information about the date, time and venue of the auction. The Property Misdescriptions Act 1991 has made it a criminal offence for an estate agent to give misleading details about a property. Even before the existence of this Act, auctioneers were expected to provide more reliable details of the lots being offered than estate agents' particulars usually gave. For this reason, and following the 1991 Act, details provided in auction catalogues are usually brief, but they can be relied upon for accuracy despite the 'saving' clauses that vendors and auctioneers often incorporate in their Conditions of Sale. Figure 2.3 shows an example of an auctioneer's particulars.

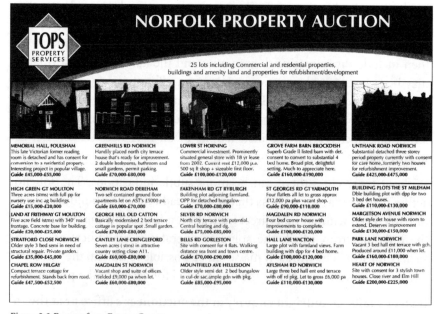

Figure 2.3 Excerpt from Estates Gazette

The catalogue

Do not be excited by the change in name! The catalogue contains the same information as the individual auctioneer's particulars but it is produced in a bound form, in lot order. In most cases these will be provided by auctioneers where there are more than three or four lots to be offered on one occasion. The lots' details are still likely to be brief but accurate. They are usually accompanied by relatively comprehensive instructions to buyers on how to proceed at the auction.

The catalogue almost always contains the particulars and the conditions of sale which are referred to in greater detail on page 50. It is this kind of comprehensive catalogue that you are likely to receive from auctioneers who maintain a mailing list and who despatch such magazines or booklets one month to three weeks before their sales.

For a basic house, you might find commentary such as:

VACANT TERRACED HOUSE FOR REFURBISHMENT	
Situation:	A–Z Map Reference 4F 51. Off Old Road.
Construction:	Brick and slate.
Tenure:	Freehold or long leasehold subject to a nominal annual rent charge.
Accommodation:	
Ground floor:	2 rooms.
First floor:	2 bedrooms, bath/wc.
Exterior:	Rear yard.
Note:	The property needs complete restoration.
Viewing:	By arrangement with the auctioneers.
Vacant possession:	On completion.
Solicitors:	Available from the auctioneers.

For a better quality house, you might easily find details such as:

LUXURY 4-BED DETACHED HOUSE IN APPROX HALF ACRE	
Situation:	A–Z Map Reference 1E 13. Travel north east along A623 for 2 miles from town centre.
Tenure:	Freehold.

Accommodation:	
Ground floor:	Porch; entrance hall with seating area; study; fully tiled cloaks with wc and vanity unit; dining room; 3 reception rooms one with fixed bar unit; kitchen/breakfast room including hob, extractor, double oven, microwave, fitted refrigerator and freezer; 4-berth sauna/solarium with shower cubicle, sun bed.
First floor:	Landing with access to balcony overlooking rear garden; 4 fitted bedrooms; fully tiled and pine ceiling bathroom with jacuzzi, shower cubicle, basin, wc, bidet; child's tiled bathroom with miniature bath and twin wash basins set in vanity units.
Exterior:	Double length garage with parking for 2 cars, fitted cupboards, sink, utility area and plumbing for washing machine; front and rear gardens with automatic flood lighting, electric fountain at rear.
Outbuilding:	Snooker room with snooker table.
Note:	This fine traditionally built family home is fitted and decorated to the highest of standards and includes all carpets, curtains and snooker table.
Viewing:	By arrangement with the auctioneers.
Vacant possession:	On completion.
Solicitors:	Available from the auctioneers.

Figure 2.4 Auctioneer's particulars and catalogue details

Understanding the jargon

The effect of the Property Misdescriptions Act has been to reduce considerably the 'estate agentese' in which all property particulars and auction particulars were previously clothed. Nevertheless, if you are accustomed to picking the detail out of sheets prepared by agents for private treaty sales, you will find no difficulty in understanding the contents of auctioneers' catalogues.

With the changes that the Property Misdescriptions Act 1991 have brought, you can be pretty sure that estate agents' descriptions do not mislead and you should find that their particulars give a clear description of the property. You are unlikely to find exceptional exaggeration or hyperbole. But do note that every single description in the particulars will have been carefully judged and 'weighed' by the auctioneers, before being included in their description.

As Home Information Packs came into use after June 2007, following the government legislation, bidders for houses may be glad to rely on them.

Scrutinise the wording carefully

You should therefore scrutinise very carefully the wording in the particulars, noting especially:

- the situation of the property;
- any descriptions of its condition, for example 'refurbishment' should be contrasted with 'modernisation' whilst 'restoration' should indicate the need for an even more extensive schedule of major repairs;
- in a property with tenants, the exact terms of tenure and any special references to irregularity or lack of payments of rent;
- the extent and nature of the accommodation and the use of adjectives rather than size to describe it;
- any other special elements that are particularly relevant to the type of property offered in the lot.

What price should my top bid be?

This is the fundamental question everyone asks themselves when bidding at auction. It is also one of the most difficult to answer. The situation partially depends upon why you are buying the property.

What type of buyer are you?

Entrepreneur: A true 'wheeler-dealer' looking to buy a bargain and make a profit.

Builder: Someone experienced in the building trade who can take advantage of his connections and knowledge to refurbish a property and sell it on at a profit, or to give him an investment with a high yield.

369 London Road, Camberley, Surrey, a four-storey building that is a restaurant and three flats, guided at £275,000 by Harman Healy, bringing in an income of £36,900, therefore producing a yield of 13.42 per cent. Could be financed over 15 years at 75 per cent of the purchase price.

Investor: An individual or company looking to 'tuck away' cash in a property which will give a strong flow of income with a commensurate yield.

Home owner: An individual seeking a property for his own occupation, which he can buy hopefully with more certainty, speed and at a cheaper price than can be bought in the normal private treaty market.

Short-term investor: A combination of an investor and entrepreneur aiming to buy cheaply, improve his income flow and resell the investment to take a profit.

Are you an entrepreneur, experienced or hoping to become experienced in property who will rely on your own opinion of value? Are you a person experienced in building or construction, who is happy to assess any likely costs of bringing the property up to a satisfactory condition? Are you an investor already deeply involved in the investment market who already has a yield in mind or are you an individual purchaser seeking to buy just one lot at one auction?

Judging the market

As an entrepreneur you will probably already have taken steps to obtain the 'feel' of the market. You may have narrowed down the type of property that interests you and perhaps researched the subject. Everyone, whether amateur or professional, can only endeavour to judge the 'right' price by comparing the lot at auction with the prices that have been paid for comparable properties in the past. This is fundamental to seeking out your bargain property. If you are an entrepreneur, you may even be prepared to make your own judgement on the condition of the building or the nature of the investment, or the likely problems that could arise on development or redevelopment. It may well be that you already have an informal chain of contacts in the various trades or professions to give you assistance.

Get a good feel for the market

If, of course, you have experience in the building trade, the assessment of structures and the ability to estimate costs, you may still need a smaller chain of contacts to make your decision, but you must still rely on that essential 'feel of the market' which can only come from research into recent, past transactions. Even then, in the phrase popular with the financial services industry: 'past performance is not necessarily a guide to future performance!'

As an investor, the eventual net yield of your investment in relation to its quality is what is going to matter to you, although other bidders may take different views from you on the quality of that investment, the yield sought and the quality of the agreement with the tenant.

All these categories of prospective bidders may feel they are experienced or entrepreneurial enough to make their own decision on price.

Key point

If you are a one-off buyer looking for your single purchase at auction, you are well advised to obtain a professional valuation.

How to decide on your top bid

The easiest way to do this is to obtain a professional valuation of your target property. The auction market is a particular test of a valuer's skill, since the competition to buy exists in the present and the purchase is immediate. You are asking the valuer to use his experience of a general market and to come to a conclusion following the results of his research of past transactions. Even when applied with maximum skill, this will not necessarily give the accurate answer you are seeking, since he is only endeavouring to put himself into the minds of two or more hypothetical bidders, with all the uncertainties that that creates. Nevertheless, his experience and assessment from past sales must be of invaluable assistance to you in making a final decision as to your maximum bid.

You should choose a Chartered Surveyor. If you can find one in the district of the property who also has experience of auctions, do obtain his assistance. You must expect to pay a non-returnable fee which will vary according to the type of report that you require. Details of the fees are given in Table 2.2.

> ### Key point
>
> If you are satisfied that you can make your own judgement as to the condition of the property, then you only need to ask your surveyor and valuer for a non-structural report on the open market value.

Valuation Range	Sample Fee Ranges		
	Non-Structural Valuation	House Buyers' Report	Structural Survey
Up to £50,000	£200–300	£150–250	£300–450
£50,001–£150,000	£300–450	£250–350	£400–550
£150,001–£250,000	£400–600	£350–450	£550–700
£250,001–£500,000	£600–800	£450–550	£700–1,000
£500,001–£750,000	£800–1,100	£550–750	£1,000–1,500
Over £750,000	£1.50 per £1,000	£1 per £1,000	£2 per £1,000

This scale is given for guidance only. Specific quotes should always be obtained prior to instructing surveyors.

Table 2.2 Fees for survey and valuation reports

A non-structural valuation report may be sufficient

You will need to provide him with as much information as you can obtain. Advise him about the exact nature of your interest and the extent of your enthusiasm for the particular lot you nominate. Be ready to put him in touch with the auctioneers. An extract of a non-structural valuation report is shown in Figure 2.5 and the general terms and conditions regarding the report are shown in Appendix 2.

Report upon the value of the property at 81 Blossom Road, Buckford

INTRODUCTION

We thank you for your recent instructions in accordance with which we have carried out an inspection of the above-mentioned property for valuation purposes.

We have not carried out any form of structural survey of the building and our inspection was intended to be for valuation purposes only. It is therefore assumed that the property is not affected by any serious defects other than those noted in this report.

In particular, we have not carried out any investigations to ascertain the presence of high alumina cement or calcium chloride additive and are unable to report whether the property is free from risk in this respect.

GENERAL DESCRIPTION

The property consists of a mid-terrace, two-storey house built in the early 1990s, part of a terrace of similar properties including both original and modernised houses.

LOCATION

Blossom Road is off Bloomfield Road, close to its junction with Charles Road (A756), a continuation of Blakemore Road which joins the A6, Blair Street at Buckford precinct.

This is a reasonably popular residential area, generally convenient for most amenities and with good communications offering access to both Manchester and Buckford City Centres.

ACCOMMODATION

Briefly, the accommodation includes:

Ground floor:
Through lounge/dining room; fitted kitchen (single-storey extension).

First floor:
Two double bedrooms, one with fitted wardrobes; bath/wc/basin.

Exterior:
Paved rear yard.

SERVICES

Mains gas, water, electricity and drainage are laid onto the property. A burglar alarm has been installed and there is an Economy 7 heating system.

TENURE

Assumed to be either freehold or long leasehold subject to a nominal annual charge.

CONSTRUCTION

Of traditional construction with external walls of brick and a pitched slate roof. The roof to the kitchen extension is partially flat and partially pitched under a mineral felt covering and was re-covered during 1992 to rectify rainwater ingress.

CONDITION

As mentioned above, our inspection was of a limited nature intended to be for valuation purposes only. We have not carried out any form of structural survey or inspected any area not normally visible without the use of ladders or opening up of any part of the structure.

The cosmetic condition of the property is generally good but we would draw your attention to the following:

1. We have referred to the reroofing of the kitchen extension and note that the underside of the ceiling shows evidence of the original leak; the bottom right-hand corner of the kitchen requires decoration to complete the work.

2. The area to the right of the first floor window to the front elevation was wet at the time of our inspection and subject to constant dampness from a leak resulting from broken guttering (photograph 1, appended).

3. A number of the slate roof tiles have slipped and require re-laying.

4. The porch area above the front door is damp, as a result of the broken gutter referred to above.

GENERAL OPINION

There are a number of houses for sale in the area, both modernised and original and prices tend to fall in the range of £50–60,000, subject to condition. Our enquiries confirm that values have fallen in the last 2/3 years, although there appears to be reasonable demand for modernised properties in mortgageable condition from first-time buyers. A number of the properties are let, either to regulated tenants who may have been in occupation for some considerable time, or assured shorthold tenancies to students at the nearby Buckford College.

VALUATION

Taking all the above facts into account, we consider the present open market value of the above-described property, with the benefit of vacant possession, to be in the region of:

£55,000 (fifty-five thousand pounds)

MICHAEL F LEWIS BA (Hons) ARICS

Figure 2.5 Extract of a non-structural valuation report

Key point

If you have any doubts at all on the quality of the structure of the property, then you have no alternative other than to ask for a full building survey.

Getting a full building survey

You should ask the surveyor to give a full building survey and an opinion of the price at which the property might sell. Your surveyor will carry out a far more detailed inspection of the building and provide you with a relatively comprehensive report on the nature of the structure and any problems that he considers might develop. An extract of a full building survey report is shown in Figure 2.6. The surveyor may suggest you obtain

BUILDING SURVEY, VALUATION, OPINION, REPORT.	**RODNEY SCHOFIELD,** F.R.I.C.S. M.C.B.A.

RODNEY SCHOFIELD, F.R.I.C.S. M.C.B.A.
FELLOW OF THE ROYAL INSTITUTION OF CHARTERED SURVEYORS.
MEMBER OF THE CERTIFICATED BAILIFFS' ASSOCIATION.

ROYLES, CHARTERED SURVEYORS
REEDHAM HOUSE, 31/33 KING STREET WEST, MANCHESTER M3 2PW.
TEL No. 061-834 2663
FAX No. 061-832 5706

Building Survey of a plot of Land and Two Storey Grade II Listed End Terraced Cottage situated and known as 3 Windy Hill, Framsham FR7 6AU.

TERMS OF REFERENCE

In accordance with your recent instructions and confirmation and Standard Terms of Reference forwarded to you recently, in which we detailed the scope and extent of the Survey we duly attended the property on 17 January 2007.

At the time of the inspection the weather was dry, cold and bright following a prolonged period of wet and inclement weather during the early autumn and winter months.

We have not inspected woodwork or other parts of the property which are covered unexposed or inaccessible and we are unable to report that such parts are free from defects; we report only on such parts which are clearly visible.

Observations are made if structural movement is suspected and comments are made on the structure, accessible roof timbers and other parts of the interior and exterior where visible. It must be noted, however, that the external survey was limited to one from ground level or via short ladders where possible.

Reference may be made as to the condition of the services but specific testing was not carried out except where stated. At the time of inspection the property was occupied and all the furniture and floor covering were in situ, and in this context it should be mentioned that in most of the rooms the carpets were nailed down or the carpets were stretched over carpet grippers and due to the placement of furnishings no inspection was possible in these areas.

The Inspection of floor and floor areas was therefore restricted to only a very limited series of spot and random checks where possible; therefore we cannot give assurances that the timbers are free from rot but from what we were able to inspect it seems reasonable to assume that the floor timbers are reasonably sound, we would suggest that once the floor coverings are removed a more detailed inspection is carried out.

INTRODUCTION

The property comprises of a two-storey listed end terrace cottage constructed in 1724; one of a terrace of three cottages within a small hamlet within a Conservation Area. The property retains many of its original features; no major additions or structural alterations have been made since construction, with the exception of the rear porch entrance which appears to be of a later construction.

Internally there has been no structural removal of walls or chimney breasts but some of the chimneys have been reconstructed or repaired in brick and the flue to the dining room appears to have been sealed at first-floor level. A smoke test revealed that this is not at present usable for an open fire and if it is intended to be used, a form of gas convector fire with a copex lining should be fitted.

The property is set within an irregular shaped plot with garden frontage and access via a small gate over which there are common rights of way; the boundaries are not strictly defined other than by the low stone walling to the gable elevation; at the rear there is a small raised garden area on which are set a number of mature trees; and an open court yard which is common to this and the other properties with Public Rights of Way and a semi-detached garage which is constructed in salvaged stone and blockwork and set with a stone tiled roof.

The property lies in a residential area and has views of open countryside and old mill properties and lies approximately half a mile from the village centre local shopping and amenities.

CONSTRUCTION

The property is constructed by traditional methods typical of the period with eighteen inch solid stone walls set on stone footings; the main elevations are faced in local random stone and have been repointed fairly recently in sand and cement mortar using a flush pointing method. These walls due to their age have a bowed appearance particularly on the gable and rear elevation and this is to some effect highlighted by the recent pointing; but no significant structural movement was noted and any deflections are to be expected in a property of this nature and age.

The floors to the ground floor are of solid construction and where exposed and visible are surfaced in asphalt. Due to the presence of fitted floor coverings, only a limited surface inspection was possible. This revealed that there were no abnormal signs of rising dampness or cold bridging, but it is not possible to tell if the floor has a damp membrane without excavation; the original floor is likely to have been constructed with stone flags. The first floors are of hollow construction and are of suspended timber type with one inch edge to edge pine boarding overlaid on timber joists which span the width of the property and are set into the gable elevation walls. The floor levels run out in the majority of the first floor area, in some places the floors have dropped some quarter to half and inch from the skirting level, this is most likely due to the general settlement which has taken place since the property was built and due to its age and the drying out of some of the timbers, and one can normally expect this in a property of this age in this locality.

Figure 2.6 Extract of a full structural survey report

approximate costs for bringing the property up to a reasonable condition in the light of the report before making conclusions about the price. You will appreciate that this procedure will take some time and both your surveyor and repair estimator must be made to realise the urgency of your request and be warned of the auction date deadline.

The House/Flat Buyers' Report and Valuation

If you are considering a one-off purchase of a house or flat, there is an

House No.	20	46	66	85
Price Paid	£200,000	£174,500	£190,000	£140,000
Repairs	+£30,000	+£40,000	+£12,000	+£35,000
	£230,000	£214,000	£202,000	£175,000
Bought In	Jan	Sept	March	June
Adjustments:				
Date	+3% +£7,000	+1% +£2,145	+2.5% +£5,050	+1.5% +£2,625
Side of Street	nil –	nil –	– –	+10% +£17,500
End of Street	–10% –£23,000	–3% –£6,435	+4% +£8,080	+10% +£17,500
Comparable Value	£214,000	£210,000	£215,130	£212,625

Adjusted comparable values

No. 20	£214,000
No. 46	£210,210
No. 66	£215,130
No. 85	£212,625
	£851,965 (divided by four)

Average comparable value	£213,000
Applied to No. 54 deduct repair costs	£60,000
Value in December	£153,000

Table 2.3 Calculating the value of a suburban house

intermediate level of report which you may consider obtaining which will cost less than the full structural survey. This House/Flat Buyers' Report and Valuation is provided by certain Chartered Surveyors, but not by all of them. The cost of such a report can sometimes be a little less than the normal valuation report and will certainly be less than the fees charged for a full building survey.

How is property valued?

Judging the value of a property is not an exact science. However, there is a number of key techniques that professional valuers use to reach an assessment of a property's value and which you can use to decide what price you should bid up to. The valuer's checklist illustrates (in a slightly simplified version) the key points you need to consider.

Valuer's checklist

1 Obtain as much preliminary information about the property as possible, in particular:
   - tenure of site; ☐
   - any tenancies; ☐
   - size and extent of accommodation and site; ☐
   - any peculiarities of the district or situation; ☐
   - recent sales, purchases or lettings of the building. ☐

2 Thoroughly inspect the property inside and out. ☐

3 Ascertain outstanding defects and deficiencies that need remedying to bring the property up to normal standards. ☐

4 Make a provisional estimate of the costs of curing those defects and deficiencies. ☐

5 Judge the effect of those costs on the mind of a hypothetical buyer. ☐

6 Obtain as many recent transactions concerning comparable properties as possible. ☐

7 Adjust those transactions for any rise or fall in the market over the period in which they have taken place. ☐

8 Compare and adjust the information from the 'comparables' so that it relates as closely as possible to the property being valued. ☐

9 For vacant properties use as far as possible transactions of vacant 'comparables'. ☐

10 For investment properties, consider rental levels as well as yields of 'comparables'. ☐

11 Allow for differing states of repair with particular reference to step 3 above. ☐

12 Come to a conclusion in the light of your analysis which you hope will equal that of a would-be buyer. ☐

How to estimate what price to pay for a house

The following example illustrates how a house in a suburban street of identical properties is valued.

Four houses in the same street have been bought with vacant possession within the last 12 months. The values of each property are affected by three items:

- the market is judged to be rising at 0.25 per cent per month;

- the even numbers in the street are more popular because they back onto a park;

- the lower numbers in the street are always thought to be the better end of the street.

The prices paid and repair costs for each house were:

House No.	Date Bought	Price Paid	Repair Costs
No. 20	January	£200,000	£30,000
No. 66	March	£190,000	£12,000
No. 85	June	£140,000	£35,000
No. 46	September	£174,500	£40,000

What price should be paid for No. 54 in December where repair costs are £60,000? Table 2.3 illustrates how to calculate what price to pay given the variable information.

Four steps are followed:

Step 1 Find the value of each property by adding the cost of repairs to the price paid.

Step 2 Add or deduct the adjustments for date purchased, side of street and the end of street the property is situated in to give you a comparable value.

Step 3 Add the comparable values of each property together and divide by the number of properties to give you an average comparable value.

Step 4 Deduct the repair costs needed to bring No. 54 up to scratch from the average comparable value and you have a valuation of the property and a good idea of what price you should bid up to.

How to calculate the rent and value of a shop

An investor is looking to purchase a shop in a prime high-street location and wants to calculate what the rental income should be and how much the shop is worth. The following information has been gleaned about similar shop investments.

1. Three shops have sold in the street in the last month.

2. These three and the one to be valued:

- are in identical positions;
- are held on identical leases;
- have been maintained in good order.

3. No adjustment is needed to compare:

- position;
- date of the transaction;
- differences in tenure;

- condition.

The shops are different in size and the quality of the covenants of the tenants varies.

Shop A

Has a floor area of 800 sq ft.
The rent is £16,000 per annum.
The tenant is a well-known multiple.
It sold subject to the tenancy for £232,000.

Shop B

Has a floor area of 1,100 sq ft.
The rent is £23,000 per annum.
The tenant is a popular local baker.
It sold for £255,000.

Shop C

Has a floor area of 1,500 sq ft.
The rent is £32,000 per annum.
The tenant is unknown and of doubtful quality.
It sold for £228,500.

Shop D

Is to be sold in auction shortly.
It has 1,253 sq ft.
It is in good repair.

Question 1: What rent can be expected for Shop D?

To work out the rent for shop D, calculate the average rent per square foot of each of the other shops (£20.74) and multiply it by the number of square feet of shop D (1,253 sq ft). Table 2.4 gives the figures needed to make the calculation.

Answer 1

Shop D 1,253 sq ft. Likely rent at £20.74 per sq. ft is £26,000 per annum.

Shop	A	B	C
Rent	£16,000.00	£23,000.00	£32,000.00
Floor area sq ft	800	1,100	1,500
Rent per sq ft	£20.00	£20.90	£21.33
Average rent	£20.74 per sq ft		

Table 2.4 Calculating the average rent

Question 2: How much is it worth?

Assuming it can be let within six months to a local retailer who has a chain of 12 shops, you need to work out what the annual percentage yield is on the investment by dividing the rent by the sale price and multiplying it by 100. The yields for shops A, B and C are given in Table 2.5.

The yield from a local retailer with a chain of 12 shops will be around eight per cent – just between the yield for shops A and B. (It is worth noting that the better the quality of covenant, the lower a yield an investor will accept. Conversely, if the tenant seems a higher risk, or poorer quality of covenant, then the investor will expect a higher yield.)

If the yield is 8 per cent and the rent £26,000, then the value is the sum that £26,000 is eight per cent of. This can be calculated by taking 100 divided by the percentage yield of 8 per cent (12.5) multiplied by the rent of £26,000.

Shop	A	B	C
Sale price	£232,000	£255,000	£228,500
Rent	£16,000	£23,000	£32,000
Yield on investment	6.89%	9%	14%
Quality of covenant	Excellent	Fair	Poor

Table 2.5 Investment yields

Answer 2

The value is therefore £325,000.

But a buyer needs to discount this amount to allow for:

• the six months he has to wait for his rent	£15,000
• his costs	£5,000
• his risk	£25,000
	£45,000
Net Value (£325,000 minus £45,000)	£280,000

Understanding the auctioneers' guidelines on price

Many auctioneers will give their opinion of the price range in which a property falls. These guidelines are occasionally published as part of the auction advertisements or part of the auction catalogue. Other firms only respond to a direct enquiry. Virtually all auctioneers will give limited guidance on the price expected.

Key point

The bottom guideline is usually relatively close to what the auctioneer has fixed or expects to fix as his reserve. The top guideline is normally a slightly optimistic forecast.

How to track what properties fetch at auction

There can be nothing more valuable to you than forming your own conclusions about the price from doing your own research. To do this, you will need to analyse the prices that have been paid for similar properties at previous auctions. Analysing past figures in the light of the present state of the market and the nature and true comparability of the properties can only come with practice. Obtaining the results of past auctions is sometimes not easy. Occasionally, auctioneers publish past results in their next catalogue and if you are on their mailing list you will be able to collate these figures.

Lot No	Full Address	Gross Income £000's	Description	1st Bid £000's	Sold [Last Bid] £000's	Remarks/ Available £000's
1	50 Glengall Rd, Peckham, London, SE15		Fh.EoT.Hse.3.Fl.17.Rm.Gdn.V.	100	228	
2	58 Maxted Rd, Peckham, London, SE15		Fh.Ter.Hse.2.Fl.5.Rm.Gdn.Ten.	Withdrawn	Prior	
3	371 Queens Rd, New Cross, London, SE14		Fh.SD.Hse.4.Fl.6.Rm.Gdn.V.	200	[344]	350
4	80 Silvester Rd, East Dulwich, London, SE22		Fh.Ter.Hse.3.Fl.AA.2.Flt.Gdn.V.	200	[265]	270
5	201 Bellenden Rd, Peckham, London, SE15		Fh.EoT.Hse.2.Fl.4.Rm.Bas.Gdn.V.	175	[227.5]	230
6	75B Friary Rd, Peckham, London, SE15	0.075	Fh.Ter.Hse.2.Fl.AA.2.SC.Flt.GR.on.Gnd.Fl.1st.Fl	75	110	
7	Flat 4, 84 East Dulwich Rd, East Dulwich, London, SE22		LL.1st.Fl.SC.Flt.2.Rm.V.	75	136	
8	6A Thorne Ter, Peckham, London, SE15		LL.Gnd.Fl.PB.Flt.3.Rm.CG.V.	60	106.5	
9	84 Westfields, Railway Side, West Fields, London, SW13		LL.Gnd.Fl.PB.SC.Flt.2.Rm.CG.V.	Refer	To	Auct'eer
10	106 Gaskarth Rd, Balham, London, SW12		Fh.Ter.Hse.2.Fl.5.Rm.Gdn.V.	275	[375]	390
11	38/38A Hosack Rd, Tooting, London, SW17	0.15	Fh.Bdg.2.Fl.AA.2.PB.SC.Flt.Gnd.Fl.5.Rm.Gdn.V.	175	235	
12	19 New Park Court, Brixton Hill, Brixton, London, SW2		LL.3rd.Fl.SC.Flt.4.Rm.V.	[]		155
13	412 Durnsford Rd, Wimbledon, London, SW19	0.1	Fh.Hse.2.Fl.AA.2.SC.Mas.GR.on.Gnd.Fl.1st.Fl.2.	100	146.5	
14	47 Burmester Rd, Tooting, London, SW17		Fh.Ter.Hse.2.Fl.5.Rm.Gdn.V.	180	[265]	270
15	166 Boundary Rd, Colliers Wood, London, SW19		Fh.Ter.Hse.3.Fl.8.Rm.Gdn.PP.3.Flt.V.	Refer	To	Auct'eer
16	131 Milkwood Rd, Herne Hill, London, SE24		Fh.EoT.Hse.2.Fl.5.Rm.Gdn.PPA.2.Flt.&.adj.Lnd.	250	[350]	375
17	21/21A Stockwell Green, Stockwell, London, SW9	12	Fh.DF.Hse.3.Fl.AA.Lwr.Gnd.Fl.Flt.2.Rm.AST.UP.	500	[600]	Refer
17A	162 Landells Rd, East Dulwich, London, SE22		Fh.Ter.Hse.2.Fl.3.Rm.Gdn.V.	140	[190]	195
17B	14 Howden Rd, South Norwood, London, SE25		LL.1st.Fl.SC.Flt.2.Rm.CG.V.	50	91.5	
18	11B Eardley Rd, Streatham, London, SW16	3.42	LL.1st.Fl.UP.AA.SC.Stu.AST.&.SC.Flt.3.Rm.V.	120	[158.5]	159
19	19 De'arn Gdns, Mitcham, Surrey, CR4		LL.Gnd.Fl.SC.Flt.3.Rm.Gdn.V.	60	98	
20	8 Tramway Path, Mitcham, Surrey, CR4		Fh.Ter.Hse.2.Fl.5.Rm.Gdn.V.	100	165	
21	10 Benhilton Gdns, Sutton, London, SM1		Fh.Det.Hse.2.Fl.5.Rm.Gdn.PP.Ext.2.Fl.V.	200	[267.5]	280
22	18 Reynolds Pl, Blackheath, London, SE3		Fh.Ter.Hse.3.Fl.5.Rm.Gdn.V.	150	210	
23	2 Newton House, Granville Park, Lewisham, London, SE13		LL.Gnd.Fl.SC.Flt.3.Rm.V.	200	239	
24	2 Point House, 18 West Grove, Greenwich, London, SE10		LL.Gnd.Fl.SC.Flt.3.Rm.V.	150	210	
25	Flat 3, Manna Mead, 17 West Grove, Greenwich, London,		LL.2nd.Fl.SC.Flt.3.Rm.V.	200	238	
26	94 Woolwich Rd, Greenwich, London, SE10		Fh.Bdg.4.Fl.PP.1.SC.Mas.&.2.SC.Flt.Gdn.PS.V.	180	310	
27	Flat 3, 8 Grange Rd, Southwark, London, SE1		LL.2nd.Fl.SC.Flt.2.Rm.V.	100	141	
28	42 St. Georges Court, Garden Row, Southwark, London,		LL.2nd.Fl.SC.Flt.4.Rm.V.	130	165	
29	87 Arica House, Slippers Pl, Rotherhithe, London, SE16		LL.10th.Fl.Flt.3.Rm.V.	80	[115]	125
29A	14 Wiseman Court, Woodland Rd, Norwood, London, SE19		LL.3rd.Fl.PB.Flt.4.Rm.V.	70	[100]	105
30	666 Old Kent Rd, Peckham, London, SE15		LL.3.Fl.SC.RUP.9.Rm.DP.SC.Flt.V.	200	[260]	Refer
31	17 Donne House, 4 Samuel Cl, New Cross, London, SE14		LL.2nd.Fl.SC.Flt.3.Rm.PS.V.	80	145	
32	147 Bradenham, Boyson Rd, Walworth, London, SE17		LL.8th.Fl.PB.Flt.3.Rm.V.	50	[75]	76
33	118 Stockwell Rd, Stockwell, London, SW9		LL.Gnd.Fl.SC.Flt.2.Rm.V.	Withdrawn	Prior	
34	Flat 3, 129 Knollys Rd, Streatham, London, SW16		LL.2nd.Fl.SC.Flt.2.Rm.V.	Sold Post	100	
35	175B Knollys Rd, Streatham, London, SW16		LL.Gnd.Fl.PB.Flt.4.Rm.V.	100	135	
36	14 Oakwood Place, Oakwood Rd, Croydon, Surrey, CR0		LL.1st.Fl.PB.Flt.2.Rm.V.	50	72.5	
37	64 Frensham Court, Phipps Bdge Rd, Mitcham, Surrey,		LL.10th.Fl.PB.Mas.4.Rm.V.	Sold Post	75	

Figure 2.7 Typical auction results

Magazines that publish auction results

The Essential Information Group (linked to the *Estates Gazette*) now provides an auction results service through its website. Further details can be obtained by calling 0870 112 3040 or by visiting its site.

Auctioneers' telephone information

Some auctioneers also provide answerphone services. In many cases, auction catalogues can be ordered by leaving your name and address on their answerphone. In other cases, auctioneers give details of their auction programme on a recorded message and, shortly before the auction, provide recorded information of lots that have been amended, sold or withdrawn.

'I have bought properties that are in some state of disrepair. They always wanted modernising and bringing up to date. In deciding what price to bid I tend to take an overall view. I check local sale prices and work out how much it will cost me to bring it up to date. I am usually prepared to pay so much at auction and if it goes for that price, I will buy it.'

Michael Roe, buyer of residential properties.

CHAPTER 3

Clearing the contracts and arranging the finance before the auction

'You must ask why the property is going for sale at auction and what (if anything) is wrong with it and satisfy yourself that you are not buying a pig in a poke. You have got to be prepared to do your own research. For example, I had to check that I was not buying a property over a coal mine. I knew the reason for sale – that the property was foreclosed and put up for auction by a building society.'

Don Lee.

As soon as you have found your chosen property, you must take a careful look at the legal and financial issues to make sure you can finance the transaction and commit to exchanging contracts as soon as you succeed in your purchase. This chapter examines these issues and other pitfalls to watch out for in the run-up to attending the auction.

When to use a solicitor

Choosing your solicitor

Your solicitor should be someone in whom you have confidence and whom you are sure will make reasonable charges for the service provided. Your solicitor should undoubtedly be someone who has experience in property conveyancing. If you can find one that has extensive experience of auction procedures, this will be a bonus. Finally, you must be sure that he can move quickly since the timescale from when an auction is announced to when it occurs is often only three or four weeks.

Lot 18 of one of Winkworths' recent auctions, a property located in Blaenau, sold for only £8,500.

Solicitors' fees

Competition between solicitors for conveyancing work has recently driven down the charges for it. Nevertheless, fees charged by solicitors vary considerably and are dependent upon the amount of work which will be necessary and the size of transaction. It is more important to have a solicitor in whom you can trust, who knows auction procedures and who will act with speed, rather than save yourself £100 in conveyancing fees. Most solicitors will give a general quotation of the price band in which their fees will fall for any specific transaction. Do ask for one before instructing them to begin work. Table 3.1 gives an example of solicitors' conveyancing fees.

Purchase at Auction (Excluding Disbursements)	Fee Range
Up to £50,000	£200–£300
£50,001–£150,000	£250–£450
£150,001–£250,000	£300–£500
£250,001–£500,000	£450–£1,200
£500,001–£750,000	£1,000–£1,500
Over £750,000	0.25%–0.35%

Table 3.1 Likely range of solicitors' conveyancing fees (depending on your choice of firm!)

Key point

You must be positive that the solicitor you choose understands the meaning of the word urgency.

What advice should I seek?

Hopefully, by the time you have absorbed the contents of this book, you will know as much or more about auction procedures than your solicitor and you will probably not need to visit or ring him to discuss what you need to do at an auction. However, as soon as you have decided to make a bid, you should immediately approach your solicitor for advice. Ideally, you should give him a copy of the catalogue and, at this first stage, discuss the conditions being applied to the sale. The conditions of sale are examined on page 50. Your solicitor will check that the conditions do not contain any unusual or surprise clauses that could penalise you. As soon as you have his reassurance that he is happy for you to go and bid, you need him to start researching the lot or lots in which you are interested.

What information does my solicitor need from me?

Your solicitor will need detailed information about your prospective property including:

1. A copy of the auction catalogue.

2. A copy of all the conditions of sale.

3. Any further details of the lots you are interested in. For example:
   - a copy of the valuation/survey/builder's report;
   - a copy of the lease (if relevant);
   - a copy of any further letters/details from the auctioneers;
   - notes of answers to queries already put to the auctioneers;
   - the name and address of the solicitors acting for the seller.
   - a copy of the Home Information Pack and any Energy Report.

4. Who is making the purchase. For example:
   - the full name and address of you and your partner;
   - partnership details, if a partnership is buying the property;
   - details of the business, if a business or limited company is buying the property.

5. Financial arrangements:
   - how the property is being paid for;
   - name and address of the mortgage provider;
   - your accountant and/or financial broker (if relevant);

- status of any sales or other assets which will be linked to the purchase.

What questions will my solicitor put to the vendor's solicitors?

Almost invariably the solicitors acting on behalf of the sellers are noted in the catalogue but, if not, the auctioneer's firm can advise you who is acting. Your solicitor should then approach them with the appropriate questions covering in particular:

The quality of the title

Copies of the title can be obtained from the internet (Land Registry) for £3. Plans cost extra. The ownership of land in England is well catalogued and formulated. Many titles and their details are recorded at the Land Registry, who provide a log-book-style document with a plan giving concise details of what a landowner holds. The log book shows:

- whether the title is freehold or leasehold (and its length);

- the current ownership;

- a brief history of the previous ownerships;

- covenants, restrictions or easements that affect the property and normally any major charge registered against the land.

In some cases, the previous purchase price is also given.

Not all titles, however, are as thoroughly catalogued and ownership of land is not always as secure. It is not unusual for auctions to be used as places for the disposal of properties where the title may be questionable and where the vendor hopes that, by submitting the property for sale in this manner, the purchaser will be less than thorough in ensuring that his solicitor makes the necessary investigations. The possibility of such a problem should not stop you from considering buying properties at auction, but should encourage you to ensure that before buying you have the title checked.

How to own property without buying it!

As a rather extreme example of the sort of problem that can arise under English law, it is possible for someone who does not initially own a plot of land or property to become its owner by occupying it for at least 12 years without anyone – and particularly the true owner – raising any objection whatsoever during that period. After 12 years, the occupier usually becomes the landowner with an appropriate title to sell.

To obtain such a 'statutory title' (also sometimes known as a 'squatter's title'), the proper procedures must be followed meticulously for the title to be perfect. If, as a buyer of such a title, you have not had the process of development of ownership thoroughly checked, it could be possible that the possessory title is not supported by suitable affidavits or has not been created because of some inadequacies in the occupation. In such extreme circumstances, a buyer at auction may find that he has purchased a property and is subsequently unable to register his title or to defend it against an original and previous owner.

The nature of any covenants, restrictions or easements

Land is frequently subject to drains, culverts or water courses underneath it; electricity, gas or similar services running on, over or under it; rights of way, bridle paths, footpaths and roads running across it and many similar 'easements'. Occasionally, one hears of people discovering that rights of way exist that run right through their garden or even right through their property. It is an unlucky bidder who discovers only after a contract has been exchanged that his lot suffers such an impediment.

Can you use your property for the intended purpose?

Covenants and restrictions on use of land can be even more complicated. If you are buying a piece of building land to develop and do not research it adequately, it might result in you buying a piece which has covenants preventing the land from being developed for the intended purpose. For example, a buyer intending to erect a multi-storey block might find covenants preventing the erection of such a building. Alternatively, the buyer of a piece of land beside a railway line or road might discover they have acquired a responsibility to erect an expensive wall or fence.

Sellers at BM lose out by playing safe

Samantha Jenkins

Vendors' nervousness about the market proved ill-founded and may have led to some of them missing out financially, according to Barnard Marcus auctioneer Chris Glenn.

Glenn was speaking after a £16.7m auction at London's Café Royal last week, where, in spite of the Tube strike, 74% of the 156 lots sold.

He said that uncertainty among some vendors had led to the prior sale of 32 lots – almost a third of the total 115 lots sold. And while he could understand the decision to take "the bird in the hand", he said there were some sellers who with hindsight "may have done better in the room".

"A few people were more nervous about the market than they needed to be," he said.

The £250,000 sale under the hammer of a vacant semi in Warwick Road, Thornton Heath, demonstrated how some vendors may have benefited by deciding not to sell prior. The lot was guided at £180,000, attracted more than 50 viewings and many legal document requests but the best prior bid was only £220,000.

A parcel of 10 assured tenancy investments were offered separately by a BES company with guides totalling £580,000. Producing rental income of £66,500 pa, they attracted very strong interest from both the established investment houses and private individuals looking for local investments. They sold for a total of £991,500.

In a "workmanlike" sale, the only disappointment, Glenn said, was the failure to sell of a vacant hotel in Collingham Place, South Kensington, W5, guided at £1.39m.

"With the level of enquiries before auction, one would have expected it to sell," he said.

Illustration 2. Estates Gazette report on a Barnard Marcus auction

Any adverse details revealed in the local search

The local search is a set of questions submitted to the local authority in which the property is situated. All sorts of planning (e.g. highway and transport plans) may affect a lot. Building or planning regulations may not have been observed when the building on a lot was erected. The local authority environmental departments may be critical of items in the buildings or on the site which could have expensive repercussions after you have bought the property. All property is subject to detailed building and planning regulations under the auspices of the local authority. The local search should reveal if any problems are present.

The solicitor acting for the seller will have obtained a local search and a Home Information Pack or be in the process of obtaining them prior to the auction. But it could be that the local search may not be available. If the local search has not been obtained, it would be wise for either you or your solicitor to enquire with the relevant local authority, if there are any adverse proposals or notices affecting the property. Appendix 1 reproduces the Enquiries of Local Authority Form listing all the questions you will need to ask them about your target property. If any planning consents affecting the lot are of interest to you, the local authority will generally provide a copy at a nominal cost or, alternatively, make available for inspection at their offices the relevant planning register.

Any other appropriate legal points

If you are unsure in your bidding or if your solicitor has been unable to obtain any details before the auction itself, you may feel it is worthwhile employing him to accompany you to the auction, to make whatever research is possible at the time and to assist you in your bidding when the lot comes up for sale. You must realise that he will charge an additional fee for such a service, probably on an hourly basis. Do obtain from him a quotation of the cost for attending the auction. You can expect such a charge to be between £80 and £200 per hour depending upon the nature and level of expertise of the person you are employing and the size, calibre and address of the firm you are using.

Key point

When you attend the auction, if you find the solicitor for the seller is present, check with him to see if there have been any subsequent alterations or changes and also to read through whatever literature he can provide.

The following checklist illustrates the stages your solicitor will go through from initial instruction through to completion.

Solicitor's checklist: Acting for a buyer

1   Request the contract, searches and replies to pre-contract enquiries plus auction catalogue and a Home Information Pack. ☐

2   Ask the client how he is financing the transaction and explain the pitfalls of buying at auction. ☐

3   Investigate title and raise any appropriate enquiries on that and any other matters and also raise such pre-contract and personal searches as may be necessary, for example a personal local search, a British Coal search, etc. ☐

4 Report to the client and establish his maximum offer and
   advise of the deposit amount he must take to the auction. ☐

5 A few days before the auction, see if there are any
   amendments with the seller's solicitors or auctioneers and,
   if so, relay those to your client. ☐

6 If the client so wishes, attend the auction with him or as his
   agent. ☐

7 Re-check the details received from the seller's solicitors and
   see if there are any amendments. If so, notify the client. ☐

8 Bid as instructed, or monitor the client's bidding. ☐

9 Ensure the contract is signed correctly and exchange of
   contracts is recorded properly. ☐

10 Obtain signed contract received by client and liaise with
   seller's solicitors, as normal, up to completion. ☐

Conditions of sale

What are the conditions of sale?

These are the terms on which the successful bidder will buy the property. They regulate not only the bidding, but also any obligations the bidder must fulfil. They give a full and definitive description of the property and prescribe what happens after your bid is successful.

Check for onerous liabilities

If you are interested in bidding for a lot, you should ask to see these before doing so – otherwise you may end up buying something that is different from what you thought. You may be left with some heavy liabilities or the property may be subject to various covenants, for example a requirement to fence the borders of the property.

It is usual for an auctioneer to draw your attention to serious matters affecting the property, either in the auction catalogue itself and/or on the day in his introductory remarks. However, his remarks are very often only a summary. It is up to you to inform yourself and look at the conditions carefully. They will always be available from the auctioneer or from the owner's solicitors.

What types of conditions are there?

The bidder at auction will usually find up to four conditions to watch out for:

- The general conditions
- The additional general conditions
- The special conditions
- Any other conditions under whatever name

These conditions may appear in several guises and in several places. You may find all the relevant conditions applicable to a lot are dealt with in the auction catalogue. Alternatively, you may find only some conditions in the catalogue, normally called 'General Conditions'. An example is shown in Figure 3.1.

Where an owner has a number of lots in an auction and he or his solicitor thinks it advisable to have certain conditions relating to all those lots or most of them over and above the general conditions, he can arrange for these to be printed in the catalogue and they will be headed 'Additional General Conditions' or something similar. An example is shown in Figure 3.2.

Watch out for hidden conditions

An owner's solicitor may need to draw up extra conditions to cover points that are not covered in the general conditions or additional general conditions, or he may find that the general conditions do not achieve what his client needs – in that case he will draw up special conditions.

Frequently, these will not be printed in the catalogue, as the catalogue will have been sent for printing before the owner's solicitor has even seen the title deeds. They will only be available from the auctioneer and the owner's solicitors.

Common Auction Conditions for Auctions of Real Estate in England and Wales – Edition 1

© Royal Institution of Chartered Surveyors
May 2002

IMPORTANT NOTE

You may use these conditions freely, but if you do:

- you must rely on your own legal advice as to their suitability for your use;

- you agree that the Royal Institution of Chartered Surveyors (RICS) and those who advised it have no liability to you or anyone who relies on the conditions;

- you must either reproduce the conditions in full or show clearly where you have made changes to them;

- you must use the title 'Common Auction Conditions (Edition 1)' and acknowledge that they are reproduced with the consent of the RICS.

The conditions have been produced for real estate auctions in England and Wales in the hope that they will be adopted by most auction houses and set a common standard across the industry.

The following introduction explains what the common auction conditions are and how they apply. The introduction does not itself form part of the conditions and auctioneers who use the conditions may adapt the introduction as part of their own guidance notes if they prefer.

INTRODUCTION

The common auction conditions have three main sections:

1. Glossary

This gives special meanings to some words used in the rest of the conditions.

2. The conduct of the auction

These conditions regulate the conduct of the auction. If you read our catalogue or attend the auction, you do so on the basis that you accept them.

3. Conditions of sale

If you buy a lot, you will sign a sale memorandum under which you agree to be bound by the conditions of sale that apply to that lot. These conditions are:

- general conditions that apply to all lots;

- any extra general conditions in the catalogue or an addendum;

- special conditions that only apply to the lot you are buying (and which may vary the general conditions).

The conditions are legally binding.

Important notice

A prudent buyer will, before bidding for a lot at an auction:

- take professional advice from a solicitor and, in appropriate cases, a surveyor and an accountant;

- read the conditions;

- inspect the lot;

- carry out usual searches and make usual enquiries;

- check the content of all available leases and other documents relating to the lot;

- check that what is said about the lot in the catalogue is accurate;

- have finance available for the deposit and purchase price.

The conditions assume that the buyer has acted like a prudent buyer. If you choose to buy a lot without taking these normal precautions, you do so at your own risk.

GLOSSARY

In the **conditions** wherever it makes sense:

- singular words can be read as plurals, and plurals as singular words;

- a 'person' includes a corporate body;

- words of one gender include the other genders;

- where the following words appear in small capitals they have specified meanings. These are listed below.

Actual completion date

The date when *completion* takes place or is treated as taking place for the purposes of apportionment and calculating interest.

Addendum

An amendment or addition to the *conditions* whether contained in a supplement to the *catalogue*, a written notice from the *auctioneers* or an oral announcement at the *auction*.

Agreed completion date

(a)   The date specified in the *special conditions*; or

Figure 3.1 Common auction conditions

(b)   if no date is specified, *20 business days* after the *contract date* but if that date is not a *business day* the first subsequent *business day*.

Approved bank

A UK clearing bank.

Arrears

Arrears of rent and other sums due under the *tenancies* but unpaid on the *actual completion date.*

Auction

The auction advertised in the *catalogue.*

Auctioneers

The auctioneers at the *auction.*

Business day

A day which is not (a) a bank or public holiday or (b) a Saturday or a Sunday.

Buyer

The person who agrees to buy the *lot* or, if applicable, that person's personal representatives: if two or more are jointly the *buyer,* all obligations can be enforced against them jointly or against each of them separately.

Catalogue

The catalogue to which the *conditions* refer including any supplement to it.

Completion

Completion of the sale of the *lot.*

Conditions

This glossary, the conditions for the conduct of the *auction,* the *general conditions,* any *extra conditions* and the *special conditions.*

Contract

The contract by which the *seller* agrees to sell and the *buyer* agrees to buy the *lot.*

Contract date

The date of the *auction* or, if the *lot* is not sold at the *auction:*

(a)   the date of the *sale memorandum* signed by both the *seller* and *buyer;* or

(b)   if contracts are exchanged, the date of exchange. If exchange is not effected in person or by an irrevocable agreement to exchange made by telephone, fax or electronic mail, the date of exchange is the date on which both parts have been signed and posted or otherwise placed beyond normal retrieval.

Documents

Documents of title (including, if title is registered, the entries on the register and the filed plan) and other documents listed or referred to in the *special conditions* relating to the *lot.*

Extra conditions

Any additions to or variations of the *general conditions* that are of general application to all *lots.*

General conditions

The conditions so headed.

Interest rate

If not specified in the *special conditions,* four per cent above the base rate from time to time of Barclays Bank Plc.

Lot

Each separate property described in the *catalogue* or (as the case may be) the property that the *seller* has agreed to sell and the *buyer* to buy.

Old arrears

Arrears due under any of the *tenancies* that are not 'new tenancies' as defined by the Landlord and Tenant (Covenants) Act 1995.

Particulars

The section of the *catalogue* that contains descriptions of each *lot.*

Practitioner

A receiver, administrative receiver or liquidator.

Price

The price that the *buyer* agrees to pay for the *lot.*

Ready to complete

Ready, willing and able to complete: if *completion* would enable the *seller* to discharge all financial charges secured on the *lot* that have to be discharged by *completion,* then those outstanding financial charges do not prevent the *seller* from being *ready to complete.*

Sale memorandum

The form so headed set out in the *catalogue* in which the terms of the *contract* for the sale of the *lot* are recorded.

Seller

The person selling the *lot.*

Special conditions

The conditions so headed that relate to the *lot.*

Tenancies

All tenancies, leases, licences to occupy and agreements for lease subject to which the *lot* is

Figure 3.1 Common auction conditions (continued)

sold, and any documents varying or supplemental to them.

Transfer

Includes a conveyance or assignment (and to transfer includes to convey or to assign).

TUPE

The Transfer of Undertakings (Protection of Employment) Regulations 1981 as modified or re-enacted from time to time.

VAT

Value Added Tax or other tax of a similar nature.

VAT election

An election to waive exemption from *VAT* in respect of the *lot*.

We (and us and our)

The *auctioneers*.

You (and your)

Someone who has a copy of the *catalogue* or who attends or bids at the *auction*, whether or not a *buyer*.

THE CONDUCT OF THE AUCTION

The *catalogue* is issued only on the basis that *you* accept these conditions relating to the conduct of the *auction*. They override all other *conditions* and can only be varied if *we* agree.

Our role

As agents for each *seller* we have authority to:

- prepare the *catalogue* from information supplied by or on behalf of each *seller*;
- offer each *lot* for sale;
- sell each *lot*;
- receive and hold deposits;
- sign each *sale memorandum*;
- treat a *contract* as repudiated if the *buyer* fails to sign a *sale memorandum* or pay a deposit as required by the *conditions*.

Our decision on the conduct of the *auction* is final.

We may cancel the *auction*, withdraw *lots* from sale, or alter the order in which *lots* are offered for sale. *We* may also combine or divide *lots*.

You acknowledge that to the extent permitted by law *we* owe *you* no duty of care and *you* have no claim against *us* for any loss.

Bidding and reserve prices

We may refuse to accept a bid. *We* do not have to explain why.

If there is a dispute over bidding *we* are entitled to resolve it, and *our* decision is final.

Unless stated otherwise, each *lot* is subject to a reserve price. If no bid equals or exceeds that reserve price, the *lot* will be withdrawn from the *auction*. The *seller* may bid (or ask *us* or another agent to bid on the *seller*'s behalf) up to the reserve price, but may not make a bid equal to or exceeding the reserve price.

Where a guide price is given that price is not to be taken as an indication of the value of the *lot* or of the reserve price. The reserve price may be higher or lower than the guide price.

The particulars and other information

We have taken reasonable care to prepare *particulars* that correctly describe each *lot*. However, the *particulars* are based on information supplied by or on behalf of the *seller* and *we* are not responsible for errors that *we* could not reasonably be expected to check.

The *particulars* are for *your* information but *you* must not rely on them. They do not form part of any *contract* between the *seller* and the *buyer*.

If *we* provide any information or a copy of any document, *we* do so only on the basis that *we* are not responsible for its accuracy.

The contract

A successful bid is one *we* accept as such.

If *you* make a successful bid for a *lot*, *you* are obliged to buy that *lot* on the terms of the *sale memorandum*. The *price* will be the amount *you* bid plus *VAT* (if applicable). *you* must before leaving the *auction*:

- provide all information *we* reasonably need from *you* to enable us to complete the *sale memorandum* including appropriate proof of your identity;
- sign the completed *sale memorandum*; and
- pay the deposit;

and if *you* do not, *we* may either:

- as agent for the *seller* treat that failure as *your* repudiation of the *contract* and offer the *lot* for sale again: the *seller* may then have a claim against *you* for breach of contract;
- sign the *sale memorandum* on *your* behalf.

Deposits must be paid by cheque or by bankers' draft drawn on an *approved bank* in *our* favour. The *catalogue* states whether *we* also accept cash, or debit or credit cards.

We may retain the *sale memorandum* signed by or on behalf of the *seller* until *we* receive the deposit in cleared funds.

Figure 3.1 Common auction conditions (continued)

If *you* make a successful bid for a *lot*:

- *you* are personally liable to buy it even if *you* are acting as an agent unless *you* obtain *our* prior agreement to *your* bidding as agent for a disclosed principal. It is *your* responsibility to obtain an indemnity from the person for whom *you* are the agent;

- where the *buyer* is a company *you* warrant that the *buyer* is properly constituted and able to buy the *lot*;

- if the *buyer* does not comply with its obligations under the *contract*, *you* are personally liable to buy the *lot* and must indemnify the *seller* in respect of any loss the *seller* incurs as a result of the *buyer*'s default.

GENERAL CONDITIONS

The *general conditions* apply except to the extent that they are varied by *extra conditions*, the *special conditions* or by an *addendum*.

1.   The lot

1.1   The *lot*, including any rights granted and reserved, is described in the *special conditions*.

1.2   The *lot* is sold subject to any *tenancies* disclosed by the *special conditions*, but otherwise with vacant possession on *completion*.

1.3   The *lot* is sold subject to all matters contained or referred to in the *documents* (except charges that are to be discharged on or before *completion*) and to such of the following as may affect it, whether they arise before or after the *contract date* and whether or not they are disclosed by the *seller* or are apparent from inspection of the *lot* or the *documents*:

(a)   matters registered or capable of registration as local land charges

(b)   matters registered or capable of registration by any competent authority or under the provisions of any statute

(c)   notices, orders, demands, proposals and requirements of any competent authority

(d)   charges, notices, orders, restrictions, agreements and other matters relating to town and country planning, highways or public health

(e)   rights, easements, quasi-easements, and wayleaves

(f)   outgoings and other liabilities

(g)   anything that is an overriding interest within the meaning of section 70 of the Land Registration Act 1925 or would be if the *lot* were registered land

(h)   matters that ought to be disclosed by the searches and enquiries a prudent buyer would make, whether or not the *buyer* has made them

(i)   anything the *seller* does not and could not reasonably know about

and where any such matter would expose the *seller* to liability the *buyer* is to comply with it and indemnify the *seller* against liability.

1.4   The *seller* must notify the *buyer* of any notices, orders, demands, proposals and requirements of any competent authority of which it learns after the *contract date* but the *buyer* is to comply with them and must indemnify the *seller* if it does not.

1.5   The *lot* does not include any tenant's or trade fixtures or fittings.

1.6   Where chattels are included in the *lot* the *buyer* takes them as they are at *completion* and the *seller* is not liable if they are not fit for use.

1.7   The *buyer* buys with full knowledge of:

(a)   the *documents* whether or not the *buyer* has read them;

(b)   the physical condition of the *lot* and what could reasonably be discovered on inspection of it, whether or not the *buyer* has inspected it.

1.8   The *buyer* is not relying on the information contained in the *particulars* or in any replies to preliminary enquiries but on the *buyer*'s own verification of that information. If any information is not correct, any liability of the *seller* and any remedy of the *buyer* are excluded to the extent permitted by statute.

2. Deposit

2.1   The amount of the deposit is the greater of:

(a)   the minimum deposit stated in the *catalogue* (or the total *price*, if this is less than that minimum);

(b)   ten per cent of the *price* exclusive of *VAT*.

2.2   The deposit:

(a)   must be paid to the *auctioneers* by cheque or banker's draft drawn on an *approved bank*;

(b)   is to be held as stakeholder unless the *special conditions* provide that it is to be held as agent for the *seller*.

Figure 3.1 Common auction conditions (continued)

2.3 Where the *auctioneers* hold the deposit as stakeholder they are authorised to release it and any interest on it to the *seller* on *completion* or, if *completion* does not take place, to the person entitled to it under the *conditions*.

2.4 If, for any reason, the deposit is not received by the *auctioneers* in cleared funds within five *business days* of the *contract date*, the *seller* is entitled to treat the *contract* as at an end and bring a claim against the *buyer* for breach of contract.

2.5 Interest earned on the deposit belongs to the *seller* unless the *conditions* provide otherwise.

3.   Transfer of risk and insurance

3.1 From the *contract date* the *seller* is under no obligation to insure the *lot* and the *buyer* bears all risk of loss or damage unless:

(a)   the *lot* is sold subject to a *tenancy* which requires the *seller* to insure the *lot*; or

(b)   the *special conditions* require the *seller* to insure the *lot*.

3.2 If the *seller* is to insure the *lot* then the *seller*:

(a)   must produce to the *buyer* on request details of the insurance policy;

(b)   must use reasonable endeavours to maintain insurance equivalent to that policy and pay the premiums when due;

(c)   gives no warranty as to the adequacy of the insurance;

(d)   must, at the request of the *buyer*, use reasonable endeavours to have the *buyer*'s interest noted on the policy where the policy does not cover a contracting purchaser;

(e)   must, unless otherwise agreed, cancel the policy at *completion*;

(f)   is to hold in trust for the *buyer* any insurance payments that the *seller* receives in respect of loss or damage arising after the *contract date*;

and the *buyer* must reimburse to the *seller* the cost of insurance (to the extent it is not paid by a tenant or other third party) from the *contract date*.

3.3 If, under a *tenancy*, the *seller* insures the *lot*, then unless otherwise agreed with the *buyer* the *seller* is to pay any refund of premium:

(a)   to the *buyer*; or

(b)   if the *special conditions* so state, to each tenant in the proportion that the tenant pays premiums under its *tenancy*, first deducting any arrears of premium due from that tenant.

3.4 Section 47 of the Law of Property Act 1925 does not apply.

3.5 Unless the *buyer* is already lawfully in occupation of the *lot* the *buyer* has no right to enter into occupation prior to *completion*.

4.   Title

4.1 Unless *general condition* 4.2 applies, the *buyer* accepts the title of the *seller* to the *lot* as at the *contract date* and may raise no requisition or objection except in relation to any matter following the *contract date*.

4.2 Where no *documents* are available before the *auction*:

(a)   if the *lot* is registered land, the *seller* is to give to the *buyer* within five *business days* of the *contract date* an office copy of the entries on the register and filed plan and of all documents noted on the register that affect the *lot*;

(b)   if the *lot* is not registered land, the *seller* is to give to the *buyer* within five *business days* an abstract or epitome of title starting from the root of title mentioned in the *special conditions* (or, if none is mentioned, a good root of title more than fifteen years old) and must produce to the *buyer* the original or an examined copy of every relevant *document*;

(c)   the *buyer* has no right to object to or make requisitions on any title information more than seven *business days* after that information has been given to the *buyer*.

4.3 Unless otherwise stated in the *special conditions* the *seller* sells with full title guarantee except that:

(a)   all matters recorded in registers open to public inspection are to be treated as within the actual knowledge of the *buyer*; and

(b)   any implied covenant as to compliance with tenant's obligations under leases does not extend to the state or condition of the *lot* where the *lot* is leasehold property.

4.4 If in the course of registering the title, the title is to consist of certified copies of:

(a)   the *documents* sent to the land registry;

(b)   the application to the land registry;

Figure 3.1 Common auction conditions (continued)

and a letter under which the *seller* or its solicitors agrees to use all reasonable endeavours to answer any requisitions raised by the land registry and to instruct the land registry to send the completed registration documents to the *buyer*.

4.5 The *transfer* is to have effect as if expressly subject to all matters subject to which the *lot* is sold under the *contract*.

4.6 The *seller* does not have to produce, nor may the *buyer* object to or make a requisition in relation to, any prior or superior title even if it is referred to in the *documents*.

5. Transfer

5.1 Unless a form of *transfer* is set out in the *special conditions*:

(a) the *buyer* must supply a draft *transfer* to the *seller* at least ten *business days* before the *agreed completion date* and the engrossment five *business days* before that date or (if later) two *business days* after the draft has been approved by the *seller*; and

(b) the *seller* must approve or revise the draft *transfer* within five *business days* of receiving it from the *buyer*.

5.2 If the *seller* remains liable in any respect in relation to the *lot* (or a *tenancy*) following *completion*, the *buyer* is specifically to covenant in the transfer to indemnify the *seller* against that liability.

5.3 The *transfer* is to be executed in duplicate and the *buyer* is to return to the *seller* the duplicate duly stamped and denoted at the *buyer*'s cost as soon as practicable after *completion*.

5.4 The *seller* cannot be required to *transfer* the *lot* to anyone other than the *buyer*, or by more than one *transfer*.

6. Completion

6.1 *Completion* is to take place at the offices of the *seller*'s solicitors, or where the *seller* may reasonably require, on a *business day* between the hours of 0930 and 1700.

6.2 The amount payable on *completion* is the balance of the *price* adjusted to take account of apportionments plus (if applicable) VAT and interest.

6.3 Payment is to be made in pounds sterling and only by:

(a) direct transfer to the *seller*'s solicitors' bank account; and

(b) the release of any deposit held by a stakeholder.

6.4 Unless the *seller* and the *buyer* otherwise agree, *completion* takes place when both have complied with their obligations under the *contract* and the total payment is unconditionally received in the *seller*'s solicitors' bank account.

6.5 If *completion* takes place after 1400 hours, it is to be treated, for the purposes of apportionment and calculating interest, as if it had taken place on the next *business day*.

6.6 Where applicable the *contract* remains in force following *completion*.

7. Notice to complete

7.1 The *seller* or the *buyer* may on or after the *agreed completion date* but before *completion* give the other notice to complete within ten *business days* (excluding the date on which the notice is given) making time of the essence.

7.2 The person giving the notice must be *ready to complete*.

7.3 If the *buyer* fails to comply with a notice to complete, the *seller* may, without affecting any other remedy the *seller* has:

(a) rescind the *contract*;

(b) claim the deposit and any interest on it if held by a stakeholder;

(c) forfeit the deposit and any interest on it

(d) resell the *lot*; and

(e) claim damages from the *buyer*.

7.4 If the *seller* fails to comply with a notice to complete, the *buyer* may, without affecting any other remedy the *buyer* has:

(a) rescind the *contract*; and

(b) recover the deposit and any interest on it from the *seller* or, if applicable, a stakeholder.

8. If the contract is brought to an end

If the *contract* is rescinded or otherwise brought to an end:

(a) the *buyer* must return all papers to the *seller* and appoints the *seller* its agent to cancel any registration of the *contract*;

(b) the *seller* must return the deposit and any interest on it to the *buyer* (and the *buyer* may claim it from the stakeholder, if applicable) unless the *seller* is entitled to forfeit the deposit under *general condition* 7.3.

Figure 3.1 Common auction conditions (continued)

9. Landlord's licence

9.1 Where the *lot* is leasehold land and licence to assign is required:

(a) the *contract* is conditional on it being obtained, by way of formal licence if that is what the landlord or the relevant lease properly requires;

(b) the *agreed completion date* is, if necessary, postponed to the date five *business days* after the *seller* has given notice to the *buyer* that licence has been obtained.

9.2 The *seller* must:

(a) use all reasonable endeavours to obtain each licence required;

(b) enter into any authorised guarantee agreement properly required under the lease.

9.3 The *buyer* must:

(a) promptly provide references and other relevant information;

(b) if properly required under the terms of the lease, execute such licence or other deed of covenant as may be required and provide guarantees, a rent deposit or other security.

9.4 If within three months of the *contract date* (or such longer period as the *seller* and *buyer* agree) all required licences have not been obtained, the *seller* or the *buyer* may by notice to the other rescind the *contract* at any time before all licences are obtained. Rescission is without prejudice to the claims of either *seller* or *buyer* for breach of this condition 9.

10. Interest and apportionments

10.1 If the *actual completion date* is after the *agreed completion date* for any reason other than the *seller's* default, the *buyer* must pay interest at the *interest rate* on the *price* (less any *deposit* paid) from the *agreed completion date* up to and including the *actual completion date*.

10.2 The *seller* is not obliged to apportion or account for any sum at *completion* unless the *seller* has received that sum in cleared funds. The *seller* must pay to the *buyer* after *completion* any sum to which the *buyer* is entitled that the *seller* subsequently receives in cleared funds.

10.3 Income and outgoings are to be apportioned at *actual completion date* unless:

(a) the *buyer* is liable to pay interest;

(b) the *seller* has given notice to the *buyer* at any time up to *completion* requiring apportionment on the date from which interest becomes payable.

10.4 Apportionments are to be calculated on the basis that:

(a) the *seller* receives income and is liable for outgoings for the whole of the day on which apportionment is to be made;

(b) annual income and expenditure accrues at an equal daily rate assuming 365 days in a year and income and expenditure relating to a period of less than a year accrues at an equal daily rate during the period to which it relates;

(c) where the amount to be apportioned is not known at *completion* apportionment is to be made by reference to the best estimate then available and further payment is to be made by *seller* or *buyer* as appropriate within five *business days* of the date when the amount is known.

11. Arrears

11.1 The *seller* retains the right to receive and recover *old arrears*.

11.2 While any *arrears* due to the *seller* remain unpaid the *buyer* must:

(a) try to collect them in the ordinary course of management but need not take legal proceedings, distrain or forfeit the *tenancy*;

(b) pay them to the *seller* within five *business days* of receipt in cleared funds (plus interest at the *interest rate* calculated on a daily basis for each subsequent day's delay in payment);

(c) on request, at the cost of the *seller*, assign to the *seller* or as the *seller* may direct the right to demand and sue for *old arrears*, such assignment to be in such form as the *seller's* solicitors may reasonably require;

(d) if reasonably required, allow the *seller's* solicitors to have on loan the counterpart of any *tenancy* against an undertaking to hold it to the *buyer's* order;

(e) not release any tenant or surety from liability to pay *arrears* or accept a surrender of or forfeit any *tenancy* under which *arrears* are due;

Figure 3.1 Common auction conditions (continued)

(f) if the *buyer* disposes of the *lot* prior to recovery of all *arrears* obtain from the *buyer*'s successor in title a covenant in favour of the *seller* in similar form to this condition 11.

11.3 Where the *seller* has the right to recover *arrears* it must not without the *buyer*'s written consent bring insolvency proceedings against a tenant or seek the removal of goods from the *lot*.

12. Management

12.1 This condition applies where the *lot* is sold subject to *tenancies*.

12.2 The *seller* is to manage the *lot* in accordance with its standard management policies pending *completion*.

12.3 Unless set out in the *special conditions* the *seller* must consult the *buyer* on all management issues that would affect the *buyer* after *completion*, such as an application for licence or a rent review under a *tenancy*, a variation, surrender, agreement to surrender or proposed forfeiture of a *tenancy*, or a new tenancy or agreement to grant a new tenancy and:

(a) the *seller* must comply with the *buyer*'s reasonable requirements unless to do so would (but for the indemnity in paragraph (c)) expose the *seller* to a liability that the *seller* would not otherwise have, in which case the *seller* may act reasonably in such a way as to avoid that liability;

(b) if the *seller* gives the *buyer* notice of the *seller*'s intended act and the *buyer* does not object within five *business days* giving reasons for the objection, the *seller* may act as the *seller* intends;

(c) the *buyer* is to indemnify the *seller* against all loss or liability the *seller* incurs through acting as the *buyer* requires, or by reason of delay caused by the *buyer*.

13. Rent deposits

13.1 This condition applies where the *seller* is holding or otherwise entitled to money by way of rent deposit in respect of a *tenancy*. In this condition 'rent deposit deed' means the deed or other document under which the rent deposit is held.

13.2 If the rent deposit is not assignable the *seller* must on *completion* hold the rent deposit on trust for the *buyer* and, subject to the terms of the rent deposit deed, comply at the cost

of the *buyer* with the *buyer*'s lawful instructions.

13.3 Otherwise, the *seller* must on *completion* pay and assign its interest in the rent deposit to the *buyer* under an assignment in which the *buyer* covenants with the *seller* to

(a) observe and perform the *seller*'s covenants and conditions in the rent deposit deed and indemnify the *seller* in respect of any breach;

(b) give notice of assignment to the tenant;

(c) give such direct covenant to the tenant as may be required by the rent deposit deed.

14. VAT

14.1 Where the *conditions* require money to be paid the payer must also pay any *VAT* that is chargeable on that money, but only if given a valid *VAT* invoice.

14.2 Where the *special conditions* state that no VAT ELECTION has been made the *seller* confirms that none has been made by it or by any company in the same VAT group nor will be prior to *completion*.

15. Transfer as a going concern

15.1 Where the *special conditions* so state the *seller* and the *buyer* intend the sale to be treated as a transfer of a going concern and this condition applies.

15.2 The *seller* confirms that the *seller* or a company in the same *VAT* group:

(a) is registered for *VAT*;

(b) has, where necessary, made a *VAT election* in respect of the *lot* which remains valid.

15.3 The *buyer*:

(a) is registered for *VAT*, either in the *buyer*'s name or as a member of a *VAT* group;

(b) has made, or will make before *completion*, a *VAT election* in relation to the *lot*;

(c) is to give to the *seller* as early as possible before the *agreed completion date* evidence of the *VAT* registration and that a *VAT election* has been made and notified in writing to HM Customs and Excise;

(d) must not revoke the *VAT election*;

and if it does not produce the relevant evidence at least two *business days* before

Figure 3.1 Common auction conditions (continued)

the *agreed completion date*, *general condition* 14.1 applies at *completion*.

15.4 The *buyer* confirms that after *completion* the *buyer* intends to:

(a) retain and manage the *lot* for the *buyer*'s own benefit as a continuing business as a going concern subject to and with the benefit of the *tenancies*;

(b) collect the rents payable under the *tenancies* and charge *VAT* on them.

15.5 Unless the *seller* obtains agreement to the contrary from HM Customs & Excise:

(a) the *seller* must on or as soon as reasonably practicable after *completion* transfer to the *buyer* all *VAT* records for the *lot*;

(b) the *buyer* must keep those records available for inspection by the *seller* at all reasonable times.

15.6 If, after *completion*, it is found that the sale of the *lot* is not a transfer of a going concern then:

(a) the *seller*'s solicitors are to notify the *buyer*'s solicitors of that finding and provide a *VAT* invoice in respect of the sale of the *lot*;

(b) the *buyer* must within five *business days* of receipt of the *VAT* invoice pay to the *seller* the *VAT* due;

(c) if *VAT* is payable because the *buyer* has not complied with this condition 15, the *buyer* must pay and indemnify the *seller* against all costs, interest, penalties or surcharges that the *seller* incurs as a result.

16. Capital allowances

16.1 This condition applies where the *special conditions* state that there are capital allowances available in respect of the *lot*.

16.2 The *seller* is promptly to supply to the *buyer* all information reasonably required by the *buyer* in connection with the *buyer*'s claim for capital allowances.

16.3 The value to be attributed to those items on which capital allowances may be claimed is set out in the *special conditions*.

16.4 The *seller* and *buyer* agree:

(a) to make an election on *completion* under section 198 of the Capital Allowances Act 2001 to give effect to this condition;

(b) to submit the value specified in the *special conditions* to the Inland Revenue for the purposes of their respective capital allowance computations.

17. Maintenance contracts

17.1 The *seller* agrees to use reasonable endeavours to transfer to the *buyer*, at the *buyer*'s cost, the benefit of the maintenance contracts specified in the *special conditions*.

17.2 The *buyer* must assume, and indemnify the *seller* in respect of, all liability under such contracts from the *actual completion date*.

18. Landlord and Tenant Act 1987

18.1 This condition applies where the sale is a relevant disposal for the purposes of part I of the Landlord and Tenant Act 1987.

18.2 Unless the *special conditions* state otherwise, the *seller* warrants that the *seller* has complied with sections 5B and 7 of that Act and that the requisite majority of qualifying tenants has not accepted the offer.

19. Sale by receiver, etc.

19.1 This condition applies where the sale is by a *practitioner*.

19.2 The *practitioner* has been duly appointed and is empowered to sell the *lot*.

19.3 The *practitioner* is the agent of the *seller*. The *practitioner* and the *practitioner*'s partners and staff incur no personal liability in connection with the sale or the performance of the *seller*'s obligations. The *transfer* is to include a declaration excluding the personal liability of the *practitioner* and of the *practitioner*'s partners and staff.

19.4 The *lot* is sold:

(a) in whatever its condition is at *completion*;

(b) whether or not vacant possession is provided;

(c) for such title as the *seller* may have; and

(d) with no covenants for title;

and the *buyer* has no right to rescind the contract or any other remedy if information provided about the *lot* is inaccurate, incomplete or missing.

19.5 Where the *practitioner* is a receiver or administrative receiver:

(a) the *documents* include certified copies of the charge under which the *practitioner* is appointed, the document of appointment by the lender and the

Figure 3.1 Common auction conditions (continued)

practitioner's acceptance of appointment;

(b) the *seller* may require the *transfer* to be by the lender exercising its power of sale under the Law of Property Act 1925.

19.6 The *buyer* understands this condition 19 and agrees that it is fair in the circumstances of a sale by a *practitioner*.

20. TUPE

20.1 Unless the *special conditions* state that *TUPE* applies, then the *seller* warrants that there are no employees whose contracts of employment will transfer to the *buyer* on *completion*.

20.2 If the *special conditions* state that *TUPE* applies, then:

(a) the *seller* has informed the *buyer* of those employees whose contracts of employment will transfer to the *buyer* on *completion*;

(b) not less than five *business days* before the *agreed completion date* the *buyer* must confirm to the *seller* that the *buyer* has offered to employ those employees on the same terms as, or better terms than, their existing contracts of employment;

(c) the *buyer* is to keep the *seller* indemnified against all liability for those employees after *completion*.

21. Environmental

21.1 This condition only applies where the *special conditions* so provide.

21.2 The *seller* has made available such reports as the *seller* has as to the environmental condition of the *lot* and has given the *buyer* the opportunity to carry out investigations (whether or not the *buyer* has read those reports or carried out any investigation) and the *buyer* admits that the *price* takes into account the environmental condition of the *lot*.

21.3 The *buyer* accepts that as a result the *buyer*, not the *seller*, is liable for any pollution on or emanating from the *lot*, including the cost of remediating it if required, and the *buyer* must indemnify the *seller* in respect of all such liability.

22. Service charge

22.1 This condition applies where the *lot* is sold subject to *tenancies* that include service charge provisions.

22.2 No apportionment is to be made at *completion* in respect of service charges.

22.3 Within two months after *completion* the *seller* must provide to the *buyer* a detailed service charge account for the service charge year current on *completion* showing:

(a) payments on account of service charge received from each tenant;

(b) service charge expenditure attributable to each *tenancy*;

(c) any irrecoverable service charge expenditure.

22.4 In respect of each *tenancy*, if the service charge account shows that:

(a) payments on account exceed attributable service charge expenditure, the *seller* must pay to the *buyer* an amount equal to the excess when it provides the service charge account;

(b) attributable service charge expenditure exceeds payments on account, the *buyer* must use all reasonable endeavours to recover the shortfall from the tenant at the next service charge reconciliation date and pay the amount so recovered to the *seller* within five *business days* of receipt in cleared funds.

22.5 In respect of irrecoverable service charge expenditure the *seller* must bear any incurred before *completion* (apportioned up to and including the *actual completion date*) and the buyer must bear any incurred after the *actual completion date*. Any necessary monetary adjustment is to be made within five *business days* of the *seller* providing the service charge account to the *buyer*.

22.6 If the *seller* holds any reserve or sinking fund on account of future service charge expenditure:

(a) the *seller* must assign it (including any interest earned on it) to the *buyer* on *completion*;

(b) the *buyer* must covenant with the *seller* to hold it in accordance with the terms of the *tenancies* and to indemnify the *seller* if it does not do so.

23. Rent reviews

23.1 This condition applies where the *lot* is sold subject to a *tenancy* under which a rent review due on or before the *actual completion date* has not been agreed or determined.

Figure 3.1 Common auction conditions (continued)

23.2 The *seller* may continue negotiations or rent review proceedings but may not agree the level of the revised rent or commence rent review proceedings without the written consent of the *buyer*, such consent not to be unreasonably withheld.

23.3 Following *completion*, the *buyer* must complete rent review negotiations or proceedings as soon as reasonably practicable but may not agree the level of the revised rent without the written consent of the *seller*, such consent not to be unreasonably withheld.

23.4 The *seller* must:

(a) give to the *buyer* full details of all rent review negotiations and proceedings, including copies of all correspondence and other papers;

(b) use all reasonable endeavours to substitute the *buyer* for the *seller* in any rent review proceedings.

23.5 The *seller* and the *buyer* are to keep each other informed of the progress of the rent review and have regard to any proposals the other makes in relation to it.

23.6 When the rent review has been agreed or determined the *buyer* must account to the *seller* for any increased rent and interest recovered from the tenant which relates to the *seller*'s period of ownership within five *business days* of receipt of cleared funds.

23.7 If a rent review is agreed or determined before *completion* but the increased rent and any interest recoverable from the tenant has not been received by *completion*, the increased rent and any interest recoverable is to be treated as *arrears*.

23.8 The *seller* and the *buyer* are to bear their own costs in relation to rent review negotiations and proceedings.

24. Tenancy renewals

24.1 This condition applies where the tenant under a *tenancy* has the right to remain in occupation under Part II of the Landlord and Tenant Act 1954, and references to notices and proceedings are to notices and proceedings under that Act.

24.2 Where practicable, without exposing the *seller* to liability or penalty, the *seller* must not without the written consent of the *buyer* (which the *buyer* must not unreasonably withhold) serve or respond to any notice or begin or continue any proceedings.

24.3 The *seller* must notify the *buyer* of any notices

served and act as the *buyer* reasonably directs in relation to those notices.

24.4 Following *completion* the *buyer* must:

(a) with the co-operation of the *seller* take immediate steps to substitute itself as a party to any proceedings;

(b) use all reasonable endeavours to conclude any proceedings or negotiations for the renewal of the *tenancy* and the determination of any interim rent, as soon as reasonably practicable, at the best rent or rents reasonably obtainable and, in the case of the renewed *tenancy*, for a term which begins on the day after the term of the old *tenancy* expires;

(c) if any increased rent is recovered from the tenant (whether as interim rent or under the renewed *tenancy*) account to the *seller* for the part of that increase that relates to the *seller*'s period of ownership of the *lot* within five *business days* of receipt of cleared funds.

24.5 The *seller* and the *buyer* are to bear their own costs in relation to the renewal of the *tenancy* and any proceedings relating to this.

25. Warranties

25.1 Available warranties are listed in the *special conditions*.

25.2 Where a warranty is assignable the *seller* must:

(a) on *completion* assign it to the *buyer* and give notice of assignment to the person who gave the warranty;

(b) apply for, and the *seller* and the *buyer* must use all reasonable endeavours to obtain, any consent to assign that is required. If consent has not been obtained by *completion*, the warranty must be assigned within five *business days* after the consent has been obtained.

25.3 If a warranty is not assignable, the *seller* must on *completion*:

(a) hold the warranty on trust for the *buyer*;

(b) at the *buyer*'s cost comply with such of the lawful instructions of the *buyer* in relation to the warranty as do not place the *seller* in breach of its terms or expose the *seller* to any liability or penalty.

26. No assignment

The *buyer* must not assign, mortgage or

Figure 3.1 Common auction conditions (continued)

otherwise transfer or part with the whole or any part of the *buyer*'s interest under this *contract*.

27. Notices and other communications

27.1 All communications, including notices, must be in writing. Communication to or by the *seller* or the *buyer* may be given to or by their solicitors.

27.2 If a communication is delivered by hand or is otherwise proved to have been received, then it is given when delivered or received. If delivered or received after 1700 hours on a *business day*, it is to be treated as received on the next *business day*.

27.3 If a communication is to be relied on without proof of its receipt, it must be sent by first-class registered or recorded delivery post to the address of the person to whom it is to be given as specified in the *sale memorandum*. Such a communication will be treated as received on the second *business day* after it has been posted.

28. Contracts (Rights of Third Parties) Act 1999

The *contract* is enforceable only by the *seller* and the *buyer* and (if applicable) their successors in title and, to the extent permitted by the *conditions*, by the *auctioneers*.

SPECIAL CONDITIONS

Lot number

Brief description of the lot

Name and address of the seller

Undisclosed. To be identified in the *sale memorandum*.

Name, address and reference of the seller's solicitors

Title

Freehold
Leasehold brief description of terms of lease

Registered or unregistered?

Registered at name of land registry
With quality of title
Title number

Unregistered commencing with describe root of title

Title guarantee

Full title guarantee
Limited title guarantee
No title guarantee, for such right and title as the *seller* may have

Deposit

Ten per cent of the *price* plus *VAT* to be held as stakeholder agent for the *seller*

Interest rate

per cent over base rate from time to time

Agreed completion date

Date

VAT

VAT is payable
The sale is a transfer of a going concern
The *seller* has not made a *VAT election*

Insurance

The *seller* is to insure and any refund of insurance payments is to be made to the tenants

The *buyer* is to insure

Vacant or let?

The sale is with vacant possession
The sale is subject to the *tenancies* listed in the tenancy schedule

Rights sold with the lot

None
Details

Exclusions from the sale

None
Details

Reservations to the seller

None
Details

What the sale is subject to

The matters set out in the *general conditions* and list existing covenants and encumbrances and any new ones to be created on sale

Amendments to the general conditions

None
The following conditions replace the *general conditions* of the same number
Details

Figure 3.1 Common auction conditions (continued)

Extra special conditions

None

Details

Transfer

The prescribed form of *transfer* is annexed
The *transfer* is to contain the following provisions:

Capital allowances

There are none
Capital allowances are available in respect of the following items, to which the value attributed is

Maintenance agreements

There are no maintenance agreements
Details of maintenance agreements are:

TUPE

There are no employees to which *TUPE* applies
Details of the contracts of employment for those employees to whom *TUPE* applies are:

Environmental

General condition 23 (Environmental) applies
The following reports have been supplied by the *seller*:

Warranties

The following warranties are to be assigned to or held in trust for the *buyer*:

SALE MEMORANDUM

Date

Name and address of seller

Name and address of buyer

The lot

The price (excluding any VAT)

Deposit paid

The *seller* agrees to sell and the *buyer* agrees to buy the lot for the price. This agreement is subject to the *conditions* so far as they apply to the *lot*.

We acknowledge receipt of the deposit.

Signed by the buyer

Signed by us as agent for the seller

The buyer's solicitors are

Name

Address

Contact

TENANCY SCHEDULE

The lot is sold subject to and with the benefit of the tenancies listed below:

Property	Date	Original landlord and tenant	Current tenant	Term	Current rent

Figure 3.1 Common auction conditions (continued)   Reproduced by kind permission of the Royal Institution of Chartered Surv

SPECIAL CONDITIONS OF SALE

AS TO LOT 1

4a-18b Keneme Drive, Barnet, Herts.

Solicitors: **Taylor Walton, Hart House, 6 London Road, St. Albans, Herts.** AL1 1NG Telephone: 01727 845245 (Ref. KNM).

1   The Property consists of:

(1)   FIRSTLY All that Freehold Property known as 4A and 4B and 6A and 6B Keneme Drive Chipping Barnet in Greater London and

(2)   SECONDLY All that Freehold Property known as 8A 8B 10A and 10B Keneme Drive Chipping Barnet Greater London and

(3)   THIRDLY All that Freehold Property known as 12A and 12B and 14A and 14B Keneme Drive Chipping Barnet Greater London and FOURTHLY All that Freehold Property known as 16A and 16B 18A and 18B Keneme Drive Chipping Barnet Greater London

2   Title to the Property FIRSTLY described is registered with Title Absolute under Title No. P162341 and Title to the Property SECONDLY described is registered at H.M. Land Registry with Title Absolute under Title No. NGL312988 and as to the Property THIRDLY described is registered at H.M. Land Registry with Title Absolute under Title No. NGL312276 and as to the Property FOURTHLY described at H.M. Land Registry with Title Absolute under Title No. NGL312777.

3   The Property FIRSTLY described is sold subject to and with the benefit of Entries Numbers 1 to 3 inclusive of the Charges Register of the said Title

and as to the Property SECONDLY described subject to Entries Numbers 1 to 3 of the Charges Register of the said Title

and as to the Property THIRDLY described subject to Entry No 1 of the Charges Register and as to the Property FOURTHLY described subject to Entry No 1 of the Charges Register of the said Title.

4.1   The Property FIRSTLY described is sold subject to and with the benefit of the following Leases:

(i)   4A - a Lease dated 23 May 1967 made between Wodehouse Estates Limited (1) John Edward Green (2) for a term of 99 years from 25 March 1967 at a yearly rent of twelve pounds twelve shillings.

(ii)   4B - a Lease dated 14 October 1966 made between Wodehouse Estates Limited (1) Sonia Elizabeth Pounds (2) for a term of 99 years from 25 March 1966 at a yearly rent of twelve pounds twelve shillings.

(iii)   6A - a Lease dated 6 September 1989 made between Ronald John Cawley Roffe Richard Jeremy Golland (1) Grainne Cecilia Jupin (2) for a term of 120 years from 25 March 1989 at a yearly rent of fifty pounds rising to four hundred pounds.

(iv)   6B - a Lease dated 30 September 1971 made between Ronald John Cawley Roffe Jack Alexander Allerton (1) William George Edwards Marion Patricia Edwards (2) for a term of 99 years from 25 March 1970 at a yearly rent of fifteen pounds seventy five pence.

4.2.1   The Property SECONDLY described is sold subject to and with the benefit of the following Leases:

(i)   8A - a Lease dated 24 May 1957 made between Frederick John Randall George Frederick Randall (1) John Porter Stretton (2) for a term of 99 years from 25 March 1957 at a yearly rent of five pounds five shillings.

(ii)   10B - a Lease dated 22 June 1983 made between Ronald John Cawley Roffe Richard Jeremy Golland (1) Susan Elspeth Laithwaite (2) for a term of 99 years from 25 March 1983 at a yearly rent of twenty five pounds rising to seventy five pounds.

4.2.2   The Property SECONDLY described is sold subject to and with the benefit of the following Regulated Tenancies:

(i)   to L M Piper with a Registered Rent of £38.00 per week effective from 13 August 1990.

(ii)   to F L Harding with a Registered Rent of £33.00 per week effective from 13 August 1990.

4.3   The Property THIRDLY described is sold subject to and with the benefit of the following Leases:

(i)   12A - a Lease dated 25 May 1984 made between Ronald John Cawley Roffe Richard Jeremy Golland (1) Paul Alexander Conway (2) for a term of 99 years from 25 March 1984 at a yearly rent of twenty five pounds rising to seventy five pounds.

(ii)   12B - a Lease dated 21 May 1971 made between Ronald John Cawley Roffe Jack Alexander Allerton (1) Alan Bell (2) for a term of 99 years from 25 March 1970 at a yearly rent of fifteen pounds and seventy five pounds.

(iii)   14A - a Lease dated 18 October 1965 made between Wodehouse Estates Limited (1) Martin Charles Curran and Patricia Curran (2) for a term of 99 years from 24 June 1965 at a yearly rent of twelve pounds twelve shillings.

(iv)   14B - a Lease dated 26 April 1985 made between Ronald John Cawley Roffe Richard Jeremy Golland (1) Susan Carol St James (2) for a term of 99 years from 25 March 1984 at a yearly rent of fifty pounds rising to one hundred pounds.

4.4   The Property FOURTHLY described is sold subject to and with the benefit of the following Leases:

(i)   16A - a Lease dated 14 August 1970 made between Ronald John Cawley Roffe Jack Alexander Allerton (1) Geoffrey Henry Howard and Jean Howard (2) for a term of 99 years from 25 March 1970 at a yearly rent of fifteen pounds fifteen shillings.

(ii)   16B - a Lease dated 24 October 1977 made between Ronald John Cawley Roffe Richard Jeremy Golland (1) Trevor William Skinner and Angela Joy Booth (2) for a term of 99 years from 25 March 1970 at a yearly rent of fifteen pounds seventy five pence.

(iii)   18B - a Lease dated 24 June 1991 made between Ronald John Cawley Roffe Richard Jeremy Golland (1) Nicola Le Moine and Raymond Vella (2) for a term of 125 years from 25 March 1989 at a yearly rent of seventy five pounds rising to four hundred pounds.

AND

18B - a Regulated Tenancy to J H Simpson with a Registered Rent of £33.00 per week effective from 13 August 2000.

5   The Vendor's Solicitors are Messrs Taylor Walton of Hart House 6 London Road St Albans Herts. AL1 1NG Telephone No 01727 845245 reference KNM). Copies of the Title Deeds, recent Local Authority Search Certificate and replies to Standard Form Enquiries before Contract are available for inspection at the offices of the Vendor's Solicitors in accordance with General Condition X.

6   Vacant Possession of the Property will not be given on completion.

7   The Vendor is not aware of any written Tenancy Agreements in respect of the Regulated Tenancies and the Purchaser shall not raise any objection or requisition thereto but shall accept as conclusive evidence a copy of the Rent Register which is available for inspection at the offices of the Vendor's Solicitors.

8   The Vendor has served no notice of disposal on the Tenants in accordance with Section 5 of the Landlord & Tenant Act 1987 and the Purchaser takes subject to the Tenant's rights under such Act. The Purchaser shall not raise any objection or requisition thereto but shall complete the Purchase of the Property notwithstanding that the Vendor has not served such Notices. Forthwith after Completion of the Purchase the Purchaser shall give Notice to all Tenants in accordance with Section 3 of the Landlord & Tenant Act 1988 (as amended by Section 50 of the Landlord & Tenant Act 1987) and shall indemnify the Vendor against any damages costs claims or other liabilities falling upon the Vendor by virtue of any delay or failure to do so.

9   The Purchaser shall in the Transfer (which shall be executed in duplicate) covenant with the Vendor to observe and perform the covenants and conditions contained in the Leases on the part of the Landlord and to keep the Vendor's estate and effects fully and effectually indemnified from all future costs claims demands and expenses in respect of any breach or non-observance thereof and if the Purchaser shall be a limited company it shall procure that at least one director of good financial standing personally covenants with the Vendor in the manner aforesaid.

AS TO LOT 2

75 Ashurst Road, North Finchley, London N12

Solicitors: **Taylor Walton, Hart House, 6 London Road, St. Albans, Herts.** AL1 1NG Telephone: 01727 845245 (Ref. KNM).

1   The Property consists of FIRSTLY All that Freehold Property known as 75 Ashurst Road Friern Barnet in the London Borough of Barnet and SECONDLY the Freehold passageway at the rear of 75/91 (odd numbers) Ashurst Road Friern Barnet in the London Borough of Barnet.

2   Title to the Property FIRSTLY described is registered at H.M. Land Registry with Freehold Title Absolute under Title No. MX193617 and as to the Property SECONDLY described Title to the Property is registered at H.M. Land Registry with Title Absolute under Title No. MX318831.

3   The Property FIRSTLY described is sold subject to and with the benefit of Entries Numbers 1 and 2 of the Charges Register of the said Title and as to the Property SECONDLY described subject to the Entries Numbers 1 to 10 inclusive of the Charges Register of the said Title.

4   As to the Property SECONDLY described the Purchaser shall raise no requisition or objection regarding the absence of the Conveyance dated 13 January 1970 referred to in Entry No 1 of the Charges Register.

5   The Property FIRSTLY described is sold subject to and with the benefit of a Regulated Tenancy to P E Watson with a Registered Rent of £210.00 per month effective from 13 August 1999.

Figure 3.2   Sample auctioneer's special conditions

Key point

You should always check to make sure that before you bid, you have seen and understand any conditions that apply to the purchase. All these conditions form the contract on which any lot is knocked down to you.

What do the general conditions mean?

The general conditions (as shown in Figure 3.1) now generally follow the recently introduced Royal Institution of Chartered Surveyors Standard General Conditions but some auctioneers are still using older conditions and therefore careful perusal is necessary. The later conditions are supposed to be written so that they are free of jargon and in understandable English. Major points to note are:

1.   the seller sells the property subject to any matters affecting it whether they are discoverable or not, either on inspection or through a local search against the property.

     For example, if the property has dry rot and you buy it, you are presumed to know about that rot. If the property has a compulsory purchase order against it, which is something that shows up on a local search, **and the vendor does not know about it**, then you are presumed to know about it.

2.   A deposit of ten per cent is payable on exchange of contracts. The general conditions will usually specify a minimum figure. For example, ten per cent or a fixed sum – often £1,500 – whichever is the greater.

3.   Risk of deterioration/disrepair should be the seller's responsibility, but the general conditions will usually alter this so the purchaser has to insure the property from the date when contracts are exchanged.

Hidden terms are no excuse to cancel a contract

4.   The purchaser is presumed to have investigated the title prior to the exchange of contracts. If the title has an oddity in it, which you discover after the contracts have been exchanged, then you cannot use this to cancel the contract. You are presumed to have examined the title

documents and know about the peculiarity. Examples of peculiarities that can arise are: someone other than the owner is claiming title to a part of the property or there is a covenant preventing you developing the site without consent from a third party.

5. There is a timetable laid down for completion. For example, no later than 2.30pm on a working day four weeks after the contract has been exchanged.

6. The purchase price must be paid by cleared funds, so a personal or building society cheque is not acceptable, whereas a banker's draft is.

Conditions about the bidding and formal paperwork

1. The owner can bid for his own lot up to the reserve or the auctioneer can do this on his behalf.

2. The bidder has formalities to complete before and after bidding. For example:

   • completing a form giving your name and address;

   • signing the memorandum of contract, which is a record of the terms on which the purchaser has bought at the fall of the gavel. (The memorandum of contract is discussed in greater detail on page 94 and an example is shown in Figure 4.2 on page 97.)

3. Bids are exclusive of VAT.

4. If the bidder fails to sign the memorandum of contract, then the auctioneer may do this on his behalf.

What do the special conditions mean?

The special conditions deal with the following:

1. The owner's identity and whether the property is being **sold** with or without vacant possession as owner, trustee or mortgagee.

2. The identity of the property. Strictly speaking, this will be found under the heading 'Particulars' but 'Particulars' tend to be presented with 'Special Conditions'.

3. Any new covenants the purchaser is to enter into with the owner (or any other party) on completion. You are most likely to come across this where a lot forms part of a larger piece of land owned by the vendor.

Special conditions imposed by a vendor

For example: A private landowner owns fields to the rear of his house. He puts these in an auction hoping that a builder will buy them. However, he wishes to protect his own comfort and so the special conditions provide that whoever buys the site must:

- erect a large fence and fast tall-growing conifers to screen off the development;

- only build private houses of a type to be approved by him;

- not use the new buildings other than as private residences.

4. Any tenancies affecting the lot.

5. Any rights the owner reserves.

    Taking the same example as in 3 above of a sale of land for development, the owner would probably want to reserve all rights of light and air so his house enjoys the level of sunshine it currently has.

Where an owner has a number of similar lots with similar concerns, many of these points may be covered in the catalogue as 'Additional Conditions'.

Are these special conditions not unlawful?

The Unfair Contract Terms Act 1977 prevents a person drawing up an agreement from inserting terms which are unfair. However, this Act does not apply to contracts for the sale of land so, **no matter how onerous the contract is, the purchaser and the owner are obliged to abide by its terms**. There are two exceptions to this principle:

1. If an interest rate or penal arrangement for payment of the price is too onerous, it may be struck out by a court as being contrary to rules in equity on penalty clauses. These are separate from the 1977 Act and are unlikely to apply to most auction contracts you will come across.

Circumstances that may allow you to cancel a contract

2. If a seller makes a misrepresentation about the property prior to the contract and then in the contract itself disclaims any liability for that misrepresentation, the disclaimer may be unlawful. You may be able to withdraw from the contract if you have placed reliance on the misrepresentation the seller has made, or sue for damages. It depends on how the disclaimer is phrased.

For example, an owner advises a purchaser that the property has planning permission for six semi-detached buildings. In fact, the planning permission is for two detached houses. In the information pack available in the auction room, there is a copy of the planning permission. There is also a set of replies to the standard enquiries which a purchaser would normally make before exchanging contracts and these reiterate that the property enjoys planning permission for six semi-detached houses. The successful bidder does not bother to read any of the information pack, nor does he speak with the auctioneer or the owner's solicitors before bidding.

Can he withdraw from the contract?

The bidder may be able to withdraw in the following circumstances:

(a) If the special conditions do not refer to the planning permission or indicate that the purchaser is presumed to buy with knowledge of the property or its use.

(b) If the special conditions do not refer to the planning permission but state:

The purchaser acknowledges that it has not entered into this agreement in reliance upon representations made by or on behalf of the vendor other than such written representations as the vendor's solicitor may have made and then save only as to such (if any) as were not susceptible of independent verification by inspection and survey of the property, by enquiry of the local authority, the local planning authority and any other

Lot 68, The Lodge, The Bourne, Southgate, London N14, sold for £116,000.

competent authority of by inspection of documents made available to the purchaser before this agreement (whether or not the purchaser has made such inspection survey search or enquiry).

In this case the owner has misrepresented information but this clause tries to prevent the purchaser claiming he has relied on that.

Does this clause work and is it lawful? The property world believes it does work and is legitimate. Usage of this clause (and similar) is widespread – **bidders beware!**

Damages will not be payable

In this example, the estate agent or auctioneer may be criminally liable under the Property Misdescriptions Act 1991 for making a misleading statement. But do remember, this does not give you any right to damages.

If you can't stand the heat, get out of the kitchen!

At this stage, before the auction, the owner is making all the rules. The buyer has no opportunity to change them and no alternative but to purchase under the conditions that are laid down.

Before bidding, every potential purchaser should make very sure that all the conditions (in whatever guise) have been read, checked and are acceptable. Since conditions are frequently clothed in 'legalese' you should take your own solicitor's advice about the significance of any conditions – particularly those that appear at all unusual.

Key point

If the conditions make the property 'too hot', whatever sort of bargain it appears, don't bid at the auction.

Hidden pitfalls to watch out for

Major arrears

Frequently the sellers of tenanted properties find that their tenants do not pay as regularly as they should. Once they have sold a property, it is relatively difficult for them to press the tenant (with whom they no longer have regular contact) for outstanding arrears. It is therefore common for a vendor to provide in the contract of sale a clause stating that the purchaser pays a sum over at completion equal to any arrears outstanding. Although this 'balances the books' for the seller, it leaves the buyer in the invidious position of having paid out money in full against the right to collect it back in arrears from the tenants. Those arrears may prove to be uncollectable or it may be necessary to spend a lot of time and money to retrieve from the tenant the cash already paid over to the seller.

Key point

Your responsibility to pay over outstanding arrears to the seller at completion may be revealed in the part of the catalogue that refers to the relevant lot or may only be mentioned in the conditions of sale.

Before bidding on any property where this condition applies, you should make detailed enquiries to establish your chances (and costs) of collecting the outstanding money from tenants. Irregularity in payments may be reflected in the outstanding arrears and it should warn you to check on the past payment record. After such enquiries, you may decide that you should trim the size of your top bid accordingly. Alternatively, you may decide not to buy because the arrears are such that you can have no confidence in the future ability of the tenants you are about to acquire to pay their rent.

Key point

In every case where you are buying a tenanted property, you should be positive before you buy that the actual tenant is in occupation of the property and has not 'done a moonlight flit'. An inspection just before the auction is always wise, whether the property is tenanted or not.

Local authority charges, public health and other notices

Where the local search reveals a local authority charge against a property, you should expect the vendor to pay off that charge at completion. You should ensure that the conditions of sale provide for this. If they do not, reduce your highest bid by the amount of the charges that you will have to pay on owning the property.

Are you required to carry out repairs?

The local search may reveal other public health and similar notices which can range from requirements to carry out certain repairs, right through to closure or demolition notices. Auctioneers encourage their clients to reveal the existence of such notices. They are usually mentioned in the sale catalogue or amendment sheets or by the auctioneer (if he is aware of them) at the time of sale. Nevertheless, you should not rely on this. Instead, you or your solicitor should ensure, by suitable enquiry to the local authority in which the property is situated, that no notices or charges are outstanding.

They should reveal if any compulsory purchase orders are in existence or pending and indicate how the property is affected by any planning proposals, warning you of any similar drawbacks to the lot.

Do not take plan sizes for granted

As plans pass between owners, solicitors and auctioneers, they are often subjected to copying and recopying. Sometimes, plans are deliberately shrunk to fit on pages for faxing, printing or other use.

Plans reproduced in the auctioneer's catalogue should never be relied upon to be accurate, even if a written scale is shown on the plan. Sometimes the auctioneer's catalogue includes a saving clause, acknowledging that plans may not be accurate. Omission of this clause from the catalogue does not mean that the plan sizes can be relied upon. If you have an opportunity to check the actual size of any land or property that you are buying, you should do so or, at worst, take suitable measurements and make your own calculations from an original of the Ordnance Survey.

View, view and view again

Viewing any lot you are thinking of buying should not be difficult. Almost invariably the auctioneer's catalogue will indicate the viewing arrangements. Occasionally, specific days and times for viewing are shown where the lot particulars are printed. Alternatively, viewing may be by direct arrangement with the auctioneer's office or by collecting the keys where it is appropriate. Occasionally, the auctioneers can only arrange viewing subject to the consent of the tenants. Whatever means of inspecting the property is provided, you should take advantage of it.

Key point

If a full inspection of your lot is reasonably feasible but is refused, you should be highly suspicious and make your decision whether or not to bid accordingly.

Financing the purchase

Will I need an accountant's advice?

An accountant may be needed at the very early stages for more general than specific advice. It is not the purpose of this book to give detailed help on accountancy and taxation matters.

Nevertheless, you will need to make an early decision once you have become interested in a property, whether you are going to buy and sell personally or through a private company or whether, by appropriate planning, you can take advantage of schemes such as self-administered pension funds, overseas companies and other measures to reduce your tax liability.

The advice and assistance that an accountant can provide you with in terms of accountancy and taxation matters depends very much on the use to which the property is to be put.

Tax allowances for investment properties

If the property is to be rented, then such income is taxable under Schedule A, unless the property is let as furnished accommodation in which case tax is charged under Schedule D, Case VI. A person is charged the tax under Schedule A by reference to the rents or receipts to which he becomes entitled in the tax year concerned. Payments that are actually made during the chargeable period may be deducted if they fall within the definition of 'permitted deductions'. These include maintenance repairs, insurance and other services which the owner was obliged to provide and for which he received no separate payment. As far as maintenance or repairs are concerned there is a whole host of types of expenditure which are normally allowable, including interior and exterior repairs and decorations, cleaning, upkeep of gardens and the costs of rent collection.

47 Tuel Lane, Sowerby Bridge, West Yorkshire, sold at auction for £12,500.

Capital allowances may also be claimed in respect of plant and machinery belonging to the landlord. These will include items of office equipment such as computers and machinery that have become part of the building, such as a lift.

Interest on a loan to purchase a property or carry out improvements may be set against Schedule A income. Where the qualifying interest exceeds the amount of Schedule A income, the excess may be carried forward and set against subsequent years' Schedule A income. Tax relief is available on interest paid on a loan to purchase an investment property provided that certain conditions are satisfied including:

- The property must be let at a commercial rent.

- In any 52-week period, the property must be let for more than 26 weeks and when not being let, the property must be available either for letting or prevented from being available because of construction work or repairs.

- The property must be situated in the UK or the Republic of Ireland.

Tax relief for holiday property

If the property being let represents furnished holiday accommodation, then it may be treated as a trade, provided certain conditions are satisfied, including the following:

- It must be let on a commercial basis.

- It must be let as furnished accommodation.

- It must be available for commercial letting to the public as holiday accommodation for at least 140 days in a 12-month period.

- It must be let for at least 70 such days.

- It must not normally be occupied by the same person for more than 31 consecutive days at any time during a period of seven months within the 12-month period.

If a property is treated as being let as furnished holiday accommodation, then interest on loans used to purchase the property and finance the lettings will qualify as an expense. If this gives rise to a loss for tax purposes, it may be offset against other taxable income. In addition, equipment and furniture and fittings may attract capital allowances. Profits from furnished holiday lettings may qualify as 'relevant earnings' for the purposes of personal pension contributions and retirement annuity premiums. For Capital Gains Tax purposes, rollover and retirement relief may also be available.

Double your exemption from Capital Gains Tax

On disposal of the investment property, Capital Gains Tax may be payable on the chargeable gains arising. However, an annual exemption can be deducted from the chargeable gains, which for the Income Tax year 2007/08 is £9,200 for each individual. If husband and wife jointly own the property, then each is entitled to this annual exemption against their proportion of the chargeable gain. It may, therefore, be advantageous to consider acquiring the property jointly between the husband and wife to benefit from this exemption. One further advantage of this is that any rental income assessable is divided between the husband and wife for Income Tax purposes. As each spouse is assessed separately for tax purposes, then subject to any other taxable income, each is entitled to set their personal allowances against the rental income. Any remaining liability is subject to the ten per cent or 22 per cent tax rate band with the remainder chargeable to higher-rate tax at 40 per cent. In this way, personal allowances and lower rate tax bands can be utilised by both spouses.

The consequences of a company acquiring the property as an investment need to be examined carefully by your accountant, as there are significant differences in the taxation treatment of companies and individuals. For example, the annual exemptions for Capital Gains Tax previously mentioned are not available to companies.

It is also possible for the commercial property to be acquired by a small self-administered pension scheme which is linked to the company, provided certain criteria are met. The Inland Revenue requirements regarding such pension schemes will need to be discussed in detail with your accountant; however, they do offer the opportunity to mitigate the incidence of tax both on a corporate and personal level.

The VAT minefield

VAT on property is a minefield. At present, most properties are sold exclusive of VAT. However, the ramifications of this tax are extensive and they should be discussed in detail with your accountant.

Key point

The acquisition of property as an investment involves both tax planning opportunities and pitfalls. It is essential that you discuss the matter in detail with your accountant before undertaking the purchase.

The deposit and balance

It is important to remember that on the day of the auction you will be required to make a deposit of ten per cent of the purchase price or a specified minimum sum. You must ensure that you are able to pay both this deposit and the balance of the purchase price 28 days later. Table 3.2 shows the different deposit amounts to be paid for sample purchase prices.

If you are using a finance broker, bank or building society to provide the funds, you should have the financing agreed, lot by lot, prior to the auction. The finance house will want to be satisfied that the valuation of the property is acceptable to them.

Price	Deposit	Balance
£350	£350	Nil
£500	£500	Nil

£1,000	£1,000	Nil
£3,000	£1,500	£1,500
£5,000	£1,500	£3,500
£8,500	£1,500	£7,000
£12,000	£1,500	£10,500
£20,000	£2,000	£18,000
£30,000	£3,000	£27,000
£50,000	£5,000	£45,000
£100,000	£10,000	£90,000
£150,000	£15,000	£135,000
£250,000	£25,000	£225,000
£500,000	£50,000	£450,000
£1,000,000	£100,000	£900,000

Table 3.2 The purchase price, deposit and balance payable

What other costs should I allow for?

You have already planned to meet the professional fees for your valuer, your solicitor and your accountant. If your bid is successful, you will have to pay the full conveyancing fees to your solicitor and if your purchase is above the relevant level, government stamp duty at one per cent of the purchase price for residential properties over £125,000; between £125,001 and £250,000 - one per cent; between £250,001 and £500,000 - three per cent; and over £500,001 - four per cent. There are dispensations on stamp duty in certain disadvantaged areas. In the April 2009 budget the minimum level at which stamp duty becomes payable will continue at £175,000 and remain unchanged until the end of the year.

The auctioneer's administration charges

As government bureaucracy has grown, so have auctioneers' on-costs. Many auction houses have not hesitated to pass these on to purchasers, payable at the time contracts are exchanged. Sometimes they are added onto the deposit cheque, but more often than not they are asked for in a separate cheque payable direct to the auction firm. These fees vary and usually have VAT added. Amounts between £200 and £600 can be expected. You can find the requirement to pay and the amount in a note in the auction brochure. Apart from these buyers' premiums, it would not be surprising if auctioneers will soon start expecting buyers to meet the cost of Home Information Packs as well.

The vendor's search fees

Almost invariably, the modern terms and conditions of sale make the purchaser meet the seller's costs of obtaining and providing the details of the local authority searches. The vendor, perhaps justifiably, feels that the searches have been obtained for the benefit of the purchaser. The buyer usually pays for these at completion. Amounts vary slightly from local authority to local authority, but they are usually in the range of £75 to £150.

Contributions to the vendor's legal conveyancing costs

This a recent element in a few auction add-on costs. Again, look for the imposition (and in my view it certainly is an imposition by greedy vendors) in the auctioneer's brochure, or in the prior oral announcements or in the amendment sheet. Different vendors impose different contributions, but they usually range from £350 to £750 per lot and will usually incur additional VAT. The whole payment is usually demanded and payable at completion.

Fees charged by government bodies

These bodies frequently charge an additional fee – often quoted as being for their surveyors' fees. This amount is usually due at completion, but can be demanded at the deposit stage. Once again, you can find reference to it in the auction brochure. A charge of one per cent or 1.5 per cent of the purchase price is very common.

How should purchasers treat all these potential add-ons? In my view you should beware of the total costs for the lot you are hoping to buy in your final bills. Vendors seem to consider these extras as a bonus or an additional benefit, but it seems to me that any wise purchaser will discount his final bid to take account of them.

The Purchase Price £	Deposit £	Balance £	Auctioneer's Admin Fee & Local Searches £	VAT if Payable on Purchase Price £	Surveyors' Fees Full Structural survey £	Plus VAT £	Solicitors Attending £	Solicitors' Fees £	Plus VAT £	Stamp Duty £	Your Expenses £	First Insurance Initial Repairs £	Making Secure £	Finance House £	Total £
£350	350	0	260	61	0	0	0	250	44	0	150	200	200	0	1,515
£500	500	0	260	88	0	0	0	250	44	0	150	200	200	0	1,692
£1,000	1,000	0	260	175	0	0	0	250	44	0	150	200	200	0	2,279
£3,000	1,500	1,500	260	525	200	35	175	325	57	0	150	200	200	0	5,127
£5,000	1,500	3,500	260	875	200	35	175	325	57	0	150	200	200	0	7,477
£8,500	1,500	7,000	260	1,488	250	44	175	325	57	0	150	200	200	0	11,649
£12,000	1,500	10,500	260	2,100	250	44	200	400	70	0	250	250	300	250	16,374
£20,000	2,000	18,000	260	3,500	300	53	200	400	70	0	250	250	300	250	25,833
£30,000	3,000	27,000	260	5,250	300	53	200	400	70	0	250	300	300	400	37,783
£50,000	5,000	45,000	260	8,750	400	70	250	450	79	0	250	350	400	600	61,859
£100,000	10,000	90,000	260	17,500	400	70	250	450	79	0	250	450	600	1,200	121,509
£150,000	15,000	135,000	310	26,250	500	88	250	500	88	1,500	350	450	800	1,800	182,886
£250,000	25,000	225,000	310	43,750	600	105	250	550	96	2,500	450	2,500	1,000	2,500	304,611
£500,000	50,000	450,000	400	87,500	800	140	300	650	114	15,000	550	4,000	1,500	4,000	614,954
£1,000,000	100,000	900,000	450	175,000	1,200	210	300	800	140	40,000	600	8,000	3,500	5,000	1,235,200

Table 3.3 *Total purchase costs*

Your cash flow is now fully prepared for the ten per cent deposit payable at the auction, for the balance of the purchase price, plus VAT if it applies, 28 days later and for all your other costs. Table 3.3 lists the possible total costs incurred for buying a property priced between £350 and £1,000,000. Depending on the individual property, there may be other costs to pay that are not mentioned here, but it gives a useful guide.

Table 3.4 is a purchase costs checklist giving all the items for which you might have to budget.

- [ ] Deposit
- [ ] Balance
- [ ] VAT on purchase price
- [ ] Credit to vendor for tenants' arrears
- [ ] Surveyors' fees and VAT
- [ ] Professional fees and VAT for attending at auction (if appropriate)
- [ ] Auctioneer's administrative charges
- [ ] VAT on add-on costs
- [ ] Vendor's legal conveyancing charges where made
- [ ] Finance house commitment fee and VAT
- [ ] Solicitors' fees and VAT
- [ ] Local search fees
- [ ] Home Information Packs
- [ ] Stamp duty (see page 77)
- [ ] Vendor's fees and costs (if charged)
- [ ] Repayment of grants
- [ ] Planning application fees
- [ ] Building regulation application fees
- [ ] Covenant buy-out
- [ ] First insurance premium
- [ ] Contractor's bill for making secure/initial repairs
  Champagne

Table 3.4 Purchase costs checklist

Financial catches to watch out for

- Remember that finance houses frequently require a commitment fee, not to mention their interest charges and their capital repayments.

- As you interpret the conditions of sale, make sure you know what amount you could have to pay for items such as tenants' arrears.

- Ensure that you and your solicitor are aware of any outstanding local authority charges or grants. These can often be made the responsibility of the purchaser to repay.

- If you are hoping to explore the planning potential of your purchase, remember that planning and building regulation applications may require the payment of a fee to the local authority.

- Be sure that you have made allowance to buy out any covenants if such a procedure is appropriate. For example, if you are buying a site for development there could be covenants preventing you from carrying out your proposals until the person holding the benefit of these covenants has agreed to your proposals and been paid a sum for his amendment.

- Finally, always leave sufficient margin for the champagne celebration after you have successfully purchased a lot at your price.

CHAPTER 4

Going for your bargain

'I went to an auction a couple of times before to get the feel for it and to see what the prices were like. I thought just before Christmas would be a good time to buy because people haven't got a lot of spare money and have other things on their mind and as it turns out I was proved right.'

Don Lee, buyer of a residential property at auction.

Doing a dummy run

Get the feel for how an auction works

Although you can be armed with the information in this guide and be made aware of what happens in an auction, nothing can be better than experiencing several auctions before you go to the first one at which you intend to bid. Doing a 'dummy run' is highly recommended. Ideally, this should extend way beyond merely calling at one or two auctions to see how matters proceed. Earlier on in the previous chapter, you read the recommendation that you approach your solicitor and accountant at an early stage for the relevant pieces of advice that they can give. You could focus your enquiries to them by indicating a general interest in a lot in an auction during your dummy run. By doing so, you will be able to develop and research the enquiries and questions you will put to them when your 'run' is for real.

Key points for the dummy run

1. Choose a specific lot to focus your interest.

2. List and rehearse the questions you would wish to ask your professional advisers.

3. Visit your dummy property and make a thorough inspection as if you were intending to buy. (You may find that you can discuss it with a surveyor without charge, if you warn him that this is a dummy run but that you are looking to develop mutual business in the future.)

4. Ask the seller's solicitor the questions that your solicitor would put to him.

5. Look at a copy of the local search or ring the relevant local authority if the search is not available.

6. Read carefully the conditions of sale, general and additional conditions and auctioneer's conditions. This will prepare you for similar research when it really matters.

7. Contact the auctioneer's office. Consider having a trial negotiation with them to practise your negotiating skills. Your experience with them in such negotiations may cast a revealing light on their approach and the reality of their guideline figures.

8. To avoid fees, you will probably not wish to ask your solicitors to research the title of the dummy lot.

No play takes place without rehearsal.

Cut out the competition and buy your bargain before auction

'I always try to do a deal beforehand because you never know what opposition you are going to come up against at auction. But you should never show your hand in case it does go to auction. The vendor is generally only going to accept a higher price before the auction.'

Michael Kirby, Chartered Surveyor.

'Chief rents' –

These rents are also known as perpetual annual rent charges which are payable by the owners of freehold land annually. In the main, the rents only exist in the Greater Manchester, Bristol and Channel Isles' districts. The period over which they can now be collected is restricted by statute.

'OPP' –

This is an acronym for 'outline planning permission'.

FRANK R MARSHALL & CO at Nantwich, Apr 7	
Shavington — Green Bank Farm, B5071 Rd. Arable/pasture farm. Hse, 10 rms, 3 attic rms, tradn bdgs, loose boxes, stores, barns. 106.10 a. F, P	400,000
BIGWOOD at Birmingham, Apr 8	
Goostrey — Buckbean Way etc. Chief rents on 57 units at £1,140 pa.	6,000
Holmes Chapel — Danefield Rd etc. Chief rents on 80 units at £1,299 pa.	6,500
DENTON CLARK & CO at Rowton, Apr 14	
Ashton — Gable Cottage, Kelsall Rd. Terr cottage, 2 bed. F, P	66,500
Cuddington — Cuddington Barn, B5069 Rd. Barn with PP conversion to hse, 4 bed, adj cottage, 1 bed. Stables/store. 2.62 a. F, P	65,000
Marbury — School Hse, School Lane. Cottage, 3 bed. Adj bdg plot with OPP 1 dwelling. F, P	60,000
Tilston — Constabulary Cottage, Church Rd. Det cottage, 3 bed. F, P	66,000
Adj garden land, 110 ft x 50 ft. F, P	8,500
Apr 15	
Helsby — Off A56 Chester Rd. Accom pasture, 13.07 a. F, P	52,000
Accom pasture, 10.73 a. F, P	26,000
Accom pasture, 28.54 a. F, P	28,500
Paddocks, 2.99 a. F, P	5,000
Manley — Manley Rd, Riley Bank. Pasture/conservation land, 27.95 a. F, P	35,000
Morley Lane, Dunham Heath. Pasture, 10.02 a. F, P	20,000

Illustration 3. Estates Gazette auction results

Move in before the auction happens!

Negotiating the purchase of a lot before auction is not at all unusual. Do remember that all the steps previously recommended should be undertaken. Before the day of the sale, you may feel confident enough to risk negotiating for the property. Lucky buyers can acquire bargains in this way but they do run the risk of 'disclosing their hand' to the auctioneers and they can be passing the initiative to them. Whether you take up such an initiative is undoubtedly a gamble. Only you can decide whether it is worthwhile in the light of your desire to buy the lot and to beat the competition that might take place on auction day. On the other hand, by revealing your interest so soon, you can lose what would otherwise be a strong position in your bidding at the auction.

Before you start such negotiations you will no doubt have decided how much you wish to pay for the property. If you are endeavouring to buy before auction, this must be either because you wish to buy the property noticeably cheaper than the amount you are ready to pay on auction day, or because you want the lot so badly that you do not want anybody else to have the opportunity to purchase and 'bid you up' on that day. The decision is entirely yours.

Key point

You must realise that disclosing your interest and your figure at this time gives the auctioneer and the seller an opportunity to adjust the reserve and take into account the amount which they believe you are prepared to bid.

Key point

By bidding before the auction you are likely to remove any opportunity of buying the property any cheaper than your pre-auction bid. But this has to be balanced against the advantages of cutting out the competition.

Contracts must be exchanged quickly for pre-auction sales

If you decide to bid before the auction, you must be prepared to negotiate quickly and if your bid is successful, to sign a contract and pay your deposit even faster. The auctioneer will require you to exchange contracts before the auction (and probably by several days in advance). **You have an even greater need for speed.** If you have decided to buy before the auction, you must be aware that there could be other people who have a similar desire to buy early. If, therefore, you have agreed a pre-auction purchase, you should not then leave your solicitor to exchange contracts or memoranda in the normal course of 'legal' time. You should press him to complete his enquiries at top speed and to exchange contracts or memoranda as a matter of urgency. You will have to provide your ten per cent deposit at the time the exchange takes place.

Many auctioneers are willing to allow you to leave your deposit with them and to complete and exchange memoranda or contracts in their office. This will speed the passage of the sale but it is not recommended unless your solicitor is satisfied with his enquiries about the title and background to the property. Only those who want a lot so badly that they are prepared to risk irrevocably committing themselves to a purchase before their solicitor is satisfied should proceed before then. Having exchanged, if you then decide to 'go back' on the purchase, legal sanctions (including loss of your deposit and other responsibilities to meet damages) will follow. The same sanctions apply if you succeed with a bid on the auction day itself and subsequently withdraw. The extent of your likely loss and damages is explained on pages 152–4.

Key point

You must realise that a purchase prior to the auction does not change any of the procedures, responsibilities or actions detailed in this book other than those that relate to attending and bidding at the auction itself.

Buyer's timetable

For most auctions, you will have about a month from the initial advertisement to the auction itself to carry out all your preparations. The following timetable provides a useful guide for buyers on when you need to make the necessary arrangements prior to the auction.

Days Prior To and After the Auction	Action
30	See advertisement and apply for auctioneer's catalogue
28	Receive catalogue
26	First inspection of property Check auctioneer's particulars
25	Instruct valuation surveyor
23	Read and understand the conditions of sale
20	Receive surveyor's report
19	Instruct solicitor Visit accountant Arrange finance

Days Prior To and After the Auction	Action
17	Second inspection of property Assess quality of tenants
6	Consider a pre-auction purchase
5	Check solicitor's report on title Check availability of finance
3	Decide on your maximum bid
1	Final visit to property prior to the sale
Auction day	Attend auction Bid successfully Exchange contracts or memoranda Pay ten per cent deposit (or minimum specified)
1	Insure property Revisit property Check security Meet tenants
1/3	If your lot was withdrawn on the day, negotiate to buy
28	Complete purchase Pay balance of purchase monies Pay stamp duty Pay solicitor's fees

Attending the auction

'You always feel a little apprehensive before you go in. You go in with nothing and come home with something else.'

Michael Roe, buyer of residential properties.

You have picked out your lots, you have done your research, you have spoken to your solicitor, accountant and other advisers and your finance is arranged. You have settled in your own mind the maximum figure you are prepared to bid for the lots you are interested in. Now you are ready to go to your auction. The next sections address the atmosphere, the nature of the auction, details of the procedures you can expect to have to follow and suggests ways you might go about the purchase of your bargain lots.

The following checklist gives the key points you should watch out for at auction. Each one is discussed in depth below.

Auction checklist: For the bargain hunter

1 Wise to attend yourself. ☐

2 Check the etiquette. ☐

3 Follow any registration procedure. ☐

4 Choose a good vantage point. ☐

5 Pay attention. ☐

6 Listen to the auctioneer's speech. ☐

7 Check for any amendments. ☐

8 Watch out for VAT. ☐

9 Check whether the auction house will be collecting an amount in addition to the bid price as a buyer's premium to cover an element of his own or the seller's expenses. This will be charged on top of the deposit and collectable at the time you sign the contract. ☐

10 Make your first bid loud and clear. ☐

11 Subsequent bids should be obvious. ☐

12 Only bid enough to buy. ☐

13 Only bid up to your maximum. ☐

14 Watch competitive bidders. ☐

15 Try to read the auctioneer. ☐

16 Be aware the auctioneer rules the roost. ☐

17 Concentrate on what is happening even if you have stopped bidding. ☐

18 Be aware of the lots you have bought. ☐

19 Sign the contract or memorandum before you leave the room. ☐

20 Expect to pay a ten per cent deposit (subject to a stated minimum). ☐

21 An unsold lot could be a bargain – move in quickly to negotiate. ☐

How to attend

Although you may expect most buyers to attend an auction in person, this is not necessary. Methods of bidding without attending are given below. But if you are to have the best opportunities of securing a bargain, you would be wise to be in the room so that you can weigh up the atmosphere, judge the approach of the auctioneer and, particularly, to out-manoeuvre your opposing bidders.

What will it be like?

As we saw in chapter one, auctions are of various types but by the time you attend you will have had every opportunity to judge the nature of the auction to which you will be going. A large and composite auction in a central city venue will have had extensive advertising and a large, high quality catalogue. You can expect a crowded room with between 200 and 1,000 potential bidders and a thoroughly organised room and reception laid out in theatre seating. With luck, you might even be offered free coffee and refreshments. There is still likely to be only a single auctioneer on the rostrum but he will probably be supported by two or three 'spotters' alongside who are there to help him pick bidders out of the large audience. Beside the auctioneer is likely to be his clerk who will record all bids as an aide-memoire during the sale. In some auctions, part of the room will be allocated as an area where contracts are signed after successful bids have been received. In other auctions there will be an area allocated for tables where solicitors, acting on behalf of owners, will be presiding ready to exchange contracts if their clients have been successful in selling.

A wonderful, Grade II-listed Regency house with three gardens and bags of charm and character, ripe for renovation, located at 42 Olive Lane, Liverpool, sold at auction for only £55,000.

Key point

You will have the choice to sit or stand but do find a position from which you are able to watch your competing bidders.

Make your first bid obvious

In such a crowd, you can expect quite a hubbub with people moving around the room. The auctioneer will have amplification equipment to assist him, but it is very probable that you will need to make a large and obvious gesture, or even to call out to attract the auctioneer's attention at your first bid for each of your chosen lots.

The size of the auction audience often comes down as the scale of the auction reduces. A composite auction, where the number of lots on offer is between approximately 50 and 100, is likely to attract an audience of between 200 and 500 people. The room and atmosphere are similar to that of larger auctions, but it will probably be easier for the bidder to attract the auctioneer's attention. Because of the size of the audience, it is possible for you to make your bids discreetly. Where auctions of this size occur outside London, it is more usual for the sellers' solicitors to attend the auction.

At smaller auctions, the audience is also frequently smaller (unless the lots offered are of overwhelming interest) with between ten and 100 people attending. For a smaller auction, the venue chosen is often a smaller sale room or hired room in a public house or local hall, instead of a large hotel or conference centre. At this size, the proceedings are a little less formal. The auctioneer does not need spotters and the sellers' solicitors usually attend. The bidding is much more discreet and you will have more opportunity to see the quality and strength of any opposing bidders.

How to behave at auction

Listed below are the key points you need to know about auction room etiquette and behaviour:

1. The auctioneer and his staff welcome anyone who swells the crowd, who is dressed reasonably presentably, regardless of his intention to bid or not and who intends to behave reasonably quietly.

2. There is always a constant to-ing and fro-ing of people. You are welcome to arrive and leave whenever it suits you, although it is usual for the audience to avoid interfering with the enjoyment of the proceedings by other people while bidding on a lot is taking place.

3. Arriving late or leaving after the lot in which you are interested is not at all unusual, although it is unwise to miss the auctioneer's opening speech and announcements.

4. Auctioneers often seem to comment on vacant seats available at the front of the auction room, despite research showing that lots are no more expensive whether you are sitting at the front of the room or standing at the back. Don't hesitate to use empty seats if you are happy to do so, but it is a useful tactic to gain a vantage point from where you can observe opposing bidders.

5. Sitting or standing is left to the choice of the attenders. If you are intending to bid, you need to be in a position where you can see the auctioneer and he can see you easily.

Arrive early and make your final checks

6. Auction rooms usually open approximately one hour before the auction commences. Most of the audience turn up in the 20 minutes before proceedings start. Auctions often start approximately five minutes late, but do not rely on this. Amazingly, it is not unusual for 90 per cent or more of the audience never to bid. If you have questions to ask the auctioneer's staff or solicitors before the auction, it is wise to arrive 30 minutes before the auction starts, if you are to avoid a crush. This will give you an opportunity to speak to solicitors, inspect local searches, deeds and leases and whatever else is available for your viewing.

7. On arrival, always check:

    *   if there have been any additions or amendments to the lots and lot details;

    *   if the lot in which you are interested has already been sold or withdrawn;

    *   if the lots are to be offered in alphabetical or numerical order.

8. If the auctioneers have a registration procedure, it is polite to adopt it and complete the appropriate forms at their request. You will not normally be asked for confidential information.

9. If the auctioneers publish in the catalogue or elsewhere any particular requirements, ensure you fulfil them in plenty of time.

10. If you are intending to bid, do not be shy about drawing the auctioneer's attention to your bid by an obvious gesture or by calling out loudly. Once you have attracted the auctioneer's attention, it is unlikely that you will need to attract his attention again for that particular lot. However, if it proves necessary, do not lose the opportunity to bid by being shy about repeating the obvious gesture or loud call.

11. Practices vary from auctioneer to auctioneer in the registration and identification of buyers. One of the more modern systems (said to have been first used at an auction of Beatles memorabilia) is the paddle system which is described in the next section of this chapter.

Auctioneer's Anecdote: A smoked salmon bomb!

On occasion, auctioneers are known to provide refreshments for their audience and a leading firm of London auctioneers decided to push the boat out with smoked salmon sandwiches which were particularly popular. At the end of the auction, they noticed a briefcase had been left behind in the refreshment area and feared it was a bomb. Curiosity overcame circumspection, however, and the briefcase was opened to reveal that it was absolutely full of smoked salmon sandwiches and a card identifying its owner. The auctioneer was delighted to note the owner's embarrassment when he telephoned him later to tell him that his briefcase had been retrieved.

How will the auctioneer know I am a bidder?

The paddle system is one method used to register prospective bidders. As the audience arrives, each person is invited (if he expresses interest in bidding) to complete a registration form (see Figure 4.1). This form will always include the name and address of the bidder or the name and address of the company or organisation on whose behalf he is bidding. The information sheet is then exchanged for a numbered bidding paddle which is not necessarily used for bidding but which is shown to the auctioneer by the successful purchaser after the gavel has fallen.

This enables the auctioneer to identify the buyer immediately and to pass instructions for the preparation of contract. Other information useful to the auctioneer is frequently sought including the name of the solicitors acting for the bidder. It is not unusual for the form to be used by the auctioneer to collect statistical data, to find out where you saw the advertisement for the lot which interests you.

Auctioneers who do not use a registration system generally have more 'spotters' on their rostrum. These spotters identify the successful bidder with the help of the auctioneer and then approach him, asking him to complete a form which details the bidder's name, address and his solicitors. The form is collected so that the necessary contract or memoranda can be prepared. The same spotter returns later to the purchaser to take him over to the table for exchange of contracts. Where the paddle system is used, it is usual for the bidder to be escorted over to the table for the exchange of contracts immediately after the gavel has fallen. If a bidder wishes to bid on subsequent lots shortly after his successful purchase, he may need to defer attending the table for exchange.

Exchanging contracts or memoranda

The full contract

In every case, buyers have to sign and exchange contracts or memoranda before they leave the auction room at the end of the sale. If they fail to do so, the auctioneer invariably has the right to sign the contract on their behalf. The contract is virtually identical to the contract which any purchaser signs to buy a property. It often follows a standard layout used by many solicitors throughout the country.

What the contract contains

- the names of the buyer and the seller;

EDWARD **mellor**

DATE: ....

NUMBER: ....

TO ALL THOSE ATTENDING THE
EDWARD MELLOR COMMERCIAL AUCTION:

To assist in your identification and to maintain privacy, please complete the details below and return this sheet to one of our staff in exchange for a numbered bidding paddle.

When a Lot is sold to you, please advise the auctioneer of your number before going across to the solicitors' table to complete the documents.

1 (a) **Your full names** ....
  (b) **Your address** ....
....
  (c) **Your telephone number(s)** ....
2 (a) **Your solicitors'** ....
  (b) **Their address** ....
....
  (c) **The person acting** ....
  (d) **Solicitors' phone number** ....

IF YOU ARE INTENDING to bid on someone else's behalf, please indicate below:

3 (a) **That person's full name** ....
  (b) **Their address** ....
....
  (c) **Their telephone number** ....
4 **Do you wish to go on our mailing list for future auction catalogues?**
  Yes ☐   No ☐

I ACKNOWLEDGE RECEIPT of a bidding paddle or number sheet and acknowledge that by signing this form I agree to participate in this auction on the basis of the Conditions of Sale published in this catalogue.

SIGNED: ....

PLEASE RETURN YOUR BIDDING PADDLE AT THE END OF THE AUCTION

Figure 4.1 Auctioneer's registration form

- the price that is being paid (the final price of the successful bidder);

- the deposit to be paid;

- the completion date;

- whether or not vacant possession is given;

- details of the property and its tenure;

- the status by which the seller will convey the property;

- brief details of the title;

- covenants that affect the property being sold;

- fixtures and fittings that are included;

- the general conditions of the published Law Society conditions referring to the relevant edition;

- the interest rate payable if the sale is delayed;

- other specific items worthy of notice.

The memorandum

The memorandum is a much briefer contract which is usually printed in the auction catalogue. An example is shown in Figure 4.2. Where full contracts are not available for signing by buyers, then the memorandum in the catalogue is used. This details:

- the contract lot number and the property;

- the price and the deposit payable;

- the name of the purchaser, declaring him the highest bidder at the sale;

- the amount of any buyer's premium or owner's additional charges.

The memorandum is not normally detached from the copy of the auction catalogue, so that the details of the property and its lot number are linked to the memorandum. A small table in the memorandum details the purchase money, the deposit paid and the balance to be paid on completion.

In the case of both the memorandum and the contract, one copy is signed and dated by the purchaser. The other copy is signed and dated on behalf of the vendors. The two documents are then 'exchanged' with the one received by the purchaser acting as a receipt for the deposit.

Key point

If you buy a property and exchange contracts, pass your copy of the contract or memorandum to your solicitor immediately.

When a contract is created

It is an interesting feature of auction law that the moment of contract is the point at which the auctioneer bangs down his gavel. The exchange of contracts or memorandum that takes place afterwards is merely a recording of the existence of the contract. The auctioneer has the legal right to sign the contract on behalf of the vendor and also the right to sign on behalf of the purchaser provided the signature takes place in the environs of the auction room within a reasonable time of the sale having taken place. The right to sign on behalf of the vendor is frequently used, but it is most unusual for the auctioneer to sign on behalf of the purchaser. However, it does leave the auctioneer in a position where he can sign either part of a contract or memorandum prior to the exchange of the parts. This is a convenient arrangement where the owner of the property is not present at the sale or where the purchaser has sent in a written bid or is at the other end of a telephone.

Auction
15th November
Memorandum of Contract

Contract Lot No. ....
Property ....
Price: £ .... Deposit: £ ....
I/We
of do hereby acknowledge that I/we:
(1) were the highest bidder(s) at the Sale by Auction this day of the lot detailed above.
(2) was/were declared the Purchaser(s) thereof subject to the Particulars and Conditions and Special Conditions of Sale at the price detailed above.
(3) have paid the deposit detailed above to the Auctioneers.
(4) agree to complete the said purchase in all respects according to the Particulars, Conditions and Special Conditions of the Sale.

Purchase money .... £
Less Deposit paid .... £
Balance to be paid on completion .... £

AS WITNESS my/our/hand(s) this day of

Signed ....
(for and on behalf of/the Purchaser(s))

We hereby confirm this sale and acknowledge receipt as agents for the vendor of the said deposit of £ .... in accordance with the Particulars, Conditions and Special Conditions of Sale.

Signed ....
(signed on behalf of the Vendor(s))

Abstract of Title to be sent to ....

Figure 4.2 Memorandum of contract

Key point

No purchaser or bidder should think they have an opportunity to renege on their bid, after the gavel has fallen, by leaving the room without completing their part of the memorandum or contract.

Financial, legal and tax traps – a last-minute check

Will the owner's solicitors be present?

Across the country, the practice of solicitors attending auction varies. It appears to be a more usual practice in the north than the south that solicitors acting on behalf of the sellers attend the auction. An enquiry to the auction firm will always give you the answer.

Key point

If the answer is yes, the vendor's solicitors are attending, you should, nevertheless, arrange for your solicitor to check the title to the property well before the sale.

Check for late information

If the vendor's solicitors are at the auction, they may have some late information or be able to show you the results of a local search. Your own solicitor may ask you to look at this essential item if he has not had the opportunity and if he thinks it will be available on the day. The vendor's solicitors may be holding other documents that you would like to see again. It is a good idea to check whatever are available and ask if any changes have occurred. These may include:

- plans of the lot being sold;
- leases and their actual wording;
- local searches;
- title details;
- a copy of the contract or memorandum;

- requirements to pay VAT.

It is not unknown for some bidders at auction to read through the catalogue as they arrive and recklessly decide to bid for a property unseen from the catalogue. If you are feckless enough to consider such a course, do at least check through whatever documents are available at the solicitors' table or at the auctioneer's clerk's table before you bid.

Auctioneer's Anecdote: Unseen is unsafe

It is not as unusual as you would think for bidders to buy lots unseen. There are investors who will tell you 'I have always had my most successful deals where I never saw the property until after I bought it'. There are those who have walked up to the auctioneer afterwards and said 'I liked the look of that lot on the slide, so I bought it. Can you tell me exactly where it is?'

There was a man with £30,000 (at 1995 values) burning a hole in his pocket who bought 27 properties in one lot at that figure in the belief that he could not go wrong getting those properties for that price. He did! They had subsided, were subject to various closure and repair notices and 15 of them were about to be purchased for clearance at a very small site value.

Watch the legal traps

It is not the purpose of this book to be a legal treatise. Nevertheless, every buyer must be aware that the contract is created at the moment that the gavel comes down. The exchange of contracts or memoranda thereafter is only a documentation of the existence of that contract. As we have already seen, the auctioneer can sign on behalf of both sides certifying that the existing contract is satisfactorily documented by the written details.

All auctioneers are aware of the Sale of Land by Auction Act 1867 which prohibits vendor's bids being made by more than one method. In property auctions, the Sale of Goods Act 1979 is partially relevant, but more important are the Estate Agents Act 1979 and the Property Misdescriptions Act 1991. These Acts regulate the propriety and behaviour of the auctioneer and his employees and business colleagues. The Property Misdescriptions Act is intended especially to ensure that auctioneers' particulars are not misleading. Details of the Property Misdescription Act are given on pages 203–6.

A Victorian townhouse in the English Marches bought prior to auction for £135,000, revalued after renovation costs of £50,000 at £295,000.

More important to the purchaser are the Auctions (Bidding Agreements) Acts 1927 and 1969. The main purpose of these Acts (as far as the bidder is concerned) is to ensure that you do not come to any agreement not to bid against anyone else at an auction unless the existence of such an arrangement and the parties to it have been declared in writing to the auctioneer before the sale begins.

Key point

The Act makes it a criminal offence for a potential bidder, who is in business as a dealer, to offer an inducement to anyone else not to bid.

How and when is the deposit paid?

Immediately the gavel has fallen, the purchaser is due to exchange his memorandum or contract and to pay over the deposit. Usually the payment is ten per cent of the purchase price, subject to a specified minimum. The amount due is indicated in the auctioneer's catalogue, generally somewhere in the conditions of sale. It is not unusual for these terms to be displayed on the walls of the sale room as well as in the catalogue and it may also be referred to in the auctioneer's opening remarks.

What is payable in addition to the deposit ?

As a purchaser, you need to find out by looking in the brochure, amendment sheets and the auctioneer's brochure whether there are any additional payments due at this time. These may well be in the following ranges:

1. Auctioneer's administrative charges: £200 to £600

2. Vendor's local search fees: £125 to £200

3. Vendor's legal conveyancing charges: £500 to £1,200

4. Local authority's surveyors' charges: one per cent to 1.5 per cent of purchase price

Be ready to hand over your money

Most auctioneers will accept a normal cheque drawn upon a recognised bank or building society. Cash is only accepted by certain auctioneers; if you intend to pay this way, check before the sale. No auctioneer has yet indicated that he will accept payment by credit card.

Certain auctioneers require certified or guaranteed cheques or banker's drafts. Personal or building society cheques are not acceptable. This does create a slight problem, since you will need to arrange for the cheque or draft to be prepared before the auction and you will not know how much the purchase price is going to be and therefore, how much the cheque should be. The only way of covering this is to ensure that the amount specified on the draft is at least ten per cent of the maximum bid proposed – and maybe a little higher to allow for a touch of indulgent bidding. It is normally sufficient for the payment order to be made out to the auctioneer's firm but, on occasion, the catalogue may specify different instructions. Where auctioneers have a practice of inviting the solicitors acting on behalf of the vendor to attend the sale, then sometimes (but not very often) the solicitors for the vendor ask for the cheque to be made payable in their name. In a few instances, where sales are being conducted for government or local authority departments or quangos, cheques are occasionally requested to be made payable to them. Cheques are normally only payable to the vendor if it is a reputable and well-known body.

The Money Laundering Regulations came into force for auctioneers on 1 March 2004. These require auctioneers to check the identities (IDs) where cash is offered for deposits in excess of 15,000 Euros (approximately £14,000). For this reason some auction houses will not accept cash deposits at all. Their catalogue will indicate their requirements.

The Money Laundering Regulations 2003

Since the introduction of these regulations, the auctioneer not only has to check the ID of the vendor before the auction, but also has to check those of the purchaser before the transaction can proceed beyond the point at which the written memorandum of the contract has been completed. Although not strictly necessary under the regulations, many auctioneers are choosing to do this themselves. Others are arranging for it to be carried out by the solicitors for the purchaser or vendor. The procedures adopted will be specified in the auctioneer's brochure.

Be prepared, if necessary, to attend the auction with proof of identity for yourself and any other individual for whom you are bidding. Companies, partnerships, trusts and other businesses need more comprehensive identification which should be checked out with the auctioneers or solicitors well before the sale.

You probably have been through these procedures already. The requirements are similar, for example, to those necessary for opening a bank or building society account.

Briefly, two pieces of evidence are required which verify your name, address, nationality and date of birth. Typical documents are listed below. One document will be required from List A and one from List B. The same document cannot be used to satisfy both lists. Originals have to be produced. Copies are not accepted.

List A

- Current signed passport.
- Current UK or EAA photocard driving licence.
- Current UK driving licence – old-style provisional driving licences are not acceptable.

- Benefit book or original notification letter from the Benefits Agency confirming your right to benefits.

- National identity card containing a photograph of the person being identified.

List B

- Current utility bill (not more than three months old and not from a mobile phone).

- Credit card or bank account statement (not more than three months old and showing the current address of the person being identified).

- Current UK or EAA photocard driving licence.

- Current UK driving licence – old-style provisional driving licences are not acceptable.

- Bank, building society or credit union statement or passbook containing your current address.

- A recent original mortgage statement from a recognised lender.

Key point

The destination of this deposit cheque and the way in which the money is held, is very important to both parties to the transaction between contract and completion.

The conditions of sale usually indicate whether the deposit money, after the exchange of contracts, is held by:

- a stakeholder on behalf of the vendor;

- a stakeholder on behalf of the purchaser;

- a stakeholder on behalf of both sides;

- the vendor.

Insist on an indemnity bond

A stakeholder can be any person, but they must be acceptable to both parties. The auctioneers or solicitors often act as the stakeholder. If the money is held on behalf of the vendor, a purchaser should insist, before exchanging contracts, that the money is covered by an insurance bond, to be held by the auctioneers or the solicitors and require that the vendor is prohibited from having access to the money until completion. The bond will protect the purchaser's money in the event of fraud or insolvency of the auctioneers or solicitors.

If the money is held on behalf of the purchaser, then there is no need to restrict control of the money further, although it is still wise to ensure that the money, whilst in the hands of professionals, is covered by a necessary insurance bond. Virtually all auctioneers and solicitors indicate the arrangements made. Once paid, the purchaser will not have access to the deposit unless the contract is cancelled.

Where the money is held by a stakeholder it is usually in the control of the auctioneers or solicitors who have been so nominated to hold it on behalf of both vendor and purchaser until completion. Again, it is wise that this money should be covered by an insurance bond and you should be satisfied that the amount is paid into an appropriate client account.

Who keeps the interest?

Where big deposit sums are payable or the period between purchase and completion is longer than usual and the amount of interest earned on the money in this period is significant, then it is important that everyone is clear who receives the interest. Normally, the interest is retained by:

- the auctioneers; or
- the solicitors; or occasionally
- the vendor; or very occasionally
- the purchaser (and then only by special agreement).

However, if the interest to be earned is large, discuss the matter with the auctioneers at least several days prior to the sale. You would be wise to make arrangements with the auctioneer's and vendor's solicitors for the interest to be credited to your benefit, making it a condition of your bidding that such an arrangement must be entered into. Alternatively, if

'S/C' –
Self-contained

'P' –
This is normally used as an abbreviation for 'Vacant Possession' which can also be noted as 'V.P.'

'L' –
Leasehold

'F' –
Freehold

'RUP' –
Residential upper part

'mais' –
Maisonette

LONDON

STRETTONS of E1 at New Connaught Rms, WC2, Apr 19

E1 — 18 Pevensey Hse, Ben Johnson Rd. S/C mais, 4 rms. L, P	30,000
50 Cephas Ave. End terr hse, 6 rms. Closing order. F, P	53,000
37 New Rd. Terr w/shop bdg. 2 floors. Let £2,068 pa. 2 floors, 388 & 410 sq ft with P. F	55,000
E3 — 104 Fairfoot Rd. Bdg plot. PP 2 flats. F, P	15,000
111 Grove Rd. Terr hse, 5 rms. F, P	54,000
13 Grafton Hse, Wellington Way. 2nd floor, S/C flat, 3 rms. L, P	17,500
E5 — 5/7 Chatsworth Rd. 2 adj shops, RUP 2 S/C flats, 4 & 5 rms. Let £3,120 PAX. Closing Order. F	40,000
4 Cricketfield Rd. S/C flat, 2 rms. L, P	25,500
19 Elderfield Rd. End terr hse, 9 rms. PP flat, mais, 2 garages. Closing order. F, P	43,000
30 Glenarm Rd. 2nd floor, S/C studio flat. L, P	15,500
103 Mount Pleasant Lane. S/C flat, 3 rms. L, P	23,000
E6 — 132 Charlemont Rd. RUP S/C flat, 2 rms. L, P	20,500
58 Dickens Rd. End terr hse, 3 bed. F, P	35,000
130 Masterman Rd. Terr hse, 2 bed. F, P	36,500
St Andrews Hall, Roman Rd. Derelict hall, site 0.10 a. Planning brief for 2 hses. F, P	31,000
E7 — 165 Capel Rd. Corner bdg, 6 rms, part used as clinic. PP 2 hses & garages on rear land. F, P	66,500
7 Neville Rd. End terr bdg as 3 S/C flats. 1 LGR, 1 studio flat & 1 x 3 rms with P. For completion F	36,500
75 Pevensey Rd. Terr hse as 2 flats, 3 rms. F, P	38,000
7 Reginald Rd. Corner shop, rear rm. RUP, 3 rms. F, P	35,000
21 Shaftesbury Rd. Terr hse, 2 bed. F, P	35,500
E8 — 234 Dalston Lane. 4 storey hse, 10 rms, 2 store rms. F, P	55,000
376C Kingsland Rd. RUP S/C mais, 3 rms. L, P	22,000
113 Shacklewell Lane. Shop, rear rm. S/C mais, 3 rms. P	28,500
E10 — 287 High Rd. Shop, rear rm, basement, mais, 4 rms, garage. F, P	60,000
E12 — 32 Salisbury Rd. Terr hse, 3 bed. F, P	36,500
E13 — 198 Balaam St. S/C flat, 3 rms. L, P	18,000
163 Grange Rd. Terr hse, 6 rms. F, P	34,500
50 London Rd. S/C flat, 2 rms. L, P	14,000
31 Maud Rd. Terr hse as S/C flat, 3 rms & S/C mais, 3 rms. F, P	41,000
Tabernacle Ave. Site 0.16 a. Planning brief for development. F, P	16,000

Illustration 4. Sample auction results

you cannot make such arrangements, allow for loss of interest when calculating the amount of your final bid.

Bids by phone require deposit payments in advance

If you intend to bid by telephone, fax or letter, then you will have to make arrangements with the auctioneer to pay the deposit before the sale. Unless you are well known to the auctioneer, he will invariably require you to pay the deposit by banker's draft, building society or personal cheque, which will have to be cleared before the sale begins. The amount will be equal to or higher than ten per cent of your proposed maximum sum. It is wise to make such arrangements well in advance of the auction, giving the auctioneer at least a week's notice.

It is imperative that funds are available to cover any cheque issued for a deposit. If a cheque or financial instrument issued to cover the deposit fails to provide the necessary funds, the vendor will exercise his rights under the conditions of sale permitting him to:

- cancel the sale at his option; and

- take civil proceedings against the purchaser for any loss or costs.

The vendor is not required to reoffer the lot by auction, but he can take any reasonable steps chosen to resell the lot. Before taking proceedings to recover any loss or costs the seller must show that reasonable endeavours have been made to resell at a proper price.

If a deposit cheque bounces, this could open up criminal proceedings. Such an offence does not remove the seller's rights to a civil claim.

Checklist: Paying the deposit

1 How much is payable?   ☐
2 Who is it to be paid to?   ☐
3 When is it required?   ☐
4 Do they require cleared funds?   ☐
5 Who receives the interest?   ☐

6   Can the interest be paid into my account? ☐

7   Is the vendor prohibited from receiving the monies until completion? ☐

8   Is there an indemnity bond? ☐

9   Is there an insurance bond? ☐

10 Are the monies being paid into client accounts? ☐

Value Added Tax

In certain circumstances VAT is payable on property or land purchases. Where a property has been registered as subject to VAT, then the purchaser will have to pay at completion VAT at the going rate in addition to the purchase price. The purchaser will receive a VAT receipt and may be entitled to reclaim that tax or part of it. Nevertheless, the incidence of the payment may well affect cash flow, financing and, possibly, the legal vehicle in which the property is bought.

Almost invariably, the auction catalogue will disclose if VAT is payable. If not, the auctioneer should publish it in the amendment sheet. He may also mention it in his opening speech and will undoubtedly mention it at the time he offers the lot.

Timing of VAT payments

VAT is almost always paid at completion of the purchase. Unless announced otherwise, the VAT will always be in addition to the price bid at the time the gavel falls.

How to find out if VAT is payable

Is VAT mentioned:

1.   in the conditions of sale?

2.   in the general preamble at the beginning of the catalogue?

3.   in the description of the lot in the catalogue?

4.   in any memoranda published in the catalogue?

5. in the auctioneer's amendment sheet?

6. in the auctioneer's opening speech?

7. at any time during the offering of the lot?

8. just before the gavel is brought down?

9. where the property on offer gives a rental income to the owner and VAT is paid by the tenants in addition to their rent?

Key point

If VAT is not mentioned in any of these contexts, then you may rest assured that it is not payable in addition to the gavel price.

How can I find out the reserve price?

Most owners are unwilling to sell their properties below a fixed figure. This is the amount which they indicate to the auctioneer as the reserve. The gavel is not brought down to create a contract for sale for any lot until there is a bid equal to or larger than the reserve figure. The auctioneer will of course encourage bidders to bid up to that price, so that he then has a sale. Usually he provides in the conditions of sale for the right to put in bids below the reserve amount on behalf of the owner who is selling.

It is not unusual for public bodies to put the reserve in a sealed envelope which the auctioneer only opens as he goes onto the rostrum, although it is quite possible that he will have discussed an appropriate amount with his client beforehand. Some owners even refuse to disclose their final reserve to their own auctioneer and sit in the audience giving a pre-arranged signal when the bidding has reached a level at which the auctioneer can sell. This practice is discouraged by auctioneers because of the uncertainty it creates for them.

Key point

The reserve is a highly confidential amount and it is most unusual for it to be disclosed to the public or to any intending bidders.

Reserves that are published

Only on a limited number of occasions – particularly where owners are thinking of selling at a low price – do auctioneers publish their reserve as part of their marketing campaign. This is done deliberately to create interest and the figure is usually published in the auction catalogue and often put into advertisements. It may be described as an 'upset price' (see Figure 4.3). This practice is frequently adopted where the instructions to sell have come from liquidators and receivers.

A published reserve puts you in the driving seat

To the auctioneer, having his reserve disclosed is rather like playing a poker hand face upwards on the table. Immediately the price at which he can sell is disclosed, then everyone in the audience is aware of whether the bids have reached a point at which the auctioneer can sell or not. He is not in a position to put pressure on people in the room to bid by going through the offering procedure on a 'mock' basis as if he were about to sell. This procedure is examined later in this chapter.

Without reserve

Very occasionally, lots are offered 'without reserve' and this literally means that if only one (even if it is excessively low) bid is received, the auctioneer has to sell. Anyone attending an auction where a property is offered at no reserve would be perfectly entitled to start the bidding at £1.

The vagaries of human nature are such that it is not at all unusual for properties offered with no reserve to attract a lot of attention and for bidders to get carried away, but it is a brave owner who would offer his property on this basis thinking he will sell at a high sum. It is a practice used more often for properties for which there is little demand or where there are large liabilities for structural repairs or other costs.

Key point

Properties offered without a reserve are not always the bargain which they may seem and should be approached with considerable care.

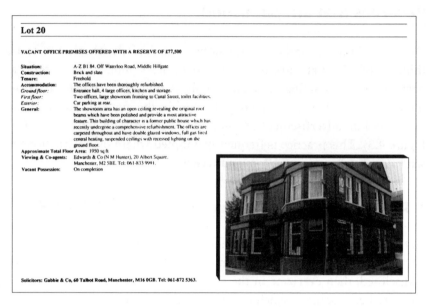

Lot 20

VACANT OFFICE PREMISES OFFERED WITH A RESERVE OF £77,500

Situation:	A-Z B1 84. Off Waterloo Road, Middle Hillgate
Construction:	Brick and slate
Tenure:	Freehold
Accommodation:	The offices have been thoroughly refurbished.
Ground floor:	Entrance hall, 4 large offices, kitchen and storage.
First floor:	Two offices, large showroom fronting to Canal Street, toilet facilities.
Exterior:	Car parking at rear.
General:	The showroom area has an open ceiling revealing the original roof beams which have been polished and provide a most attractive feature. This building of character is a former public house which has recently undergone a comprehensive refurbishment. The offices are carpeted throughout and have double glazed windows, full gas fired central heating, suspended ceilings with recessed lighting on the ground floor.
Approximate Total Floor Area:	1950 sq ft
Viewing & Co-agents:	Edwards & Co (N M Hunter), 20 Albert Square, Manchester, M2 5BE. Tel: 061-833 9991.
Vacant Possession:	On completion

Solicitors: Gabbie & Co, 60 Talbot Road, Manchester, M16 0GB. Tel: 061-872 5363.

Figure 4.3 Auction catalogue illustrating an upset price. This was a property where the vendor had the building on the market for quite a long time before the auction, at an asking price noticeably higher than the upset price quoted. She felt that by publishing the upset price, it would be an indication to people who had previously been interested that the vendor would be willing to sell at a noticeably lower figure than had previously been asked in the market. As it happened, the property offered still did not sell at the auction.

A cautionary tale

Mr Black is after a cheap property that he can 'do up and rent out' to bring him a small income. He calculates that if he buys something under £5,000, refurbishes it for £10,000 and then rents it out at £4,000 a year, this would represent a really good investment.

Don't get carried away by 'no reserves'

He is delighted to see a property at a local auction at no reserve. It looks a little run-down in the picture but does not seem too bad and he dashes to the auction without doing any checking. Before Mr Black had even collected his wits at the auction, the bidding had started at only £5 for the lot which interested him and seemed to be going fast and furious until it slowed down at £2,700. He quickly jumped in with £2,800 and was delighted when the gavel fell on his first bid, particularly since he felt he had saved himself £2,200 already.

His solicitor's charges of £500 seemed rather expensive and he was even less pleased on seeing the property for the first time the day after the auction to discover that it suffered from subsidence, rising damp, was infected with woodworm and had suffered from an arson attack which had burnt out the back of the building. A surveyor estimated it would take around £35,000 to put it right.

The local council, having had their attention drawn to the property by the auction publicity, sent around their building inspector, who condemned it. Mr Black failed to respond to the request that he demolish it and they carried out the work for him submitting a bill for £3,200 including 15 per cent establishment expenses plus VAT.

Lot 26
23 Vale Street, Clayton
AT NO RESERVE
VACANT SEMI DETACHED HOUSE IN NEED OF COMPLETE RESTORATION

Situation: A-Z 2F 51. Off North Road, Ashton New Road (A662)
Tenure: Long leasehold subject to a ground rent of £4 pa.
Accommodation: *Ground floor:* Hall, lounge, kitchen. *First floor:* 3 bedrooms, bathroom/wc *Exterior:* Gardens front and rear, space for car
Viewing: Keys available from the auctioneers
Note: The property is boarded up. The entire property is in need of thorough overhauling and refurbishment.
Vacant Possession: On completion
Solicitors: Davies Wallis Foyster (Mr I Osborne) 37 Peter Street, M2 5GB

Figure 4.4 An auction lot offered at no reserve

Mr Black still owns an empty site which cost him over £7,600 and no one wants to buy, but upon which a lot of people seem to want to 'fly-tip' rubbish

In Figure 4.4, the derelict nature of the property is obvious and, furthermore, was spelt out in the auctioneer's description. Defects in properties offered at no reserve are not always so obvious.

Disclosing when the reserve has been reached

Auctioneers will go to great lengths to prevent the audience from realising which bids are made on behalf of the sellers and which bids have been made by people in the room. Therefore, there is usually no obvious indication when the auctioneer 'reaches' or 'passes' the reserve. Thereafter, certain auctioneers like to disclose that the bidding is higher than the reserve and will use such phrases as 'the property is in the market' or 'at this price I shall sell if I receive no higher bid' or simply indicate that the reserve has been reached. Other auctioneers only disclose this information on certain lots where they feel it will encourage the bidding.

Key point

Many auctioneers never disclose that the reserve has been reached and it is only known when either the gavel falls for the sale or the gavel does not fall and the lot is withdrawn.

Discovering the reserve price

If you are able to discover, by fair means or foul, the level of the reserve, you are in a stronger position than other bidders competing against you. To discover reserves, bidders must resort to their ingenuity. In most cases, the reserve figure will be known to the auctioneer and to some of his senior and junior staff who may be led into disclosing the actual figure. Close acquaintanceship with the auctioneer might or might not help but, undoubtedly, a 'quick peek' at his auction catalogue (if he has an unguarded moment) could reveal the figure.

Can I tell what the reserve is from the starting price?

There is no fixed theory about the relationship between the price that the auctioneer first asks for, the figure at which he takes the first bid and the reserve price. It is worth considering the psychology of the auctioneer and weighing up his style and practice as the auction proceeds. There are several factors in his mind:

- On the papers in front of him for each lot, he will have the reserve 'writ large'. His note of the reserve figure will not only be in large numerals but also in a bright colour so he cannot miss it. He is striving to encourage the bidding to reach this reserve figure. As he starts off each lot, this amount will be uppermost in his mind as his target. It is not unusual that the first figure he mentions in seeking the opening bid could well be that reserve amount.

- The auctioneer likes to receive bids in the room and be seen to be taking them. On the other hand, if he has a considerable number of lots to sell and is in a hurry to complete the sale, he will wish to start the bidding not too far below the reserve. Table 4.1 illustrates possible opening bids and increments against given reserve prices.

Reserve	Likely Opening Increments with Responsive Bidding	Possible Opening Bid with Unresponsive Bidding	Possible Opening Bid
£10,000	£1,000	£6,000	£4,000
£20,000	£1,000	£15,000	£10,000
£30,000	£2,500	£20,000	£15,000
£50,000	£5,000	£30,000	£20,000
£100,000	£10,000	£60,000	£50,000
£200,000	£10,000	£150,000	£100,000
£300,000	£25,000	£200,000	£150,000

Table 4.1 Opening bids, reserves and increments

- If the auction is going well, and the auctioneer is receiving responsive bidding from the floor, then he is likely to start the bidding closer to his reserve than otherwise. If there is very little response and not many bids forthcoming, he may try a starting bid that is particularly low to encourage enthusiasm from the audience. Unfortunately, there is no proven formula; but as you become used to your auctioneer's style you may be able to spot a pattern in his behaviour.

'The auction itself was run very well. I had been before so I knew they were good and entertaining – it's the best bit of free entertainment in Manchester.'

Don Lee, buyer of a residential property at auction.

CHAPTER 5

Bidding and winning your bargain

'Buying at auction is very straightforward. If I could see houses that were being sold at comparable prices in comparable areas, I would buy privately. But buying at auction is a way of ensuring I don't have to pay more than I need to pay. You want to make sure you acquire your property at a bargain level and auctions are the way.'

Michael Roe, buyer of residential properties,

How does an auctioneer conduct an auction?

The auctioneer's opening speech

Bearing in mind that auctioneers are individualists, you can expect all their opening speeches to vary considerably. They do, however, frequently contain important information and it is wise to be at the auction before the start and before the auctioneer's introductory remarks. If you are only going to be interested in a lot towards the end of a long day of selling, ensure that you hear the opening speech, even if you then decide to take a break from listening to the sale of some of the earlier lots.

The speech will usually contain:

1. A polite welcome.

2. An indication of how the sale will be run with advice on any lots that have been withdrawn or that will be sold out of numerical or alphabetical order. For example, the auctioneer may decide to split a lot into two or put two lots together and sell them as one. Alternatively, he may decide to offer a lot as it stands and if it does not sell, then to split it into two. For some reason the vendors may decide that they want to vary the order of sale and the auctioneer will indicate that he will sell lot 2 before lot 1 or make a variation such as lot 10 will only be offered at the end of the auction rather than after lot 9.

Announcements of changes

3. Details of any late amendments to the information published in the catalogue. (It is very common for auctioneers to issue amendment sheets which detail these variations.) Amendments may include corrections to addresses or descriptions or may be more fundamental. Quite often, the published details state the wrong terms or starting dates or the rents payable under leases. Even more frequently, review dates on leases seem to need variation.

This property in Stockton-on-Tees was sold at £71,000. This substantial building, that had been converted into eight flats, each let on ASTs for £55 per week. When sold, only five flats were let but this still generated £14,300 pa. When fully let, the property would earn £22,800. £71,000 meant the buyer had an immediate 20 per cent yield with the potential for over 30 per cent.

4. Comment on the auctioneer's right to bid on behalf of vendors and on behalf of people who have left bids with him, or his firm or his employees. The phrase in the speech may be:

    'On behalf of the auctioneers, I give notice that they reserve the right to bid, through me or otherwise on behalf of purchasers who have left bids with them, or on behalf of vendors, or as agents, or as principals for any lots.'

You will see that this comment coupled with the conditions of sale leaves the auctioneer to take bids:

- on behalf of people who are not present but who have made proxy bids;
- made by people who are bidding by telephone;
- on behalf of people who have already instructed him by letter, fax or similar instruction to bid up to a specific sum on a specific lot;
- on behalf of the vendor;
- on behalf of himself or his firm.

5. The procedures that follow during the auction for:

- methods of bidding;
- obtaining the details of purchasers;
- the arrangements for signing and exchanging contracts or memoranda;
- the amount of the deposit and how it is to be paid.

6. The completion date of each lot.

Persuading, cajoling and bullying for the highest bid

Auctioneers come in all shapes and sizes and ages; their charisma and charm vary throughout the range, but almost invariably they are frustrated actors! There is no doubt the performance of a good auctioneer on the rostrum is the equivalent to that of a high quality professional actor on the stage. This performer on the rostrum sets out to use all his abilities to make the most of the competition engendered in the auction room and to persuade, cajole, lead or bully bidders into paying more than their common sense would suggest.

The auctioneer has the benefit that the entire audience must concentrate on him. Many newcomers to auctions fear that their slightest move might be interpreted as a bid and they will finish up buying a property they did not intend to take home.

Key point

This fear is not justified and all auctioneers take care not to 'knock down' lots to individuals in the audience who make involuntary (or even voluntary non-bidding) gestures.

What the auctioneer is thinking

The auctioneer runs the auction on three levels of consciousness. Uppermost in his mind will be the level of bidding at or above the reserve that he is striving to reach to effect a sale. For this reason, auctioneers often unconsciously seek to start the bidding at the reserve amount. If the bidding does not begin at this price, the auctioneer may ask for lower starting prices.

At the second level the auctioneer has a regular rhythm of patter relating to the bid that he has received and the next bid he is seeking. Auctioneers often have an almost monotonous mantra-like recitation of amounts.

At the third level he is hawkishly seeking movements or sounds in the audience which betray the existence of bidders.

Auctioneer's Anecdote: Bidders are like the opposite sex

Quote from the Manchester Evening News: 'Bidders are like the opposite sex. We can't do without them. Too often the low bidder is jeered, the tentative bidder chivvied and the reluctant bidder chided. Remember always, all bidders need encouragement and more encouragement until they thrive and smile and multiply and bid and bid and bid. Auctioneers should always ensure positively that the final bid they accept before the climactic bang of the gavel is a bid. No auctioneer earns merit from accepting as his last bid a smile, the response to a neighbour's joke, a nervous twitch or sneeze or a salutation across the sale room to a colleague.'

How large do the bids jump?

Having found a bidder or bidders, the auctioneer will aim to dictate the increments in the bidding. He will seek to make them as large as possible, probably in the range between two and a half per cent and five per cent of the bids. The increments may initially be in quite large amounts but as the price rises they will almost invariably reduce when the bidding slows down and the sale price nears.

Bidding Range	Main Increments	Intermediate Increments	Possible Final Increments
£1,000–£20,000	£1,000	£500	£250
£20,000–£50,000	£2,500	£1,000	£500
£50,000–£100,000	£5,000	£2,500	£1,000
£100,000–£250,000	£10,000	£5,000	£2,500
£250,000–£500,000	£25,000	£10,000	£5,000
£500,000–£1,000,000	£100,000	£50,000	£25,000

Table 5.1 Bidding ranges and increment sizes

Table 5.1 gives examples of increment sizes in line with bidding prices. Most auctioneers aim to encourage a regular rhythm of bidding by their audience. It is common for them to concentrate on only two bidders at a time moving on to other bidders only when one of the original pair drops out. Occasionally, auctioneers will take their bids in turn from three bidders. By following this practice of using their audience in pairs or trios they are able to ensure that the bidders are aware when it is their turn to participate.

The personal style of each auctioneer varies, but a typical offering and bidding scenario is as follows:

AUCTIONEER: I now wish to offer lot number six, a charming and desirable residence with vacant possession, 16 Acacia Road, Lewisham. Where may I start the bidding? £50,000?
(*Silence.*)

AUCTIONEER: Well, ladies and gentlemen, it is in your hands not mine as to where we start the bidding. Should it be £45,000?
(*Silence.*)

AUCTIONEER: Will £35,000 tempt someone to bid? Thank you sir, I have your bid (*as bidder number one waves his catalogue vigorously in the air*).

AUCTIONEER: I am bid £35,000. Do I see £37,500? £37,500 anywhere?
(*Bidder number two coughs and raises a tentative finger in the air.*)

AUCTIONEER: £37,500 bid. £40,000 anywhere?
(*Bidder number one nods his head discreetly.*)

AUCTIONEER: £42,500?
(*Bidder number two shakes his head.*)
(*Bidder number three shouts £42,500!*)

AUCTIONEER: £42,500. £45,000 may I say?
(*Bidder number one nods his head.*)

AUCTIONEER: £47,500?
(*Bidder number three winks.*)

AUCTIONEER: £50,000?
(*Bidder number one looks away.*)
(*Bidder number three waves his catalogue.*)

AUCTIONEER: I have your bid, sir, at £47,500 which is your bid. £50,000 anywhere? Any further bid? I am bid £47,500. I am looking for £50,000. Have you all done? Has the bidding finished? At £47,500 for the first time. For the second time ...
(*Bidder number four shouts out incomprehensibly.*)

AUCTIONEER: I have a new bidder at £50,000. £52,500 anywhere? Have you all finished at £50,000? Will a bid at £51,000 tempt anyone at this stage?
(*Bidder number one raises his finger in the air.*)

AUCTIONEER: I have £51,000. £52,000 may I say?
(*Bidder number four nods her head.*)

AUCTIONEER: I am bid £52,000. £53,000 anywhere? £53,000 may I say? Have you all now finished at this price? At £52,000 then for the first time, £52,000 for the second time (*pointing at bidder number four*). It is your bid, Madam, at £52,000. Any further bid? £53,000 anywhere? (*The auctioneer lifts his gavel and holds it threateningly in the air and after a pause brings it down.*)

AUCTIONEER: Sold at £52,000.
(*Looking at bidder number four pointedly.*)

AUCTIONEER: May I see your paddle number, madam?
(*Bidder number four shows her paddle number.*)

AUCTIONEER: Sold to 142 at £52,000. And for my next lot ...

Key point

However charming and encouraging the auctioneer is, it should always be remembered that his responsibility is to obtain a sale for the owner of the property at the highest price possible.

Watch out for changes to the lot details

The auctioneer's firm will always indicate whether any lots have been sold prior to the sale and whether any lots have been withdrawn. They may have posters on the wall or at the entrance indicating lots sold prior. The information may also be recorded on amendment sheets that are issued.

Occasionally, lots are split or amalgamated for the purpose of a sale. It may be that the order of the sale has been changed or there are changes in the details of some of the lots. This is likely to be announced in the auctioneer's speech and detailed in any amendment sheets issued. A typical amendment sheet is shown in Figure 5.1.

Lots Sold: 4, 5, 6, 8, 14, 15, 17, 25, 30, 32, 36

7	This property has recently had gas central heating installed and full rewiring.
12	The solicitors' correct address is 229 Burnage Lane.
13	This lot is freehold not leasehold as described in the catalogue.
25	The solicitors acting are Addleshaws, Dennis House, Marsden Street, Manchester. Tel: 0161 832 5994.
29	One of the lifts is in working order but the other is not.
30	Two bedrooms should read three bedrooms.
31	Special Conditions of Sale are available for inspection at the office of the auctioneers. The total weekly income is £696.15 and not as printed in the catalogue. The following is a schedule of occupiers' agreements as at 9.7.05.

Occupier	Weekly Rent	Agreement Date	Expiry Date
World Book & Childcraft International	£140.00	01.10.06	31.12.07
TA Wise (t/a Tour inc Production Agency)	£46.15	04.08.06	05.09.07
Amjad Dar (t/a First Call)	£60.00	02.08.06	31.08.07
Elaine Chadwick	£140.00	01.06.06	30.09.07
Julian Stein	£50.00	01.06.06	30.09.07

Associated Homecare Limited	£220.00	18.08.06	17.02.08
Madman Movies Limited	£40.00	23.08.06	19.09.08
34	We have recently been advised that the tenant of the shop has not paid rent for nine months. The purchaser will be required to pay the arrears of £1,800 outstanding over to the vendor at completion.		
35	The solicitors acting are Alsop Wilkinson (Jill Worthington dealing), 11 St James Square, Manchester M2 6DR. Tel: 0161 834 7760.		

Figure 5.1 An amendment sheet

Key point

If any lot in which you were interested has been withdrawn, you do NOT have any right to claim any expenses or damages against the auctioneer, his firm or the vendors.

How to make your bid

Use your own style

Any auctioneer will reminisce over the variety of styles adopted by bidders. Many of the stories may be apocryphal but tales are recounted of buyers who bid in mirrors, with their toes, their fingers, their nose, by winking or by proxy.

Key point

There is no need for you to adopt any sophisticated style. The important part of bidding is to ensure that the auctioneer's attention is drawn to you at the stage where you are making your first bid. A bold raising of the hand, waving of the catalogue or paddle, or even a shout may be necessary to draw the auctioneer's attention to you in the first instance.

Keep your eye on the auctioneer

Once he knows you are interested, then your movements can be a matter of your own style as long as they are sufficient to show your interest. It is wise during this period to keep looking directly at the auctioneer. Your bidding should always be confident. Act as if you attend auctions every other day. Make all your gestures strong and firm. Should the price become too high for you, then stop the movement and look away from the auctioneer. Many bidders specifically indicate with a shake of the head that they are no longer interested and occasionally some of those change their mind and start bidding again.

Key point

There is no point in trying to unsettle or disturb the auctioneer, particularly since you need him 'on your side'. Much more important is the impression you create in the minds of competitors bidding against you.

Auctioneer's Anecdote: The bidder is not always the decision-maker

Not surprisingly, husband and wife teams often sit together in auctions. Occasionally, a group of three or even four board members or partners may attend an auction together. In these cases, it is frequently very obvious to the auctioneer which member of the team is the decision-maker and, for some reason, it is most unusual for that decision-maker to be the actual bidder. The wife decides but the husband bids! The managing director decides but the company secretary bids! The auctioneer, on his rostrum, is frequently in a position to see these decisions being passed 'down the line' and is always intrigued to see the look of surprise on the husband's or company secretary's face when the auctioneer appears to take the bid off him before he has even made his gesture. No auctioneer would ever admit that he does not have a heightened sense of ESP.

Bidding by telephone

Many of us have seen the telephone bid used, particularly at the leading chattel auction sales on television. Most auctioneers of property are willing to make the telephone available for bidding, but this does have certain disadvantages to the buyer. You need to establish your credit with the auctioneer several days before the auction, and he will probably require you to send him a cheque before the auction representing the ten per cent deposit of the maximum sum that you are willing to bid.

This has two disadvantages. First, the auctioneer is aware of the maximum you will pay and if he is unscrupulous, he may take advantage of this knowledge by increasing the reserve. Second, it prevents you from making any bids higher than 'the first number you thought of' at the time you dispatched the cheque. For some reason, perhaps because they disturb the auctioneer's rhythm of bidding, telephone bids always come over weakly in the room and seem to have less impact on opposing bidders. The audience may believe they are a ploy of the auctioneer to increase the number and level of bids.

Auctioneer's Anecdote: Long-distance bidding

A well-known firm of provincial auctioneers decided to run an auction in the provinces and in London at the same time. They installed an auctioneer and solicitors in each room and linked the rooms up with three telephone lines. Microphones at each end conveyed the proceedings in each room to loud-speakers in the other. The first eight lots were all sold in a room in the provinces and although one or two bids came through on the loud-speakers from the London end, the city bids were few and far between. As the bidding rose higher for the ninth lot, over the loud-speakers in the provinces were heard the bids taken by the second auctioneer in London from a bidder in that room. The lot was sold to the London buyer. This immediately provoked a strong murmur and comment from the provincial audience which the auctioneer in that room immediately picked up on and said 'You didn't really think there was anybody at the other end, did you?' to nods of assent all round the room.

Can I employ someone to bid for me?

Having read this guide, you will be well equipped to tackle an auction yourself. But there is no reason why you should not seek out an auctioneer, solicitor or other professional experienced in the sale room to act on your behalf. It may be that the valuer who has assisted you in the earlier stages will be willing to join you in the room for an appropriate fee. He may charge a specific fee of between £150 and £300 or may charge at an hourly rate of between £80 and £200 per hour. You may want to discuss with him the tactics that you might both use to upset the opposition. But in the end, you will have to appreciate he can only bid up to the price you specify and that any different decision by you will need transmitting to him quickly if he is to enter a bid above your authorised amount. There are no other agencies that specialise in bidding on a purchaser's behalf.

Bidding by proxy

A final method of submitting your bids is to notify the auctioneer's firm by letter, fax or email. As with the telephone bid, you will need to cover the ten per cent deposit. Bidding by proxy has the same disadvantages as the telephone bid, but if you resort to it then it is important that you instruct the auctioneer in writing to bid up to your chosen maximum price. All reputable auctioneers will accept this instruction, but again you have the disadvantage of not being able to vary your maximum price having gauged the atmosphere in the auction room. Also, the auctioneer is aware of the maximum figure that you are willing to pay and might adjust his increments accordingly.

Key point

The best method is to attend the auction in person and, having obtained suitable advice, bid yourself.

Bidding tactics to beat the competition

'I didn't start the bidding. There were one or two other bidders lower down. I let them have their say and then came in at the end. I bid twice and the second time it stopped, my bid being the highest bid. I thought the auctioneer might withdraw it because it was only slightly higher than we had bid before the auction. I thought it probably hadn't reached the reserve. But then the gavel came down and I knew it was ours.'

Michael Kirby, Chartered Surveyor.

Use a jump bid to put off the competition

Although you will hear the auctioneer dictating the bids he is seeking, if the bidding is well below the price you have decided to pay, you may elect to make a jump bid shouting out a figure which is higher than that for which the auctioneer has just asked. The auctioneer will not be too upset by your disturbance of his bidding rhythm and it may be that an opposing bidder will be put off their stride. You should set out to convince your opponents that you will cap their bids regardless of how high they go and so discourage them from putting in any more bids.

How to reduce the size of the auctioneer's increments

The auctioneer's aim is to dictate the increments in the bidding and to make them as large as possible. He will have more opportunity to do this at the cheaper levels than in the middle range. Thus, with bidding at the £10,000 to £15,000 level, the auctioneer in his early stages may be able to take the bidding to £10,000, £11,000, £12,000, £13,000, £14,000, £15,000. As he comes closer to his reserve and the prices get higher, you may find him reducing the increments to £500 to encourage the bidding and to indicate to his audience that he is coming closer to the reserve. The bidding might then proceed at £15,500, £16,000, £16,500, £17,000. Some auctioneers, having reached their reserve or being very close to it, might bring their increments down to £250 or even £100 or £50 a time. Knowledgeable auctioneers resist this knowing full well that by keeping the increments as large as possible they will obtain a final bid higher than they might otherwise achieve, thus obtaining more for their client.

A useful gambit is to try to reduce the size of the auctioneer's increments in the bidding figures at an early stage. An experienced auctioneer may be wise to this move and refuse to accept low increments but others will accept a reduction in the increment sought, if they are convinced you will give them a bid at that amount. By reducing the increments much earlier than the auctioneer would choose and making your opponents bid innumerable times, you will make them think that you have reached a high amount, enabling you to move in and catch the last bid at a lower level than it might otherwise reach. The following example illustrates this in practice:

Bidding the price down – in practice

AUCTIONEER: I now wish to offer lot number six. A charming and desirable residence with vacant possession, 16 Acacia Road, Lewisham. Where may I start the bidding? £50,000?
(*Silence.*)

AUCTIONEER: Well, ladies and gentlemen, it is in your hands not mine as to where we start the bidding. Should it be £45,000?
(*Silence.*)

AUCTIONEER: Will £35,000 tempt someone to bid? Thank you, sir, I have your bid (*as bidder number one waves her catalogue vigorously in the air*).

AUCTIONEER: I am bid £35,000. Do I see £37,500? £37,500 anywhere?

BIDDER NUMBER TWO: £35,500.

AUCTIONEER: I am looking for £37,500. Will you make it £37,500?

BIDDER NUMBER TWO: No. £35,500.

AUCTIONEER: Your bid at £35,500. I will accept £36,000?
(*Bidder number one nods her head.*)

AUCTIONEER: £36,500.
(*Bidder number two winks.*)

AUCTIONEER: £37,000?
(*Bidder number one waves her finger.*)

AUCTIONEER: I am bid £37,000. I am seeking £37,500. Any further bid? £37,500 anywhere? Any further bids? At £37,000 then for the first time. For the second time. (*The auctioneer lifts his gavel and holds it threateningly in the air and, after a pause, brings it down.*) Sold at £37,000. May I see your paddle number, madam? (*The bidder shows her paddle number.*)

AUCTIONEER: Sold to 142 at £37,000. Now for my next lot …

How to reduce the increments even more …

Bidders have been known to bid in the 'and £100' style, quite specifically interjecting a rhythm of 'and £100 and £100 and £100'. If the auctioneer will wear it, our scenario would go as follows (the auctioneer has a reserve of £40,000):

'And 100' – in practice

AUCTIONEER: I now wish to offer lot number six, a charming and desirable residence with vacant possession, 16 Acacia Road, Lewisham. Where may I start the bidding? £50,000?
(*Silence.*)

AUCTIONEER: Well, ladies and gentlemen, it is in your hands not mine as to where we start the bidding. Should it be £45,000?
(*Silence.*)

AUCTIONEER: Will £35,000 tempt someone to bid? Thank you sir, I have your bid (*as bidder number one waves his catalogue vigorously in the air*).

AUCTIONEER: I am bid £35,000. Do I see £37,500? £37,500 anywhere?
(*Bidder number two coughs and raises a tentative finger in the air.*)

AUCTIONEER: £37,500 bid. £40,000 anywhere?
(*Bidder number one nods his head discreetly.*)

AUCTIONEER: I have £40,000.
(*Bidder number two shakes his head.*)

BIDDER NUMBER THREE: And £100.

AUCTIONEER: £40,100. £42,500, may I say?
(*Bidder number one nods his head.*)

AUCTIONEER: £42,500 I am bid.

BIDDER NUMBER THREE: And £100.

AUCTIONEER: £42,600. Do I see £45,000?
(*Bidder number one looks away.*)

AUCTIONEER: (*pointing at bidder number three*) I have your bid, madam, at £42,600 which is your bid. £45,000 anywhere? Any further bid? I am bid £42,600. I am looking for £45,000.
(*Pause.*)

AUCTIONEER: Can I perhaps tempt anyone at £43,000?
(*Pause.*)

AUCTIONEER: Have you all done?
(*Pause.*)

AUCTIONEER: Has the bidding finished?
(*Pause.*)

AUCTIONEER: Very well, then, at £42,600 for the first time (*pause*), for the second time …(*pause*), and for the final time at £42,600 …
(*The auctioneer lifts his gavel and holds it threateningly in the air and after a pause brings it down.*) Sold at £42,600.

(*looking at bidder number three pointedly*) May I see your paddle number, madam. (*Bidder number three shows her paddle number 142.*)

AUCTIONEER: Sold to 142 at £42,600. For my next lot ….

Auctioneer's Anecdote: How to make big numbers sound small

An auctioneer selling a piece of land for a local authority had instructions that his reserve was any bid over £1,000,000. He wanted to take his increments in £100,000 jumps, so that because of the reserve, the minimum price at which he would sell would be £1.1m. From a psychological point of view, he wanted the increments in the bidding to appear as small as possible although he was determined that, at that stage, they would be not less than £100,000. He is reputed to have tested out on a variety of people whether £1.1m would sound less to a bidder than £1,100,000 or whether he should fall back on the 'and £100' formula discreetly forgetting to mention that the £100 really related to the £100,000 that he was seeking. He decided that he would start the bidding at £600,000 so that the £100,000 increment pattern would be developed well before he reached his reserve. To the auctioneer's horror, having started the bidding at £600,000, and taken a second bid at £700,000, an astute builder 'jump bid' to £1,000,000 hoping to frighten off the opposition. The auctioneer could not sell at £1,000,000 and had lost his initiative in establishing the £100,000 increments. After the bid of £1,000,000 it looked as if the jump bid had succeeded, no other bidders were forthcoming and the silence was ominous. The auctioneer was in a quandary: he could not sell at £1,000,000 and he could not take a bid on behalf of the vendor since that would be in excess of his reserve. The room was silent for what seemed like an age, in an endeavour to regain the initiative the auctioneer changed the coloured slide which gave a second view of the piece of land that he was selling. With the tension broken, the bidding resumed (in £100,000 increments!), the professionals in the room were carried away and the land sold at £3.5m – which you must confess sounds much less than three million, five hundred thousand pounds!

Stoke Newington 313 Amhurst Rd 5-storey terr prop as in need of imp Fgdn (gp£375,000) F V . 487,000	**'Fgdn'** – Front garden
Stoke Newington 158 Green La 3-storey mid-terr off sc flat over in need of imp (gp£275,000) F V prior 285,000	**'imp'** – Improvement
Stratford 63 Borthwick Rd 2-storey s-d prop as Fgdn let £23,400pa PP for conv 2 x 2-bed flats & 1 x 1-bed flat (gp£300,000) F av	**'F'** – Freehold
Stratford 145 Chandos Rd 2-bed terr d-h in need of mod Fgdn (gp£120,000) F V . 167,000	**'prior'** – Sold before auction
Stratford 79 Crownfield Rd 3-bed terr d-h cellar in need of imp Fgdn (gp£130,000) F V . 171,000	**'PP'** – Part vacant possession
Stratford 79 Chandos Rd 2-storey end-terr prop as let AST £16,380pa (gp£210,000) F w 209,000	**'av'** – Available, i.e. unsold
Tottenham 55a Scales Rd 1-storey end-terr studio flat Fgdn (gp£85,000) F V . 85,000	**'mod'** – Modernisation
	'V' – Sold with vacant possession
	'gp' – Auctioneer's guide price
	'w' – Withdrawn unsold
	'85,000' – Sold at the auction at £85,000

Tricks the auctioneer will use against you

Watch out for the auctioneer bidding on behalf of the vendor

It is virtually always mentioned in the auctioneer's conditions of sale and often in his introductory speech that he reserves the right to bid on behalf of various parties. These parties always include the person selling the lot. It can sometimes happen that an auctioneer has only one bidder at some stage in his offering of a lot and where the level of bidding has not reached the reserve or upset price. As the auctioneer cannot sell below his reserve figure, he will use his right to take a bid on behalf of the vendor. This right is enshrined in the Sale of Land by Auction Act 1867 and is included in the auctioneer's conditions of sale.

How the auctioneer bids the price up – in practice

An example of how this works in practice follows (the auctioneer has a reserve of £45,000):

AUCTIONEER: On behalf of the auctioneers, I give notice that they reserve the right to bid, through me or otherwise on behalf of purchasers who have left bids with them, or on behalf of vendors, or as agents, or as principals for any lots.

AUCTIONEER: I now wish to offer lot number one, a charming and desirable residence with vacant possession at 10 West Road, Lewisham. Where may I start the bidding? £50,000?
(*Silence.*)

AUCTIONEER: Well, ladies and gentlemen, it is in your hands and not mine as to where we start the bidding. Should it be £45,000?
(*Silence.*)

AUCTIONEER: Will £35,000 tempt someone to bid? Thank you, sir, I have your bid (*as bidder number one waves his catalogue vigorously in the air*).

AUCTIONEER: I am bid £35,000. Do I see £37,500? £37,500 anywhere?
(*No one moves in the room.*)

AUCTIONEER: £37,500 I am bid.

Note: This is a bid which the auctioneer has interjected on behalf of the seller. The bidding level is well below the reserve of the lot but the auctioneer wishes to keep the momentum of the bidding going and has seen no signs of anyone else wanting to bid in the room and has therefore exercised his right to bid on behalf of the owner.

AUCTIONEER: £40,000 anywhere?
(*Bidder number one nods his head discreetly.*)

AUCTIONEER: £42,500?
(*No one moves in the room.*)

AUCTIONEER: I am bid £42,500.

Note: This is the second bid that the auctioneer has made on behalf of the seller because there is still no momentum in the bidding and the reserve has not been reached.

BIDDER NUMBER TWO: £45,000.

AUCTIONEER: £45,000 I am bid. £47,500 may I say?
(*Bidder number one nods his head.*)

AUCTIONEER: £50,000?
(*Bidder number three winks.*)

AUCTIONEER: £50,000, I have your bid sir. £52,500 anywhere? Any further bid? I am bid £50,000. I am looking for £52,500. Are you all done, has the bidding finished? I am bid £50,000 for the first time, for the second time.

Note: The auctioneer is now above his reserve. He cannot take a further bid on behalf of the owner/seller and is therefore about to bring his gavel down if there are no other bids from people in the room.

AUCTIONEER: Sold at £50,000 (*looking at the successful bidder pointedly*). May I see your paddle number, sir?
(*Bidder number three shows his paddle number as 142.*)

AUCTIONEER: Sold to 142 at £50,000 and for my next lot …

Watch out for bids that are 'off the chandelier'

In bidding parlance, in the better quality auction rooms, if the bidding has stopped more than one increment below the reserve, the auctioneer can then take a bid off the chandelier on behalf of the vendor. In slightly lower quality salerooms this is known as taking a bid off the wall! This right is a vital part of the auctioneer's armoury.

The auctioneer may continue to interject bids on behalf of the vendor in between genuine bids from the floor. He may therefore reach the point where his last bid, which was made on behalf of the vendor, is just one increment beneath the reserve. This will not stop the auctioneer then going through his first and second time patter to suggest that he is about to sell (despite being unable to do so because the bid was made on behalf of the vendor and it is below the reserve).

If he is competent, no one in the room should be able to judge from his demeanour, his body language or his tone of voice that a bid has been made by anyone other than someone in the room. If the auctioneer is not exceptionally competent, you may be able to judge that a bid was off the chandelier and there is no competition other than the vendor and so act accordingly. At that point, you may decide to bid no further, let the lot be withdrawn and bargain to buy it cheaply after the sale.

Stop bidding and make your offer after the auction

An interested bidder who wishes to follow this brinkmanship behaviour needs to be very sure that the opposing bid was taken off the chandelier before the lot was withdrawn and was not from an opposing bidder who made tiny movements that were only obvious to the auctioneer.

Key point

If the last bid was made on behalf of the vendor and is below the reserve, the auctioneer will not bring down the gavel. Instead, he will announce that the lot has been withdrawn.

A lot that gets withdrawn – in practice

The bidding for a lot that is withdrawn might be as follows (the auctioneer has a reserve of £55,000):

AUCTIONEER: I now wish to offer lot number six, a charming and desirable residence with vacant possession, 16 Acacia Road, Lewisham. Where may I start the bidding? £50,000?
(*Silence.*)

AUCTIONEER: Well, ladies and gentlemen, it is in your hands not mine where we start the bidding. Should it be £45,000?
(*Silence.*)

AUCTIONEER: Will £40,000 tempt someone to bid? Thank you sir, I have your bid (*as bidder number one waves his catalogue vigorously in the air*).

AUCTIONEER: I am bid £40,000. Do I see £42,500? £42,500 anywhere?
(*Bidder number two coughs and raises a tentative finger in the air.*)

AUCTIONEER: £42,500 bid. £45,000 anywhere? Do I hear £45,000?
(*Silence.*)

Note: The reserve is £55,000. The bidding appears to have stopped at £42,500. The auctioneer now chooses to interject a bid taken off the wall on behalf of the vendor.

AUCTIONEER: I am bid £45,000. £47,500?
(*Bidder number one winks.*)

AUCTIONEER: £50,000?
(*Bidder number two nods.*)

AUCTIONEER: I have a bid at £50,000. £52,500 anywhere? Any further bids.
(*Nobody moves.*)

AUCTIONEER: I am looking for £52,500. £52,500 I have.

Note: This is a bid made on behalf of the vendor.

AUCTIONEER: Have you all done? Has the bidding finished at £52,500. For the first time at £52,500, for the second time. £55,000 anywhere? (*The auctioneer lifts his gavel and holds it threateningly in the air as if he is going to bring it down but does not do so.*)

AUCTIONEER: Any further bids? Well, ladies and gentlemen, I regret that we have not quite reached the reserve. The owner is looking for a slightly higher price than has been bid. I regret that I cannot sell the property at £52,500 and I must therefore withdraw it from sale. If anybody would like to discuss a purchase of this lot after the auction with me, please do not hesitate to come up and see me.

Note: The property has been withdrawn. The last bid of £50,000 made from the floor was two increments below the reserve. The last bid was of £52,500, interjected by the auctioneer on behalf of the seller. No one bid thereafter. The reserve of £55,000 had not been reached and therefore the auctioneer could not sell from the rostrum.

What an auctioneer is not permitted to do

An experienced auctioneer will not:

1. Show by his demeanour that a bid has been taken off the wall.

2. Take a bid on behalf of the seller (off the wall) at the reserve price.

3. Take a bid on behalf of the seller from more than one source during the bidding for any lot.

What an auctioneer is permitted to do

An auctioneer is permitted to:

1. Take bids either:

   - off the seller; or

   - off a single representative on the floor acting on behalf of the seller; or

   - himself on behalf of the seller.

   However, he can only take one of these courses for any particular lot.

2. Interject bids either:

   - on behalf of the seller in between bids from potential buyers on the floor; or

   - made by the seller in between bids from potential buyers on the floor; or

   - from a single individual representing the vendor in between bids from potential buyers on the floor.

   However, he can only take one of these courses for any particular lot.

3. Interject bids on behalf of other potential buyers (in addition to those on behalf of the seller) up to the maximum amounts that they have specified in their proxy instructions.

4. Accept bids from individuals who are acting by proxy on behalf of potential buyers, where those instructions to bid have been given in writing or are being transmitted over the telephone.

Watch out for subtle changes in the auctioneer's behaviour

It is always worth analysing an auctioneer's pattern of performance in the early lots to see if you can detect subtle changes in the auctioneer's demeanour for lots that are sold, compared with those that are unsold, and for evidence in the auctioneer's behaviour that he has (or has not) reached his reserve. The anecdote below indicates one way in which an auctioneer's behaviour discloses a reserve price. However, there is much to be said for not trying to be too clever, but instead to be well satisfied with a purchase at or below your top figure where the gavel has come down on your bid. You then know for sure that the purchase is yours from that moment.

Auctioneer's Anecdote: A coded reserve

It is known amongst the dealers of one particular provincial town that a well-known auctioneer remains seated until he has reached his reserve and that he then stands up. This has been his practice for many years and the result is that, as soon as the auctioneer stands up, the knowledgeable bidders reduce the bidding increments to minimal amounts in the knowledge that they will be buying the property at, hopefully, very little more than the previous bidder.

Bids on behalf of the vendor

Once you are aware of the logic of the auctioneer's right to bid on behalf of the vendor, it should not disturb you, as owners of property will nearly always wish to specify the minimum sum at which they are willing to sell. Nevertheless, Parliament in 1867 was very concerned about auctioneers using 'puffers' in the audience to inflate artificially the price of the lot. Evidently, at that time, even property auctions had developed the sort of notoriety that mock auctions developed in the 1950s. The 1867 Sale of Land by Auction Act re-enforced the vendor's right to bid but was very insistent that he could not have 'two bites of the cherry'. Vendors can bid for themselves or someone in the audience can be appointed to bid on their behalf or the auctioneer can bid on their behalf but only one of these methods of bidding is permitted. Bids on behalf of or by the vendor can only be up to one bid below the reserve and will not be above the reserve price.

Key point

No person attending an auction need fear that there are three or four individuals conveniently positioned in the audience to 'puff up' the price.

Bidding with a vendor in the audience – in practice

The scenario for the bidding with the vendor in the audience might then go as follows (the auctioneer has a reserve of £54,000):

AUCTIONEER: I now wish to offer lot number six, a charming and desirable residence with vacant possession, 16 Acacia Road, Lewisham. Where may I start the bidding? £50,000?
 (*Silence.*)

A commercial property bargain. Lot 2 of a TOPS' sale was this retail premises. It included ground floor and basement space and sold for a bargain price. Why rent when you can buy at this kind of money?

AUCTIONEER: Well, ladies and gentlemen, it is in your hands not mine as to where we start the bidding. Should it be £45,000?
 (*Silence.*)

AUCTIONEER: Will £35,000 tempt someone to bid? Thank you sir, I have your bid (*as bidder number one waves his catalogue vigorously in the air*).

AUCTIONEER: I am bid £35,000. Do I see £37,500? £37,500 anywhere?
 (*Bidder number two coughs and raises a tentative finger in the air.*)

AUCTIONEER: £37,500 bid. £40,000 anywhere?
 (*Bidder number one nods his head discreetly.*)

AUCTIONEER: £42,500?
 (*Bidder number two lifts his finger.*)

AUCTIONEER: £42,500. £45,000 may I say?
 (*Bidder number one nods his head again.*)

AUCTIONEER: £45,000 bid. £47,500?
 (*Auctioneer points in a general direction to his left and takes a bid off a member of the audience who is actually the vendor.*)

AUCTIONEER: £47,500 bid (*the bid made on behalf of the vendor*).

AUCTIONEER: £50,000 anywhere?
 (*Bidder number one looks away.*)
 (*Bidder number three waves her hand.*)

AUCTIONEER: I am bid £50,000. I am looking for £52,500. £52,500 anywhere? Have you all done? Has the bidding finished? At £50,000 then for the first time, for the second time …
(*Bidder number four shouts out incomprehensibly.*)

AUCTIONEER: I have a new bidder at £52,500. £55,000 anywhere? Have you all finished at £52,500? Will a bid at £53,000 tempt anyone at this stage?
(*No one moves. Auctioneer takes another bid off the vendor in the audience.*)

AUCTIONEER: I have £53,000 (*the bid made on behalf of the vendor*).

AUCTIONEER: £54,000 may I say?
(*Bidder number three nods her head.*)

AUCTIONEER: I am bid £54,000. £55,000 anywhere? £55,000 may I say? Have you all now finished at this price? (*Pause.*) At £54,000 then for the first time, £54,000 for the second time (*pointing at bidder number three*). It is your bid, madam, at £54,000. Any further bid? (*Pause.*) £55,000 anywhere? £55,000 do I see?

AUCTIONEER: Then for the last time …
(*The auctioneer lifts his gavel and holds it threateningly in the air and after a pause brings it down since the reserve of £54,000 has been bid by someone in the room.*)

Sold at £54,000.

(*Looking at bidder number three pointedly.*) May I see your paddle number, madam?
(*Bidder number three shows her paddle number.*)

AUCTIONEER: Sold to 142 at £54,000. My next lot is …

'I waited until the other bids had been made and then came in at the end. I only made one bid, and that was the last bid that succeeded. I was pleased to get it.'

Michael Roe, buyer of residential properties.

How to act and bid at the auction

If you are going to bid at auction for the first time, the following checklist will help you:

1. Sit where you and the auctioneer can see each other clearly. Stay calm, acknowledge you are nervous (so is the auctioneer!).

2. Concentrate, listen and be aware of what is happening around you. Remember your homework and analyses of the lot(s), the auction, the auctioneer and other bidders.

3. Concentrate and listen harder when your lots come up.

4. Look the auctioneer in the eye.

5. Wait for a short pause in which to enter the bidding at or below your maximum figure.

6. Indicate your first bid at the price for which the auctioneer is asking by attracting his attention by a major movement (a wave of the catalogue, a paper, the hand or a bidding paddle).

Shout, wave and stand up if necessary!

7. If this fails, shout the figure of your bid and wave at the same time.

8. If necessary, stand up to attract his attention.

9. Make subsequent bids in the rhythm and pattern sought by the auctioneer. Violent movements should not be necessary. Subsequent bids can be made by anything like:

    *   a raised finger;

    *   a nod of your head;

    *   a flick of the catalogue;

    *   raising the paddle;

    *   a wink or raised eyebrow.

10. If you wish to bid less than the increment asked for by the auctioneer, state your bid loudly. He may or may not accept it.

11. Keep looking the auctioneer in the eye until the lot is yours or unless you wish to stop bidding.

12. To stop bidding, withdraw your gaze and cease movements or speech. If you wish to be polite, indicate your lack of further interest by a shake of the head next time the auctioneer looks at you.

13. If you decide to come back into the bidding, go back to number 4!

14. If you decide to stop, still continue to analyse your competitors and the auctioneer, as the lot may be withdrawn and you may be competing against them later in negotiations by private treaty.

Do not:

1. Bid higher than the price you have fixed as your maximum.

2. Get carried away by the crowd and the auctioneer's enthusiasm (well, not by more than one bid anyway!).

3. Be shy about bidding – the auctioneer will love to have you doing it.

4. Be frightened by anyone else in the room into not bidding.

5. Accept payment from someone else in the room for not bidding.

6. Be frightened by tales of dealers' rings as:

   • they don't usually exist in property auctions;

   • they can't force you into bidding higher than what you fix as your maximum figure.

7. Be bullied by the auctioneer into paying more than your maximum or a greater increment than you choose (but do be realistic about your choice of increment in relation to the price level of the bidding).

8. Be shy about stopping when the bidding is higher than you choose to pay.

9. Buy a lot you have not researched just because it 'looks nice', 'seems cheap', 'is at no reserve', etc.

Auctioneer's Anecdote: The big bang

A London auctioneer, who is now a household name, recalls how in one of his first auction sales he was particularly nervous. A point that had been made to him in his training was the importance of timing. To ensure he did not dwell too long on any particular lot, he carefully removed his watch and placed it on the rostrum where he could clearly see it. On the very first lot, with the joy of passing his reserve and the enjoyment in working competitive bids, he promptly brought the hammer down with a large bang only to find that this had landed on his watch. So much for timing!

How quickly do the lots sell?

Auctioneers come in all shapes and sizes. They also offer lots at greatly different speeds. Many originally learned their rostrum techniques selling chattels and furniture and it is not unusual for chattels of moderate value to sell at 100 to 120 lots per hour. In the composite auction of property, the bidders are paying larger sums that are considerably more important to them. Although the bidding takes a little longer in a property auction, the numbers of bids are less than one sees for chattels because the increments are so much higher. Furthermore, in an auction of property there may be elements of the lot which the auctioneer chooses to highlight and the bidding can be slower.

Expect to see properties sell at 20 to 30 lots per hour

The auction catalogue may give an approximate guide of how long the auction will take. In a day-long sale, it is quite common for the catalogue to indicate starting times for various batches of lots. As the size of the auction reduces, the human nature of auctioneers leads them to draw out the proceedings. In a local pub or hotel where there are five or six lots to offer, the proceedings may take up to one hour. When all is said and done, vendors have to be convinced that the auctioneer has had a really good go at selling their property and has promoted it in its best light. This applies particularly where domestic owner-occupied properties are being offered and the rate of sales tends to be a little slower.

Auctioneers are usually consistent in their individual speed of selling. If you want to judge the rate at which an auctioneer sells, the best way of finding out is to attend one or two auctions in person. Even then, auction houses may put different auctioneers on the rostrum or have different qualities of properties to sell at different speeds. Furthermore, it generally takes longer to sell a lot than it does to offer and withdraw it. But, in a difficult market, the auctioneer is more likely to linger over trying to persuade bidders to add to their last price so that he can reach his reserve.

Key point

Whoever the auctioneer is and wherever the sale is taking place, you can guarantee that as the bidding gets closer to the end, it will always become slower.

Will I always have the chance to make a bid?

If you are unable to make your offer at the early stages in the bidding, do not worry. Every auctioneer of merit will give you an opportunity to slip your bid in before the gavel comes down. Phrases such as 'going for the first time', 'going for the second time' or even the time-honoured phrase of 'going, going, gone' are virtually always used. The auctioneer will invariably incorporate in his patter phrases which indicate that he is about to sell. What is more difficult to ascertain is whether he is going to withdraw rather than sell because he has failed to reach his reserve.

In the auction room, the auctioneer is God

You will always see in the auctioneer's conditions that the auctioneer reserves the right to regulate bidding and to refuse undesirable bids. Furthermore, the auctioneer also reserves the right to resolve any disputes over bidding. There have been one or two celebrated court cases where two bidders have been neck and neck and the unsuccessful buyer has disputed the sale. But in each case it has been held that the auctioneer's decision is final.

The view of certain solicitors and auctioneers is that the legal position could be changing and that the interpretation of an auctioneer's position may depend upon the wording of the conditions of sale published in the brochure.

Your response is simple. Avoid the issue. When you are bidding make absolutely sure that the auctioneer is aware of your presence and of your bid. If you are at all unsure, make your bid again, even more visibly. Check, of course, that he is not treating it as a bid above your last sum!

> **Key point**
>
> If a dispute arises, the auctioneer has absolute jurisdiction.

It is unusual for an auctioneer to bring down the gavel before he has identified the actual bidder. A variety of phrases is used. The auctioneer may specifically indicate to the final bidder, looking him directly in the eyes, that they are the final bidder while going through the 'first time, second time' patter. The buyer may be identified by an article of his clothing or the colour of his clothing or his position in the room; 'the gentleman in the brown suit on the aisle', 'the lady on the back row', 'the couple in the front row in the matching raincoats'. The identity of the last bidder may be emphasised when the auctioneer refuses to take consecutive bids from the same individual where that person is raising his hand too enthusiastically.

Even if the gavel has fallen, the auctioneer is entitled to reoffer the property, in the event of a dispute, as long as he does it immediately. Where bidding paddles are used, then immediate identification of the buyer is easy and will enable any other bidder who feels that he was the buyer, to raise the question immediately.

This will not happen to you because you will have been bidding obviously and confidently and will have made the auctioneer very aware of your interest and determination to bid.

The auctioneer's code of conduct

The Royal Institution of Chartered Surveyors produced, during 1994 (and subsequently revised in 2004), a recommended code of conduct for auctioneers. It does not have the force of law nor even the force of the bylaws or regulations of this august body. Nevertheless, it is a set of guidelines which their members are expected to follow and which, in the future, may be incorporated in whole or in part in local government or central government regulations or legislation. It is available from the Royal Institution of Chartered Surveyors (tel: 0870 333 1600).

Specifically, the preamble to the guidance notes indicate that they serve three purposes:

1. To act as an aide-memoire to points that should be considered by all members of the profession intending to conduct public auctions of real property in England and Wales.

2. To help the vendors of such property (being the clients of the auctioneer).

3. To provide guidance to members of the public (who may be potential purchasers) attending auctions about the background to and the procedures to be followed at auction.

The code is divided into the pre-auction, auction and post-auction periods and, apart from indicating many details of the recommended procedure for auctions, is intended to give considerable comfort and assistance to bidders and successful purchasers.

What happens if the lot is withdrawn or remains unsold?

'You can sometimes get a better deal at auction especially from lots that get withdrawn. Once you have reached your highest price you hope that the property hasn't reached the vendor's reserve and you can do a deal afterwards. You can get quite good deals that way.'

Michael Kirby, Chartered Surveyor.

Check before you attend that your lot is still for sale

There are many reasons for lots being withdrawn and on occasion vendors have been known to withdraw them without reason. It is always wise to check with the auctioneers, approximately 24 hours before the auction takes place, to see if the lot or lots which interest you are still going to be offered. This will certainly necessitate a telephone call. Some auctioneers maintain a pre-recorded message which gives the information on a special number. This will be shown in the auction catalogue.

	118 Northfield Avenue, Ealing, London W13 9RT
	Telephone: 020 8810 1213 Fax: 020 8566 2348
Robertson Smith & Kempson	Email: auction.admin@rskhomes.co.uk
	Website: www.rskhomes.co.uk

PUBLIC PROPERTY AUCTION
to be held at
THE RAMADA HOTEL, EALING COMMON, LONDON W5 3HN
on 27th February 2007, commencing at 2pm
Nearly 50 lots offering a variety of property, to include:

LEASEHOLD INVESTMENTS	7 Tees Avenue, Greenford	Site at 244/246 Chalvey Grove, Slough
135a High Street, Hounslow	18 Inverness Road, Hounslow	12 Poplar Road, New Denham
135b High Street, Hounslow	6 Brunswick Park Gardens, N11	Site at 11 Chiltern Close, Worcester Park
135c High Street, Hounslow	24 Alexandra Road, Hornchurch	Land at Syon Lane, Isleworth
16 Chalfont Court, NW1	7 Livingstone Road, Hounslow	COMMERCIAL
5 Bay Court, Popes Lane, W5	28 Denham Road, Feltham	The Advertising Hoarding, Pinner Rd,
22 Archer House, W13	VACANT FLATS	Harrow
VACANT HOUSES	37 Longfield House, Ealing W5	112 Laird Street, Wirral
Spring Cottage, Hounslow	Flat 8, 53 Westwood Hill, SE26	1 Wharfside, Alperton
96 West Way, Hounslow	Rex Court, Hampton Road West, Feltham	FREEHOLD INVESTMENTS
1 The Green, Hayes	57 Harris Close, Hounslow	Flats 1-17, Fairview, Caveness, Scotland
9 The Greenway, Hounslow	29 Foxlees, Sudbury	499 Sipson Road, West Drayton
24 Hardings Lane, Penge, SE20	9 Ashmore Court, Heston	33 Lowfield Road, Acton, W3
8 Coniston Avenue, Greenford	1 Gatton House, W13	1 Essex Road, W3
53 Evering Road, London, N16	29 Medway Parade, Greenford	10 Brougham Road, Acton, W3
34 Matthews Road, Greenford	13 Ashbourne House, Slough	84 Maple Close, Yeading
96 Oswald Road, Southall	LAND	86 Maple Close, Yeading
7a Berrymead Road, Chiswick, W4	Site at St Mary's Place, Upminster	52 Hencroft Street South, Slough

Why lots get withdrawn

Since you may have spent money and time in researching a lot, it is perhaps most unreasonable for vendors to withdraw lots. Nevertheless, they can do this without any responsibility to you for your abortive costs. Their reasons may include:

The property has been sold before the auction

1. Sellers aim to dispose of their properties at a price which is acceptable to them. They are concerned more about an auctioneer's ability to market the property than his ability to sell the property on the auction day itself. The marketing may have been so successful that vendors receive an offer they are willing to accept. Some vendors are glad to sell at any price. Others do not want to lose the chance of a sale at a reasonable price as 'a bird in the hand is worth two in the bush'. It is not unusual for vendors

to sell prior to the auction if they feel they have received a figure that exceeds considerably the amount which they expect to receive in the auction. If vendors did not think that the auction was the best way of obtaining a sale at the highest price, they would not decide to use this method in the first place. This thinking must influence their attitude to accepting or refusing pre-sale bids.

Incorrect details

2. A lot does not have to be sold to be withdrawn. Auction catalogues have to be prepared at speed and under pressure. Whilst particulars are being prepared, information is frequently at a premium. Owners are not necessarily forthcoming with all the facts required for a catalogue and their solicitors may not be able to provide accurate information in a hurry. In many circumstances, therefore, the auctioneer's catalogue does not contain full details or contains inaccurate details. In these cases the firm may decide not to offer the property until the full information can be made available. Alternatively, it may be the solicitor who decides that it is not possible to provide sufficient evidence on the title or background to the property for it to be safely included in a contract of sale in time for the auction. The solicitor may insist that the lot is withdrawn until everyone is sure the information is correct.

Change of mind

3. Owners of property quite often change their mind and decide not to sell a property or decide that the moment is not opportune. They may feel that the marketing prior to the auction has not produced the amount of interest they expect and that withdrawal at this stage is better than having the property offered and withdrawn at a disappointing bid.

These are just some of the reasons why lots may be withdrawn prior to auction. In each case, you have no entitlement to damages or compensation for your abortive costs, from either the vendor or the auctioneer.

Unsold lots

There have been recent discussions amongst auctioneers about how unsold lots should be treated. The code of conduct for auctioneers indicates very specifically that auctioneers should disclose in unequivocal terms when a lot has not been sold and should not bring the gavel down.

This practice known as 'buying in' is most unlikely to be seen and heard in the sale room of any respectable auctioneer.

Key point

A past practice amongst certain auctioneers of bringing down the gavel, even though the reserve price has not been reached, is now very strongly discouraged.

'For a house or a plot of land that is good you can be outbid if people get carried away. The professional who is buying property will not get carried away but the average punter can tend to get carried away quite easily.'

Michael Kirby, Chartered Surveyor.

CHAPTER 6

After the auction – what happens next?

'I bought another house at the end of 2005 and was surprised when it was knocked down to me for £24,000 as I was expecting to pay up to £25,000. I did think at one stage that I might not get the property although I was prepared to bid £1,000 more than I paid for it. For this second house, similar properties in the area are costing almost twice as much. I was surprised it went for what it did do. I was well pleased with it.'

Don Lee, buyer of a residential property at auction.

What to do when you have got your lot

Is the property insured and secure?

The very first thing you must do is arrange for the property to be adequately insured through your insurance broker or company. You should then pass the copy of the contract or memorandum that has been signed by the vendor or his agent to your solicitor so they can start preparing for completion.

Next, inspect the property again immediately and arrange with the vendor to make it physically secure. You may decide that the keys to the buildings have been so widely distributed in the pre-auction period that the locks should be changed and doors made thoroughly secure. You must expect to have to meet any security requirements imposed as a condition of your insurance cover. It may be appropriate to board up windows, remove any physical objects lying around that could be used by vandals and have any fences and other security arrangements overhauled immediately. All these actions will need the vendor's agreement which can be obtained through either the auctioneers or their solicitors.

Speak to your finance house

Your finance should already be arranged. Whether it is through a building society, a finance house, merchant bank or bank, they must be told without delay that you have been successful in your purchase and be warned of the date you are proposing to complete. Tell your finance house which firm of solicitors you are using. Ask them to liaise directly with your solicitors and provide the loan in time for the completion date.

You will be expected to complete quickly

You will normally be expected to complete 28 days after the auction. At that time, you will have to pay the balance of the purchase monies, stamp duty and any other costs that fall due. Occasionally, contracts allow a shorter or longer time for completion, which the special conditions of sale will have revealed.

If VAT is charged on the purchase price, then this must be paid in full at completion. You or your solicitor should ensure that you obtain a VAT receipt to reclaim the amount if your accountant advises that this is appropriate.

It is usually prescribed in the conditions or special conditions of sale that the conveyance is to be for the entire lot as it was described and is to the original buyer or bidder. If you wish to have the lot conveyed in pieces and to people other than yourself, you are unlikely to succeed in getting the vendor to do this for you unless this was specially arranged with the auctioneer and the vendor's solicitors before the auction started.

A residential opportunity in the expensive North London area of Crouch End was offered as lot 22 by Harman Healy and the selling price of £100,000 for this one-bedroom flat was a long way short of market value; an agent would have been selling for £120,000. This was a good value purchase.

If you wish to have the title to the property split between different owners and this has not been pre-arranged with the auctioneer and the vendor's solicitors, then you will have to meet the extra costs and delay in using your solicitor to prepare new and separate conveyances of the individual pieces to the separate buyers. The cost will increase your solicitor's charges and may involve the separate purchasers paying stamp duty on their own behalf, if the sale prices are above the minimum figure at which stamp duty is due.

What to do after the auction

1. Pass your copy of the contract or memorandum (signed by the seller or his agent) to your solicitor.
2. Arrange insurance.
3. Arrange security.
4. Revisit the property.
5. Tell your finance house you have bought the property.
6. Check for major misdescriptions of the lot (and discuss immediately with your solicitor, if there are any).
7. Meet the tenants (if any).
8. Arrange for future management and rent payments.
9. Prepare to complete 28 days after the auction.
10. Check your finances.
11. Recheck your cash flow.
12. Check the position on VAT.
13. Meet your accountants.
14. Confirm the date for completion with your solicitor, insurers and finance house.
15. Obtain a statement of funds due from your solicitor.
16. Pay and complete.
17. Collect a VAT receipt at completion (if appropriate).

18. Pay all your outstanding fees and costs.

19. Prepare to enjoy your new acquisition.

What happens if I decide not to complete?

Losing your deposit

When the gavel falls the contract is made. A condition of the contract is that the successful bidder exchanges contracts or memoranda and pays a deposit immediately. The conditions of sale indicate how much the deposit should be, but it is usually ten per cent of the purchase price or £1,500 (whichever is the greater). The position is the same whether you buy at auction or by private treaty.

Key point

It does not pay to change your mind after the gavel has fallen. If you renege on the contract, your deposit is forfeited, in full.

You may lose more than your deposit

If you renege on the contract, the seller can take the deposit and is then entitled to resell the property. The resale might be at a lower price than the original. If the new proceeds (after deduction of all the new costs and expenses that the seller has been involved in) are less than the original price (minus the deposit), then the seller is entitled to charge you his extra loss. However, if the net proceeds (less costs and expenses) are more than the original price (minus the deposit), then the seller does not have the right to proceed against you for more money, but he is not responsible to repay any part of the deposit.

Key point

If the original sale price minus the deposit is less than the net proceeds on the resale, then the seller claims the shortfall from the original buyer.

Key point

If the original sale price minus the deposit is more than the net proceeds on the resale, then the seller keeps all of deposit as well as net proceeds.

The following examples illustrate how it works.

How a seller claims for a shortfall

Example 1

Original sale price	£250,000
Deposit of ten per cent retained (£25,000)	
Resale at a lower price	£220,000
Less costs of resale	£10,000
Net proceeds of resale	£210,000
Original sale minus deposit	
£250,000 – £25,000	£225,000
Resale minus costs	
£220,000 – £10,000	£210,000
Shortfall claimed by seller from original buyer	£15,000
Seller also retains deposit of £25,000	

Seller receives		
New sale proceeds		£220,000
Minus resale costs		£10,000
Net new sale proceeds		£210,000
Plus original deposit	£25,000	
Plus shortfall	£15,000	
		£40,000
Seller receives total of		**£250,000**

How a seller retains the deposit in full

Example 2

Original sale	£250,000
Deposit of ten per cent retained (£25,000)	

Resale at only a slightly lower price	£240,000
Less costs of resale	£10,000
Net proceeds of resale	£230,000
Seller receives	
New sale proceeds	£240,000
Minus resale costs	£10,000
Net new sale proceeds	£230,000
Plus deposit	£25,000
Seller receives total of	**£255,000**

Is there a get-out?

Misdescribing the property

You may discover, after a successful bid, that there is a major misdescription of the lot in the catalogue or (less likely) by the seller or auctioneer. Auctioneers and vendors always aim to remove the right of buyers to withdraw from their purchase despite a major misdescription, but the Unfair Contract Terms Act 1977 can prevent such conditions from being enforced. In recent court cases, several judges have held that auctioneers have a duty of care to purchasers to describe lots accurately. This case law is distinct from the criminal offence which auctioneers and estate agents can commit under the Property Misdescriptions Act by giving misleading particulars.

Case study: How a purchaser cancelled a contract because of a misdescription

A builder decided that he had land which was surplus to his requirements in spite of owning it for almost 25 years. Just after the builder bought the land, he obtained planning consent for a development of 60 two-bedroomed flats. He did not start building; no work was carried out that was covered by the planning consent and five years after it was issued, the consent lapsed.

Six years after that, following pressure by environmental groups, the planning policy was changed for the district. Planning consent was now only available to build houses at low densities. A 60-flat development would no longer gain consent. Six months before the builder instructed the auctioneers, a new outline planning consent was granted for the land, allowing for a low-density development of 15 houses. The consent was granted and in existence at the time of the auction.

Misleading particulars can get you out of a contract

Unfortunately, due to staff errors at the builder's office and the auctioneers, the catalogue referred to the earlier consent for 60 flats and did not indicate the date of the consent or that it had lapsed. The successful bidder at the auction assumed, without checking, that the information in the auctioneer's catalogue was correct and based his highest bid on the feasibility of carrying out a high-density development.

Only after he had paid his ten per cent deposit and exchanged contracts did he then research the planning position by contacting the local planning authority and discover to his horror that the land was only worth 50 per cent of what he had paid to use for the construction of 15 houses. The planning authority indicated the policy established for the district and said they would resist any application to renew the planning consent for a high density development.

The purchaser took legal proceedings to have the contract cancelled maintaining, quite justifiably, that the auctioneer's catalogue contained a major misdescription that resulted in the bidder paying far more than the land was worth. The auctioneers pleaded in the case that the general conditions of sale excluded them from the responsibility to describe the property correctly and that the purchaser was not entitled to seek a rescission of the contract.

The judge held that the conditions were in breach of the Unfair Contract Terms Act. He also held that there was a major difference in the value of the land with existing planning consent compared with that which had lapsed. He gave the decision that the purchaser was entitled to cancel the contract, to the return of his deposit and his costs in taking the action.

Had the Property Misdescriptions Act 1991 been in force, it is probable that if the purchaser or anyone else had chosen to complain to the local weights and measures office, the auctioneers would have been found guilty of a criminal offence by giving a misleading description, unless they could prove that they had shown 'due diligence' in their research prior to the auction and the misleading particulars were in no way their fault.

How a purchaser failed to cancel a contract due to a misleading description

An industrial property was offered by auctioneers in Lincoln. In their catalogue they described the floor area as 3,980 sq ft. A successful bidder did not check this floor area before the auction but discovered the week afterwards that the floor area was only 3,880 sq ft. At the same time, he decided that the building was not quite what he wanted and that he would like to renege on the contract.

Minor discrepancies will not count

In the subsequent court case for rescission of the contract, he was unsuccessful because the judge decided that the difference in floor area was only small and not of a sufficiently significant amount to cancel the contract. The successful bidder had to proceed to completion and also had to meet the costs of the vendor.

Key point

If there has been a major misdescription of the lot in the catalogue, it is very probable that you will be able to support a case to have the contract to buy cancelled (and your deposit returned) or the purchase price adjusted to take into account the diminution in value of the property between its real value and the value as originally described.

Negotiate before you complete

If your research before the auction does not reveal a major misdescription, but after making the purchase you discover one exists, you should reveal the extent of the misdescription to your solicitor immediately. Ask his advice about having the contract set aside (cancelled) or seeking a reduction in the purchase price. These negotiations must be carried out before you reach completion of the purchase. Never consider completing the purchase subject to your right to claim an adjustment of the purchase price afterwards, in spite of the requirement that you complete at the end of 28 days. If an argument develops over whether a property has been misdescribed or not, you should not allow completion to occur until the argument has been resolved. If you do complete, then the vendor receives all the purchase price and is under no pressure to discuss the point. Furthermore, it will be up to the purchaser to decide whether or not to start an action. You are in a much stronger position if the vendor is waiting for his money and you leave the vendor in the position where he has to commence an action to complete the purchase.

If you wish to claim a misdescription:

- do it quickly;

- pursue the negotiations to a conclusion before completing;

- never complete, reserving the right to argue afterwards.

Wait until the auction is over to pick up a better bargain

After the auction, the bargain buyers move in. There is no reason why you should not be amongst them if the price you are willing to pay for certain lots proved to be less than the reserve and no one else stepped into the bidding to buy. If the bidding for any lot which interests you goes above the price that you are willing to pay and is withdrawn, do not despair of buying it later. As soon as you stop bidding, listen and watch very carefully to try to assess the quality of any opposition there may be against you. It is possible that an opposing bidder, on seeing that a property has been withdrawn, will not be willing to repeat that bid after the excitement and urgency of the auction has passed.

Make your offer when the vendor is 'down'

It is probable that the property was withdrawn at a figure that is close to the vendor's reserve. Almost invariably the last bid that the auctioneer took on a withdrawn lot was made on behalf of the vendor and taken 'off the chandelier'. The seller may have fixed an optimistic reserve with high expectations and hope that the ambience of the sale room would encourage reckless bidding. In his despair of seeing the lot withdrawn after the auction, that is the time for you to move in and he may succumb to a lower bid from you.

Key point

Do not hesitate, if your lot is withdrawn, to negotiate to buy it at your price afterwards.

The auctioneer may nominate some of his staff to remain in the room and conduct negotiations on withdrawn lots. If so, he is likely to have mentioned this at the time he withdrew them. Even if he didn't, it is always worthwhile approaching senior staff to start negotiations immediately. They are as keen to sell as you are to buy. Remember, there may be other people in the room who are as experienced or more experienced than you, who will also be moving very quickly to see whether they can pick up withdrawn lots at cheaper prices. The auctioneer generally remains on or close to his rostrum after the auction. Do not hesitate to go up to the auctioneer and start negotiating straight away.

Find out the reserve, if you can

The auctioneer or his staff may be willing to disclose the reserve at this stage or it may be possible to read it on literature in front of them. If you can establish the reserve price, this will help you decide what private offer to make. If you make an offer and it is accepted, exchange contracts or memoranda straight away and pay your deposit so that the purchase is yours and no opportunist has the chance to acquire the property before you.

Buying immediately after the sale may not appeal to you because:

- you may feel you want to consider a little longer the price that you are willing to pay;

- you may feel you want to go and visit the lot again before you start negotiations to buy the property privately; by delaying, you run the risk that someone else may buy before you.

On the other hand, if you approach the auctioneers a week after the sale and the lot is still unsold, it is possible that the sellers will be beginning to lose their optimism and enthusiasm and will be willing to consider a lower offer than they would have taken at the sale. Either way, there is no reason why you should not make an offer to the auction house and negotiate for any withdrawn lot at a reasonable time after the sale. Before you do so, check that the property is in the same condition as it was when you originally looked at it. After that, your bargaining can begin. It is probably the second oldest adage in the property profession that 'a buyer's first bid is never his final bid' and you should negotiate accordingly.

> **Auctioneer's Anecdote: The oldest adage in the property profession**
>
> There are only three matters that should really concern you regarding a property: 'position, position and position'.

How to buy a bargain from withdrawn lots by private treaty

1. Do not despair of buying at your price, however high the bidding went.

2. Listen and watch the auctioneer and other bidders immediately after you have stopped bidding.

3. Try to judge how much genuine opposition there is against you. Were there any other actual bids?

4. Try to assess the likely figure of reserve from the auctioneer's comments, actions and body language.

5. Remember the last bid and the amount at which the lot was withdrawn. This may be a future guide to your negotiations.

6. Speak to the auctioneer's staff immediately after the lot is withdrawn and find out if they are in a position to negotiate a post-auction sale there and then.

7. If not, or if you are unsuccessful with the staff, move quickly up to the auctioneer on the rostrum after the auction and negotiate with him immediately.

8. Try to discover the reserve as a guide to your chances of success in that negotiation.

9. If negotiations fail at the auction, visit the property again, review your past research and reconsider your figure.

10. Try to negotiate again the next day.

11. If these negotiations fail, try again later – perhaps in a week. The vendor's resolve can and often does weaken as time goes by.

12. Be persistent in your attempts to negotiate a purchase.

13. In your negotiations, remember the auctioneer will act on the assumption that your first offer is lower than you are finally willing to pay. Do not disappoint him!

14. If you agree a post-auction purchase, complete any outstanding research, pay your deposit and exchange contracts as quickly as you can.

Keep your solicitor on his toes

If you are successful in your negotiations, then you and your solicitor need to be just as speedy as if you were negotiating a purchase before the sale. If you agree a private treaty purchase after the sale, make sure your solicitor does not go to sleep on the paperwork, research and enquiries. It may be that his research and enquiries are complete and that he is satisfied with the title. In this case, consider exchanging contracts or memoranda at the auctioneer's office rather than waiting for your solicitor to do it with his opposite number acting on behalf of the seller. You will have to pay the ten per cent deposit to the auctioneers or the vendor's solicitor at the agent's instruction.

Key point

If you buy through private treaty negotiation after the auction, the procedures are exactly the same as when you exchange contracts before the sale or at the auction itself.

The best bargains can be found even later

Some of the best property bargains are bought not at the auction itself, but much later. By keeping a close eye on auction results, it is possible to spot which properties were withdrawn and did not sell immediately afterwards and then move in to pick them up at a bargain price. It is a technique used by many entrepreneurs and dealers, but there is no reason why anyone cannot find their home in this way.

Key point

It pays to research auction results for withdrawn lots.

Auctioneer's Anecdote: How to make £90,000 from one bargain

A well-known dealer who frequents London auctions relies almost entirely on buying lots after the sale. A well-known firm prepared their details in a hurry and the vendor was too busy to check the draft that they sent him. The owner's solicitors had no physical knowledge of the property. Only half the accommodation of the building was listed in the catalogue. The dealer was aware of this but no one else seemed to notice it. The vendor fixed a high reserve for the property. The dealer was unwilling to bid up to that reserve and the lot was withdrawn. The vendor was dis-spirited by the lack of interest in the auction and a week later he told the auctioneer he would accept a price 20 per cent less than his reserve for a quick sale. Coincidentally, on the very same day, the dealer checked through the list of unsold lots and noticed it was still available. He rang the auctioneer and was told of the price reduction. He bought the property for £140,000. Shortly after completion, he obtained planning consent to split the property into two individual units, carried out the moderate amount of building work necessary at approximately £20,000 and then sold off the front and back portions of the property at £130,000 and £120,000 respectively making a handsome profit of £90,000. The deal started that buyer on a property career which has made him a multi-millionaire and he is still an avid searcher through the lists of withdrawn lots.

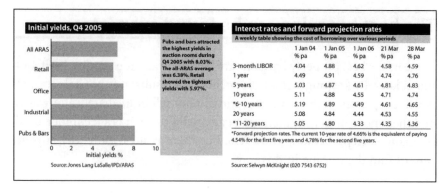

Figure 6.1 Auction statistics from 1 April 2006 in the Estates Gazette

How to find your bargain property

Property Auction News

The best source for finding out when and where property auctioneers are based and the districts their auctions cover.

The Estates Gazette

The *Estates Gazette* is a good source of property information.

Auction house reports

Virtually all auction houses produce schedules of their results shortly after each sale. They are frequently available on a mailing list. They usually indicate which lots have been withdrawn and, more usefully, list the prices at which the unsold lots are available. These figures are generally the original reserves. Remember that at this stage sellers are at their lowest ebb so even these quoted figures could be negotiable. Usually in the days immediately after a sale auctioneers find their phones hot with enquiries about the unsold lots so you could be in competition. Don't hang about. Move quickly!

Barnard Marcus identifies its bidders at £29m sale

Estelle Maxwell

Barnard Marcus launched a register of the room at its latest auction, in an effort to stay in touch with bidders after the sale.

Auctioneer Chris Glenn said the scheme would help the firm to track established and potential investors and entice them to future events. Visitors to April's auction will be required to pre-register.

He said: "By doing this, we will know a lot more about our bidders than previously. It will help novice buyers to recognise a friendly face and enable us to monitor potential money-laundering activities, which we are required to do by law."

Glenn was pleased with the day's results. Forty-eight out of 213 lots sold prior, sales totalled £29.27m, and the success rate was 77%, with investors' thirst for land with potential for planning permission powering the prior sales. Bidding from owner-occupiers and developers was strong.

Though the final take was reduced by difficulties with legal documentation for a portfolio in Colwyn Bay, North Wales, levels of interest prior to the event indicated that demand for stock was high, Glenn said.

"There was no shortage of money and people are desperate to find somewhere for it," he said. "The difficulty for us is trying to deliver the right kind of stock, because there is the appetite for it among bidders.

"We offered more than 230 properties on RightMove, which was visited 550,000 times in three weeks. Some lots had 6,000 hits, so we knew the appetite was likely to be exceptional."

Star performers included a freehold house divided into flats in Walthamstow, E17. It was bought for £90,000 three years ago and sold for £175,000.

Figure 6.2 Auction news in the Estates Gazette

Local and national news items

You can only discover them by reading those local newspapers that feature auction news. Some national newspapers such as the *Financial Times* and the *Daily Telegraph* occasionally carry auction news but it is not as comprehensive as the journals such as the *Estates Gazette*. It is unusual for any articles to refer to unsold lots.

Key point

It is most unusual for the identity of any purchaser to be revealed in any of the literature related to the publication of results. Auctioneers have a strict code of not revealing the names and addresses of purchasers unless specific consent is granted.

CHAPTER 7

The insider's guide to an auction house

'I would definitely buy another property at auction and have no hesitation recommending others to buy at auction provided they understand the risks and have no worries.'

Don Lee, buyer of a residential property at auction.

The auctioneer's timetable – sale day is A-day

This chapter gives you an inside view of what happens in an auction house in the three to four months before A-day (auction day) and in the months afterwards.

In a busy auction house where composite auctions are organised on a monthly basis, the auction team will be organising a regular round of two to three auctions at a time. Each auction has its own three-monthly programme overlapping the others. The organisation of an auction may be in the hands of one individual or a team. A standard auction programme spans three months from the preparation period through to post-auction. To ensure the programme runs smoothly, the auctioneer has built-in standards, routines and procedures. Even so, each programme has its periods of relative quiet and frantic activity. Some days proceed smoothly with routine administration, inspection and preparation of the catalogue whilst others are frantic, making arrangements and negotiating with vendors, buyers and potential bidders.

At the same time, the accountancy team will be concerned with keeping records of sales, ensuring bills are rendered for entry fees and sales commissions, collecting in amounts due and being positive that deposit and purchaser's cheques are dealt with in accordance with professional rules and held in appropriately secure and insured accounts.

In a firm that holds auctions less frequently the programme will be similar.

Entry fees

Nine to ten weeks before A-day

It is a universal practice for auctioneers to separate their charges into two elements. These are an entry fee when instructed and a separate fee when contracts are exchanged.

The entry fee charged depends on a number of factors:

1. **Situation of the auction house**

    A major London firm may charge three times the entry fee that a local provincial firm will charge for the same service.

2. **Advertising**

    The extent of promotion and marketing necessary varies considerably from lot to lot and area to area. Firms may recommend supplementary advertising in addition to that covered by their normal entry fee where special lots justify it.

3. **Quality of the catalogue**

    The catalogue may be in an expensive, glossy and coloured style produced at an enormous cost which the auctioneers seek to cover by entry fees. Alternatively, it may be of lesser quality at a cheaper cost justifying a smaller entry fee.

4. **Size of mailing list**

    Many of the principal auction houses maintain a mailing list of over 10,000 names which may be expanded further for especially attractive lots. Other firms may only maintain mailing lists of between 300 and 3,000 names which can be serviced at a cheaper cost and which justify a smaller entry fee.

Key point

Entry fees can vary from £250 to £2,500 (excluding supplementary advertising). (See pages 189–90.)

Similarly, commissions on sales vary. They are frequently quoted as a percentage of the sale price obtained in a range from one and a half per cent to six per cent. Auction houses generally specify a minimum sale fee. Some firms specify as low as £500, a norm for provincial firms is around £700, while in London it can be around £2,500.

Under the Estate Agents Act 1979 and subsequent regulations, auctioneers are required to provide details of their charges. Failure to do this puts them in a very weak position when claiming fees after a sale has taken place. A sample of an auctioneer's auction terms is shown in Figure 7.1 and analysed in more detail in chapter 8.

At this stage, the ball is firmly in the court of the seller to return the entry form and fee promptly and to provide the fullest and most accurate details possible of the property that is to be sold. The auctioneer may provide an auction details sheet similar to the one in Figure 7.2. Often those basic details will need amplification depending upon the nature of the property being sold. For example, the details of the tenancies may be extensive for a commercial investment. The accommodation may be more than can be covered in the space available on the form. Nevertheless, the form does provide the vendor with an aide-memoire to the vital details required.

Wise auctioneers forcefully encourage vendors to disclose known defects in properties such as outstanding repair or sanitary notices, major arrears of rent, structural failings now existing or which ought to have been remedied in the past. Auctioneers always stress that properties should be described 'warts and all'.

Most auctioneers have a deadline date for the entry of lots in a particular auction but quite frequently they can be persuaded to adjust this date by two or three days.

AUCTIONEER'S AUCTION TERMS

1 Following the receipt of instructions and the full entry fee as communicated, the Auctioneers will take all reasonable steps to include the property described in these instructions (hereinafter referred to as 'the property') in their next suitable and available composite public auction (hereinafter referred to as 'the auction').

2 Entry fees which are to cover the costs of advertising and promotion are non-returnable and are due as a debt from the owner/agent to the Auctioneers upon the signing of the instructions.

3 By signing this instruction form, the owner/agent gives the Auctioneers absolute irrevocable authority to act as sole selling agents to negotiate and enter into a contract for the sale of the property:

(a) from the date hereof until the auction at a price authorised by the owner/agent;

(b) at the auction at the highest genuine bid at or above the reserve price;

(c) at any time up to eight weeks after the auction at the reserve price;

and by so signing this instruction form the owner/agent warrants to the Auctioneers that he has the authority to give such absolute irrevocable authority.

4 Upon unconditional exchange of any such contract for sale entered into the Auctioneers shall become immediately entitled to three per cent plus VAT of the contract price for the sale of the property or the minimum sale fee plus VAT, whichever is the greater, from the owner/agent and the Auctioneers and their duly authorised agents shall be entitled to deduct that sale fee plus VAT from any deposits received on, before or after exchange of any such contract for sale from the intending purchaser without further authority.

5 The balance of any such deposits will be held to an insurance bonded clients' account up to completion of such contract for sale, but any interest earned on such deposits held by the Auctioneers shall be held to their credit and not to the credit of the owner/agent and shall at all times be the absolute property of the Auctioneers.

6 Should any such contract for sale be exchanged but not completed the Auctioneers shall become immediately entitled to a commission payment from the owner/agent of one and a half per cent of the contract price, or 50 per cent of the minimum sale fee, whichever is the greater, plus VAT, without deduction.

7 The owner/agent hereby confirms his understanding that the effect of appointing the Auctioneers as sole selling agents as set out above is inter alia to prevent the owner/agent whether by himself, his servants or agents or otherwise whatsoever:

(a) from negotiating or entering into a contract for sale of the property from the date hereof until 12 weeks after the date of the auction otherwise than through the Auctioneers;

(b) from negotiating or entering into a contract for sale of the property from the date hereof at any time with a person introduced to him by the Auctioneers other than through the Auctioneers.

8 The owner/agent further confirms that he has been provided with and read the Auctioneers' 'Information for Vendors' catalogue.

9 If, in breach of the Auctioneers' rights as sole agents, a contract for sale of the property is negotiated otherwise than through the Auctioneers and such contract for sale is entered into or exchanged at any time up to 12 weeks after the date of the auction, or at any time with a person introduced to the owner/agent by the Auctioneers, the Auctioneers shall on exchange of such contract become immediately entitled to payment from the owner/agent of liquidated damages equal to:

(a) where the contract price is revealed by the owner/agent to the Auctioneers three per cent of the contract price, or the minimum sale fee, whichever is the greater, plus VAT;

Figure 7.1 Auctioneer's auction terms

(b) where the contract price is not revealed to the Auctioneers and no reserve price has been fixed for the property three per cent of 110 per cent of such reserve price, or the minimum sale fee, whichever is the greater, plus VAT;

(c) where the contract price is not revealed to the Auctioneers and no reserve price has been fixed for the property three per cent of the Auctioneers' estimate of the market value of the property, or the minimum sale fee, whichever is the greater, plus VAT.

10 If the property is withdrawn by the owner/agent other than by reason of a sale made pursuant hereto before the auction, the Auctioneers shall on such withdrawal become immediately entitled to a commission payment from the owner/agent equal to:

(a) where a reserve price for the property has been fixed one and a half per cent of the reserve price, or 50 per cent of the minimum sale fee, whichever is the greater, plus VAT;

(b) where no reserve price for the property has been fixed one and a half per cent of the Auctioneers' estimate of the market value of the property, or 50 per cent of the minimum sale fee, whichever is the greater, plus VAT;

save that should a contract for sale of the property thereafter be negotiated otherwise than through the Auctioneers and such contract for sale be entered into or exchanged at any time up to 12 weeks after the date of the auction (or at any time with a person introduced to the owner/agent by, or contacted by, the Auctioneers) the Auctioneers shall be entitled to claim liquidated damages under Clause 8 hereof in lieu of their claim to a commission payment under this clause, and should a claim for commission payment under this clause have already been made by the Auctioneers and paid by the owner/agent they will nevertheless be entitled to claim from the owner/agent the difference between the sum paid hereunder and the sum they are entitled to under Clause 9 above.

11 The minimum sale fee described in there auction terms shall be £600 plus VAT.

12 The reserve price will be notified to the Auctioneers by the owner/agent either verbally or in writing at least three working days before the date of the auction. If it is not, or in the event of the owner/agent fixing a reserve price which in the opinion of the Auctioneers is too high, then the Auctioneers may at their discretion choose not to offer the property at the auction. In such an instance the owner/agent will not have any claim whatsoever against the Auctioneers and will still be liable for the entry fee whether paid in advance or not. In the event of the owner/agent notifying the Auctioneers of the reserve price, which in the opinion of the Auctioneers is lower than they themselves would recommend, then in the absence of a suitable explanation from the owner/agent as to why such reserve price is suggested the Auctioneers may within 14 days of such notification notify the owner/agent that such reserve price is lower than the Auctioneers would recommend and shall not be regarded as the reserve price for the purpose of Clauses 9 and 10 herein.

13 The Auctioneers require the owner/agent:

(a) to instruct solicitors to act on his behalf:

(i) to deduce full and proper title to the property;

(ii) to provide full contract of sale documents together with any additional and special conditions necessary;

(iii) to attend at the auction to render details of the title, and provide a copy of an up-to-date local search if available;

(iv) to exchange contracts if so required by the Auctioneers;

(v) to indicate that all deposits paid may be received and held as agents for the owner/agent in accordance with the terms hereof;

(vi) to take full responsibility for the preparation and use of the memorandum of contract in the catalogue if it is used by the owner/agent or by the Auctioneers.

Figure 7.1 Auctioneer's auction terms (continued)

(b) to indemnify the Auctioneers and their agents against any claims made because of faulty title or information provided by the owner/agent or any other failures by the owner/agent or his solicitors or other agents.

14 For the avoidance of doubt the Auctioneers will be entitled to receive VAT in accordance with the law in addition to all commissions and entry fees payable.

15 The Auctioneers will use their best endeavours to obtain a signed memorandum and deposit from the successful bidder at the auction but cannot be held responsible to the owner/agent if the successful bidder will not comply with these requirements. In the event of a failure of a successful bidder to supply his name and address and, if appropriate, the name and address of the person or company on whose behalf he has been bidding, the Auctioneers are authorised to resubmit the property for sale at their total discretion at any time during the course of the same or future auction sessions within 12 weeks thereof.

16 The Auctioneers have the owner/agent's authority to refuse to accept any bids in the Auctioneers' absolute discretion. Even though this shall only be done in the best interests of the owner/agent, exercise of the discretion shall not in any way render the Auctioneers liable to the owner/agent.

17 The Auctioneers are authorised to accept payment of deposits by cheque.

© **Howard R Gooddie 2007**

Figure 7.1 Auctioneer's auction terms (continued)

The inspection and the preparations

12 to 13 weeks/eight to nine weeks before A-day

Sellers need to help the auctioneers at this stage to make it easy for them to inspect the property. They need to provide:

- keys that fit and enable access to all portions of the building;

- letters of authority for production to tenants to allow entry;

- an accurate description of how to reach the property;

- plans showing the extent of the boundaries with details of any easements;

- full details and telephone numbers that may be necessary for access or to cover emergencies;

- details of burglar alarm provisions and how they may be switched on and off.

If a Home Information Pack is needed, these provisions will need to be made 12 to 13 weeks before A-day. Otherwise, it will be eight to nine weeks before.

AUCTION DETAILS SHEET

Property Address: _____

_____

Description (eg tenanted house, _____
vacant semi, commercial investment) _____

Route to Property: _____

_____

Construction Materials:

Tenure: Freehold/Leasehold   (Please delete as appropriate)

Chief or Ground Rent: (Please delete as appropriate)

Tenants' Names:

Rent or Rents Receivable:

Outgoings Payable:

Period of Lease:

Rent Reviews: **Rent Review Formula:**

Approximate Site Area:

Accommodation: **Ground Floor:**
                   First Floor:
                   Exterior:
                   Additional:

Viewing Arrangements:

Any Co-Agents:

General Comments:

Solicitors: **Name of Firm:** _____

               Address: _____

_____

               Person Dealing: _____ **Phone No.** _____

Reserve Price:

BLUE - Retained by Vendor   GREEN - Auctioneer   WHITE - Auction Co-ordinator

Figure 7.2 Auction details sheet

During the following week, the auctioneer's team:

- inspects the properties;
- organises photographs;
- prepares catalogue details;
- obtains plans and copies of planning consents (see Figure 7.3);
- gains details of building regulation consents;
- obtains copies of leases;
- collates any other items necessary for the catalogue.

The catalogue details

Eight weeks before A-day

With the details organised, the catalogue is now prepared in draft, the auctioneers taking great care that they are not in breach of the Property Misdescriptions Act 1991. They may ask the vendor, their solicitors, co-agents and anyone else who has provided information to co-operate in ensuring that the catalogue details are correct.

During this period, if they have not already been instructed by the vendors, the solicitors who are acting on their behalf are warned of the proposed sale, asked to check the catalogue details, check the property details in it, apply for a local search and prepare a contract for sale. They need at least four weeks' warning and prefer more if possible.

Final copy

Seven weeks before A-day

This is a hectic period when all the details have been collated and approved and are merged into the copy ready for submission to the printers. At this stage, the photographs, plans and other material are chosen and redrawn, edited, cropped or changed in scale to fit the style of the catalogue and the nature of the property being offered.

Town and Country Planning Act 1971 (as amended)

PLANNING PERMISSION

Name and address of applicant: Name and address of agent (if any):

   Mr & Mrs Turner,   Jenkins Technical Services,
   28 Kings Road,   The Business Centre,
   Kilbyfield,   Kay Street,
   Kilner,   Bury,
   KL1 7BC.   BL9 6BU.

Part 1 – Particulars of application

Date of application: Application no.
14 April 2007   17/28/307

Particulars and location of development:
Two storey rear extension to residential home, Kings Road, Kilner.

Part 2 – Particulars of decision

The Rossendale Borough Council hereby give notice in pursuance of
the Town and Country Planning Act (as amended) that **permission
has been granted** for the carrying out of the development referred
to in Part 1 hereof in accordance with the application and plans
submitted <u>subject to the following conditions</u>:

1. The development must be begun not later than the expiration of
   five years beginning with the date of this permission.

2. Car parking, servicing and manoeuvring facilities shall be
   provided within the application site, and thereafter laid out
   and surfaced to the satisfaction of the local planning
   authority before any building which is hereby permitted is
   first occupied for the purposes of this permission, or at such
   other time as may subsequently be agreed, in writing, with
   that authority.

3. Samples of the proposed reconstructed stone to be used for the
   construction of all external walls shall be submitted to and
   approved by the local planning authority before any
   development is commenced.

<u>The reasons for the conditions are:</u>

1. Required to be imposed pursuant to section 41 of the Town and
   Country Planning Act 1971 (as amended).

2. In order to ensure that sufficient car parking and servicing
   space is provided within the application site thus ensuring
   that visiting vehicles are not encouraged to park on the
   carriageway of adjoining highways thereby causing obstruction
   to same.

3. For the avoidance of doubt.

Figure 7.3 Planning consent

Engineering and Planning Department,
Stubbylee Hall,
BACUP, Lancashire, OL1 something

ENGINEER AND PLANNING OFFICER
Date: **15 JUN 2007**

(See over for general information and guidance on post-decision procedures)

IMPORTANT NOTICE
This is an approval under
PLANNING ONLY

GENERAL INFORMATION FOR APPLICANTS INCLUDING GUIDANCE ON POST-DECISION PROCEDURES

1. If the applicant is aggrieved by the decision of the local planning authority to refuse permission or approval for the proposed development, or to grant permission or approval subject to conditions, he may appeal to the Secretary of State for the Environment in accordance with section 36 of the Town and Country Planning Act 1971 (as amended), within six months of receipt of this notice. (Appeals must be made on a form which is obtainable from the Department of the Environment, Tollgate House, Houlton Street, Bristol, BS2 9DJ.) The Secretary of State has the power to allow a longer period for the giving of a notice of appeal but he will not normally be prepared to exercise this power unless there are special circumstances which excuse the delay in giving notice of appeal. The Secretary of State is not required to entertain an appeal if it appears to him that permission for the proposed development could not have been granted by the local planning authority, or could not have been so granted otherwise than subject to the conditions imposed by them, having regard to the statutory requirements.

2. If permission to develop land is refused or granted subject to conditions, whether by the local planning authority or by the Secretary of State for the Environment, and the owner of the land claims that the land has become incapable of reasonably beneficial use in its existing state and cannot be rendered capable of reasonably beneficial use of carrying out of a development which has been or would be permitted, he may serve on the Council of the district in which the land is situated a purchase notice requiring that Council to purchase his interest in the land in accordance with the provisions of Part IX of the Town and Country PLanning Act 1971 (as amended).

3. In certain circumstances, a claim may be made against the local planning authority for compensation, where permission is refused or granted subject to conditions by the Secretary of State on appeal or on a reference of the application to him. The circumstances in which such compensation is payable are set out in section 169 of the Town and Country Planning Act 1971 (as amended).

4. (Applicable only to cases where planning permission or reserved matters approval has been granted). This permission refers only to that required under the Town and Country Planning Acts and does not include and consent or approval under any other enactment, bylaw, order or regulation; not will it operate as a listed building consent in respect of any works described in the permission for the alteration or extension of a listed building. Such works should be the subject of a separate application for listed building consent in that behalf. In particular, the applicant should take note that it may also be necessary to seek

Figure 7.3 Planning consent (continued)

building regulation approval to carry out the works described in plans accompanying this application pursuant to the provisions of the Building Regulations 1976. The applicant should take further note that it is necessary for him to ensure that all relevant permissions or consents are obtained including, where applicable, an order to divert or stop public footpaths, <u>before</u> any development is commenced.

5. In cases involving the erection of a building, or any extension to an existing building, the applicant should take note that the provisions of section 31 of the County of Lancashire Act 1984 will, as appropriate, apply to any concurrent or subsequent submission for building regulation approval for such development insofar as the provision, or, as the case may be, the retention of adequate means of access to the building (or any extension thereto), or to any neighbouring building, for the fire brigade is concerned.

Figure 7.3 Planning consent (continued)

Each catalogue contains the following information for each lot:

- Address

- Nature of property

- Tenure

- Summary of fundamental terms of any leases

- Brief description of accommodation

- Viewing arrangements

- Any co-agents

Human nature being what it is, it is inevitable at this stage that certain responses have not been received from vendors or their solicitors or co-agents who will need chasing up.

Printing and first advertising

Five to seven weeks before A-day

The final copy is read, checked and approved.

Printers' programmes vary but auctioneers look to their printers to organise the catalogue being printed, collated and returned to their office within six to ten working days. During this period, the auctioneer's office is not quiet since the advertising programme has to be organised, the first advertisements submitted and For Sale boards organised. The mailing list, which is on constant update, is run off ready for the despatch of the catalogues immediately after they are received from the printers. These catalogues may be sent out by a mailing house if this method of mailing is used. Addresses from enquirers responding to the advertisements are added to the mailing list.

Computer programs are ideally suited to deal with the registration of enquiries, their assessment, analysis and organisation, whether received by telephone, letter, fax or answerphone. Some auctioneers maintain free mailing lists; others maintain annual subscription lists at costs from £20 to £100 per annum and a limited few run dedicated telephone numbers where the caller pays. Figure 7.4 shows how an auctioneer's mailing list is structured.

The mailing of the catalogue should allow you to have at least four clear weeks in which to assess the lots in the auction and organise your research and enquiries. The catalogue is also dispatched to all vendors, vendors' solicitors, landlords, tenants and anyone else (other than all those already registered on the mailing list) whom the auctioneers feel will be interested in the property. Owners of land or buildings which adjoin lots may well be interested in the expansion of their ownership by buying next door and will receive a copy. Because of their potential as buyers they are frequently targeted in auctioneers' mailing shots.

Co-agents (other firms of estate agents who may have been employed by either the auctioneers or the vendor to promote the sale of the property at the same time as the auctioneers) have to be given a good supply of catalogues to issue from their offices.

Enquiries frequently include requests for guideline prices. These figures are usually a pessimistic and an optimistic estimate by the auctioneers (agreed in conjunction with the vendors) of the prices that might be realised for the lots. They are only guidelines but they need to be available from the moment the first enquiries start coming in. On occasion, auctioneers publish them in their advertisements or in the catalogue. The fixing of guidelines (and the philosophy behind them) is explained in more detail on pages 208–10.

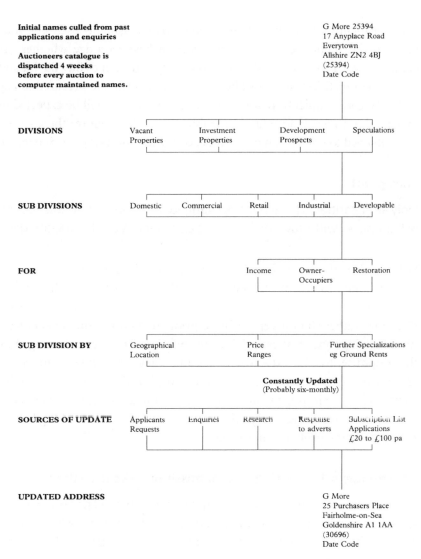

Figure 7.4 *Auctioneer's mailing list structure*

Enquiries and offers before the auction

During the next 30 days, the auctioneer's office deals with all the initial enquiries and, shortly after the catalogues go out, starts to receive offers from potential buyers who would like to negotiate the purchase prior to the auction. Negotiating to buy a lot before auction is common. Many potential buyers feel confident enough to risk negotiating before the auction. This cuts out the competition by preventing others from making a bid on auction day. By initiating negotiations, you gamble disclosing your hand to the auctioneers before the sale. You have to judge whether the gamble is worthwhile depending on how badly you want to buy the lot and beat the competition. You must be sure how much you are prepared to pay and to negotiate quickly. If your offer is successful, you will be expected to exchange contracts before (and probably several days before) the auction. You will need to pay the ten per cent deposit when contracts are exchanged.

Key point

Only after contracts have been exchanged on a sale prior to the auction will the seller withdraw the lot from being offered on the auction day.

Sellers will make up their own minds, in consultation with the auction team, whether to accept offers before auction. In the light of the interest shown, they may be encouraged to revise the reserve in an upward direction, rather than accept a figure prior to auction. Auctioneers have mixed feelings about offers prior to the auction. They are encouraged by the response to the advertisements but they are often tempted to encourage vendors to accept on the 'bird in the hand' philosophy. Nevertheless, their judgement is put to the test in advising the seller about the merits of accepting or rejecting a prior bid rather than risking having to withdraw the property on the day.

Auctioneer's Anecdote: 'I cannot possibly make it on the day'

It is an acknowledged fact in auctioneers' circles that all people, without fail, when making offers before the auction state categorically that they 'will not be able to attend on auction day'! Their reasons frequently emphasise human beings' originality.

Enquiries are notoriously difficult to analyse. Some enquirers do not disclose their hand at all and merely ask for catalogues to be sent to them. Other enquirers disclose the interest they have in types of property in general or sometimes in specific lots. These enquiries frequently stretch to asking the auction house what price a particular lot might reach. The enquirer's response to the guidelines that are then quoted can give the auctioneers some opportunity to define the strength and quality of the applicant's interest at that stage.

Vendors frequently want to know the amount of interest that has been shown in their lots. The number of applicants wishing to view particular properties can indicate the degree of interest. Nevertheless, every auctioneer will tell stories of properties that fail to sell, despite tremendous interest and other lots that sell with considerable competitive bidding, despite little interest being shown before the auction. Although many buyers deny it, it is common to see individuals who have been unsuccessful in buying prior to the auction day, attend and bid. However, no wise auctioneer relies on this happening.

Key point

In the light of interest shown and offers received, guidelines and reserves are frequently reviewed.

Immediately before the auction

Three to five days before A-day

During this period, pressure needs to be exerted on buyers (and frequently on buyers' and sellers' solicitors) to exchange contracts on any sales that are agreed prior to the auction. If such contracts have not been exchanged by the day of the sale, then the lot is offered.

An amendment sheet is prepared giving any changes to the details and describing the lots and the order of selling. Steps are taken to advise interested parties and enquirers where lots are sold prior to the auction.

At this point, reserves are agreed with sellers in the light of the amount of interest shown in the properties and offers received. Many auctioneers require the reserves to be confirmed in writing by the vendors (to be received before the auction commences). Government bodies frequently detail their reserves in a confidential letter to the auctioneer, only to be opened just before the auction starts.

One day to go

Last minute negotiations and revisions of reserves and guidelines continue whilst the auctioneer and his staff prepare for the auction and organise their support material and equipment. The auctioneer checks the last details in the amendment sheet and prepares his auction brief, schedule of reserves and his speech.

The auction

A-day

The auction passes in a flurry of hectic activity. What happens on the day is explained in chapters 4 and 5. The work of the staff does not finish with the auction. Immediately after it, negotiations with potential buyers start on withdrawn lots. These potential buyers fall into three categories:

1. Bidders or intending bidders who were not willing to bid at prices equal to the reserve. They will be hoping to buy the property after the auction at their maximum figure or may be having second thoughts and hoping that by negotiating a little higher they will be successful. Alternatively, they may sense that the owner of the property is willing to reduce the price, having been disheartened by the lack of success at the auction.

2. Bargain hunters who are looking to pick up cheap lots.

3. Potential buyers who were perhaps not sufficiently researched or prepared or did not have their finance in place to buy at the auction but who hope that their arrangements can be completed shortly.

This is a good, sound, secure commercial investment. Lot 36 of an Allsop's commercial auction consisted of the ground floor lease and the upper floors' ground rents of this impressive building in the centre of Chiswick, West London. The income was £31,200, which equated to a yield of 8.6 per cent on a purchase price of £361,000. There was a rent review shortly and there could have been other advantages to owning the freehold.

All three types of potential buyer will be encouraging the auctioneer to disclose his reserve. If they succeed in persuading the auctioneer to reveal the reserve, they will start negotiating from that figure having discovered the price at which the vendor is willing to sell.

The schedule of the results has to be prepared for immediate transmission to relevant publishers such as the *Estates Gazette*. Cheques are collected, banked and 'express' cleared as appropriate. Press releases are submitted to the *Estates Gazette* and whichever local newspapers and financial press the auctioneers feel might be willing to publish their results.

Immediately after the auction

The week after A-day

If a number of lots has been withdrawn, this period is particularly hectic with continuing negotiations for sales. These negotiations do not stop the routine work being carried out of preparing and issuing bills for the auctioneer's fees, transferring the deposits and payments for fees, and updating the records for filing and preservation. All vendors, regardless of whether they have attended the sale or not (and the majority don't), are advised of the results of the sale as far as their lots are concerned. The solicitors for both sellers and purchasers need to be contacted. The boards erected under the advertising programme need to be updated with SOLD slips, where appropriate, and subsequently removed.

Auctioneer's Anecdote

For one provincial auctioneer, a SOLD indication is insufficient on his boards which can be seen adorned round his town with a blurred gavel against the words 'Going, Going, Gone'!

After the auction

Two to four weeks after A-day

Now the final tidying takes place. The sales of any remaining lots (those withdrawn and unsold) are still promoted. The final fee notes are rendered as the remaining pre- and post-auction private treaty sales are completed. Sellers who have been unfortunate enough not to sell their lots are approached to see if they wish to offer them in a subsequent auction. Completion of all the sales should then take place approximately one month after the auction.

The Auctioneer's Programme	
9 to 10 weeks before A-day	Receive lots, confirm terms. Demand and collect entry fees.
8 to 9 weeks before A-day	Obtain full details from vendors. Inspect photographs and catalogue.
8 weeks before A-day	Draft catalogue, check details and arrangements with vendors and solicitors.
5 to 7 weeks before A-day	Final copy prepared and submitted to printers. Guidelines agreed with vendors. Solicitors apply for local searches and organise draft conditions and contracts. Catalogues printed, For Sale boards erected, adverts prepared, mailing list run off, enquiries recorded.
4 weeks to A-day	Catalogue mailed. Details of auction published.
4 weeks to 5 days	Enquiries dealt with, viewings arranged and made, offers prior to auction negotiated and solicitors instructed on contracts.
3 to 5 days before A-day	Press for exchange of pre-auction contracts, agree reserves with vendors.
1 day to go A-day	Last preparations for auction room. Auction takes place, deposits banked.
The week after A-day	Negotiate on unsold lots, arrange invoices, transfer fees, publish results.
2 to 4 weeks after A-day	Liaise with solicitors leading up to completion, hand over balance of deposits, remove For Sale boards.

CHAPTER 8

Thinking of selling your property?

There may come a time when you wish to sell your property. This chapter takes you step by step through the key points, ensuring a smooth passage to a successful sale at auction.

To auction or not?

The traditional property, which auctioneers encourage vendors to sell by auction, is one where the lot is so unique that the auctioneers expect an exceptional demand and the final valuation is difficult to judge. However, many sellers find auctions a quick and successful method of selling almost any type of property. The types of property that are offered at auction fall into three groups.

1. The exceptional property seeking an exceptional price

The types of property that can benefit from the ambience of the auction room and where competition can be brought out into the open and fostered are:

- the thatched cottage overlooking the trout stream;

- the retail investment let at a good rent to a company whose payment is impeccable;

- the mews home in an area of exceptional demand;
- the plot of building land on which all the local builders are convinced they can sell houses at high prices exceptionally quickly.

Surprisingly, these lots probably make up less than five per cent of what is being offered in the sale room at the beginning of the 21st century.

2. Properties forming the main auction market

Vendors have discovered that the auction room is also a successful place from which to market the more run-of-the-mill properties. They benefit from having the competition out in the open following good advertising and widespread exposure to the market. The circumstances where a contract exists when the gavel falls is a very worthwhile benefit. No wonder more than 65,000 properties a year are offered for sale in the auction rooms of England.

3. Properties for a quick disposal

The third type of property sold by auction is that which a vendor is seeking to dispose of quickly. It may be that the seller has been trying to sell the property by private treaty for a long time and has now reached the end of the line. Such disposals are often provoked by pressure from financiers or follow repossession or liquidation.

> **Key point**
>
> Many bargains exist where properties need to be disposed of quickly.

Seek the auctioneer's advice

All auctioneers are willing to discuss the advantages and disadvantages of auction. If you are looking to sell, they will be able to advise you if the sale room is the place to offer your property or not, depending upon your circumstances.

Advantages of selling by auction

1. The contract exists immediately the gavel falls.
2. Auctions have extensive and exciting marketing and advertising.

3. The marketing period is short.

4. Purchasers can see the competition that exists.

5. Competitive bidding results in a sale at market price.

6. The seller and purchaser know where they stand immediately – there is no renegotiation or gazumping.

7. The national average success rate from the offering of properties for sale by auction was just under 72 per cent in 2008.

The types of auction houses

Auctioneer's offices

With over 80 auctioneers offering their services throughout the country, choosing the firm to use may not be easy. The range of firms to choose from falls into the following groups.

* Firms around London that specialise in the property offered.

* Firms in London that cover a wide range of properties both in general, composite auctions and in specialised ones. Consider where your buyers are likely to be based. Local firms are best for locally based bidders. City firms are best if your lot will appeal to major investors or speculators. Do you want a local or a national market?

* Firms based in London that conduct auctions throughout the UK. (Those that do not have an office relatively close to your property should be rejected unless they cater for an important specialisation.)

* Firms based in the larger towns throughout the country that run regular composite auctions.

* Local firms that run smaller auctions frequently on demand.

How to choose your auction house

1. Find a newspaper that advertises auctions in your area or your specialisation and collect the various catalogues.

2. Subscribe to *Property Auction News* for a full listing of forthcoming sales and collect auction catalogues (see page 18 for details).

Do your research thoroughly

3. Research the catalogues and the advertisements and prepare a shortlist of the firms. Select those that offer plenty of properties similar to yours or that appear to have a niche in the style of property you are offering.

4. Research the advertisements and publicity which the auction houses offer to help you decide the style and media choice appropriate for your lot. For example, if you are selling a major commercial investment nationwide, advertising in the *Estates Gazette* is imperative. On the other hand, for a desirable cottage in the country your publicity is better placed in local newspapers and magazines that have plenty of articles on country affairs. The golden rule is to plump for the media and auction houses that will give you maximum exposure amongst your likely bidders.

5. Which firm is most successful in selling property like yours? Your own experience from visiting auctions and word of mouth is probably the best guide. If you are looking at success rates from sales, rely more on your own experience than on published figures in news items which frequently tend to be 'hyped'. Don't forget to take into account sales prior to and after the auctions.

Pick an efficient firm

6. When approaching firms, make a note of how efficient they are. Were you dealt with promptly, courteously and efficiently? Remember, when you ask for catalogues or information, you are using the same services as a potential bidder.

7. Don't base your decision on the auctioneer who quotes the highest likely selling price or guidelines. He can only give you his impression of the market and at the first meeting may deliberately be a little optimistic. What really matters to you is how high actual bidders can be encouraged to go on auction day, not an auctioneer's valuation.

Don't go for the cheapest

8. Don't be persuaded to employ an auction house that quotes a low commission or entry fee. An extra £250 in commission can be easily paid for by an auctioneer who is sufficiently good on the rostrum or in his pre-auction publicity to gain just one extra bid. Auctioneers that regularly use large bidding increments in the sale room can procure a final bid far in excess of the saving a reduced rate of commission brings.

Checklist: How to choose your auction house

1 Analyse catalogues. ☐

2 Visit some auctions. ☐

3 Which firms offer your type of property in plenty? ☐

4 Which auction house has the right style of publicity and media choice to suit your lot? ☐

5 Which auctioneer is most successful in selling properties like yours? ☐

6 Which firm deals with you most efficiently? ☐

7 Which auction firms have a specialisation that may be an advantage to you? ☐

8 Do you want a local or a national market? ☐

9 Where are your buyers likely to be based? Local firms are best for locally based bidders. ☐

10 Don't base your decision on the auctioneer who quotes the highest likely selling price or guidelines. ☐

11 Don't be swayed by a low commission or entry fee. ☐

12 Which auctioneer has the charisma to charm bidders 'out of the trees'? ☐

13 Which auctioneer insists on large increments at the end of the bidding? ☐

Agreeing the auctioneer's terms

All auctioneers publish agency terms, but those terms vary from firm to firm. It is usual for auctioneers to charge an entry fee. They may recommend supplementary advertising and promotional elements which are specified at the beginning. Thereafter, there are various other features of the terms to note:

When are the fees payable?

The entry fee is usually due at the time of instruction. Sales fees are due in the following circumstances:

1. When contracts are exchanged or at completion.

Fees may be due if you do not complete

2. The auctioneer may be entitled to a fee or a reduced fee where contracts are exchanged but completion does not follow.

3. A fee or reduced fee may be payable where the property is withdrawn by the vendor before the auction. The amount is usually calculated on either the reserve price fixed or the figure that the auctioneer reasonably judges to be a realistic reserve.

4. A fee or reduced fee is normally payable if the seller withdraws the property from the sale, either because it has been sold elsewhere or merely on a whim.

5. Most auctioneers require a fee to be paid where a lot is sold before, at or even after the auction during a specified period. The auctioneer's terms usually provide a formula for calculating the fee if a sale price is not disclosed by the vendor and the property sells by private treaty, not through the auction house.

What type of agency?

Most auctioneers provide a sole agency agreement specifying how long they have the right to sell the property. Under these terms, the owner is responsible for paying the auctioneer the entry and sale fees laid down, however the lot is sold during that period. These fees are payable, even if the property is sold by another agent or by the owner direct. On occasion, auctioneers agree to joint sole agency terms where they act in tandem with another agent. The agents agree between each other how the entry and sale fees are to be split.

Key point

Under sole agency the seller has to pay a fee, however the property is sold, during the period specified.

It is very unusual for auctioneers to accept an agency agreement where the owner is not liable to pay them a fee if the property has been sold privately or through another agency.

Right to collect the fee

It is normal for auctioneers to reserve the right to collect their sale fee from the deposit that is paid after the exchange of contracts or memoranda. It is usual for auctioneers to claim the right to retain any interest earned on deposits whilst they are held in their accounts.

What level of fees can a seller expect to pay?

Entry fees and sale fees vary depending upon the quality of the catalogue, the amount of advertising and the extent of the services which are provided by the auctioneer. The major auction houses can charge up to £2,500 entry fee for each lot. For this amount, the vendor can expect to see his property extensively advertised and included in a high quality catalogue. Sale fees are normally between one and a half per cent and three per cent of the price at which the property is sold, subject to a minimum fee which may be between £600 and £2,500. On occasion, auctioneers may recommend additional expenditure on specialised advertising, if they feel such an approach justifies it. Table 8.1 illustrates the range of fees payable.

Sale Price	Entry Fee	Minimum Fee	1.5%	2%	2.5%	3%	VAT	Total Cost	Comment
					Sales Fee At:				
Up to £20,000	£600	£600	–	–	–	–	£175	£1,175	
Up to £25,000	£600	£600	–	–	–	–	£175	£1,175	
	£600	–	–	–	£625	–	£179	£1,179	
	£600	–	–	–	–	£750	£201	£1,351	
Up to £30,000	£600	£600	–	–	–	–	£175	£1,175	
	£600	–	£600	–	–	–	£175	£1,175	
	£600	–	–	–	£750	–	£201	£1,351	
	£600	–	–	–	–	£900	£228	£1,528	
Up to £50,000	£600	–	£750	–	–	–	£201	£1,351	
	£600	–	–	£1,000	–	–	£245	£1,645	
	£600	–	–	–	£1,250	–	£289	£1,939	
	£600	–	–	–	–	£1,500	£332	£2,232	
Up to £75,000	£600	–	£1,125	–	–	–	£267	£1,791	
	£600	–	–	£1,500	–	–	£332	£2,232	
	£600	–	–	–	£1,875	–	£398	£2,673	
	£600	–	–	–	–	£2,250	£464	£3,114	
Up to £110,000	£600	–	£1,500	–	–	–	£332	£2,232	
	£600	–	–	£2,000	–	–	£420	£2,820	
	£600	–	–	–	£2,500	–	£508	£3,408	
	£600	–	–	–	–	£3,000	£595	£3,995	
Up to £150,000	£600	–	£2,250	–	–	–	£464	£3,114	Supplementary
	£600	–	–	£3,000	–	–	£595	£3,995	advertising usual at
	£600	–	–	–	£3,750	–	£726	£4,876	and above a selling
	£600	–	–	–	–	£4,500	£858	£5,758	price of £150,000
Up to £200,000	£600	–	£3,000	–	–	–	£595	£3,995	
	£600	–	–	£4,000	–	–	£770	£5,170	
	£600	–	–	–	£5,000	–	£945	£6,345	
	£600	–	–	–	–	£6,000	£1,120	£7,520	
Up to £250,000	£600	–	£3,750	–	–	–	£726	£4,876	
	£600	–	–	£5,000	–	–	£945	£6,345	
	£600	–	–	–	£6,250	–	£1,164	£7,814	
	£600	–	–	–	–	£7,500	£1,383	£9,283	
Up to £500,000	£600	–	£7,500	–	–	–	£1,383	£9,283	
	£600	–	–	£10,000	–	–	£1,820	£12,220	
	£600	–	–	–	£12,500	–	£2,258	£15,158	
	£600	–	–	–	–	£15,000	£2,695	£18,095	
Up to £750,000	£600	–	£11,250	–	–	–	£2,039	£13,689	
	£600	–	–	£15,000	–	–	£2,695	£18,095	
	£600	–	–	–	£18,750	–	£3,351	£22,501	
	£600	–	–	–	–	£2,250	£4,008	£26,908	
Up to £1,000,000	£600	–	£15,000	–	–	–	£2,625	£17,625	
	£600	–	–	£20,000	–	–	£3,570	£23,970	
	£600	–	–	–	£25,000	–	£4,445	£29,845	
	£600	–	–	–	–	£30,000	£5,320	£35,720	

Table 8.1 Auctioneers' fees

Key points

The Estate Agents Act 1979 and its subsequent regulations require estate agents to specify their terms in writing to all vendors.

If current government intentions are fulfilled, all sellers' auctioneers will also be required, by statute, to provide a Home Information Pack (HIP) including an Energy Report for every house (with certain limited exceptions).

The legal clauses to watch out for

The terms might include the following clauses:

Payment in advance

1   Following the receipt of instructions and the full entry fee as communicated, the Auctioneers will take all reasonable steps to include the property described in these instructions (hereinafter referred to as 'the property') in their next suitable and available composite public auction (hereinafter referred to as 'the auction').

The auction house is confirming that their entry fee is payable in advance. This sample term has been culled from a document issued by a company which runs composite public auctions. A number of lots is offered in one place on one day. The number of lots may range from two to 302 or more.

Non-returnable fees

2   Entry fees which are to cover the costs of advertising and promotion are non-returnable and are due as a debt from the owner/agent to the Auctioneers upon the signing of the instructions.

This term again confirms the entry fee is due in advance and that no part of it is returnable. Some auctioneers do allow all or part of the entry fee to be used in payment of the sale fee due, if the lot is sold.

Authority to sell

3 By signing this instruction form, the owner/agent gives the Auctioneers absolute irrevocable authority to act as sole selling agents to negotiate and enter into a contract for the sale of the property:

   (a) from the date hereof until the auction at a price authorised by the owner/agent;

   (b) at the auction at the highest genuine bid at or above the reserve price;

   (c) at any time up to eight weeks after the auction at the reserve price.

By so signing this instruction form, the owner/agent warrants to the Auctioneers that he has the authority to give such absolute irrevocable authority.

This term emphasises that a sole agency has been entered into and that the person instructing has authority to sell the property. Not only are the auctioneers given authority to negotiate a sale but also to enter into a contract for its sale on behalf of the vendors in the following circumstances:

- in the event of a pre-auction sale at a price the owner agrees; or

- to a genuine bidder at the reserve or above it on auction day; or

- at any time up to eight weeks after the auction at the reserve price.

Since the vendor will be committed to a sale entered into by his sole agent, it is necessary that the auctioneer's authority is irrevocable. Both the auctioneer and the vendor need to be positive that the latter has not entered into a contract at a price which the owner does not like and, therefore, the terms very specifically define the price at which the auctioneers can sell. Section 3(a) underlines

Lot 16 of a Harman Healy sale was the first of a group of residential lots. A two-bedroom flat in this block in Edgware, Middlesex, sold for £116,000. This was roughly an eight per cent to ten per cent saving on the market and it currently yields 7.8 per cent.

the fact that the auction house will have to obtain the vendor's specific authorisation to the price before the sale. Section 3(b) emphasises the procedure which takes place in the auction itself where the auctioneer is aware that he can only enter into a contract by bringing down the gavel at the highest bid providing it is at or above the reserve. Section 3(c), apart from giving the auction house a reasonable time to sell after the auction, stresses that during this time the owner accepts that he is willing to sell at the reserve. Although the terms of agency specifies this final point in the procedure, it is not unusual for the auctioneer and the vendor to discuss the price at which the property can be sold after the auction. The seller may be willing to vary this agreement and advise his agents that a lesser price than the reserve will be acceptable.

Some sellers are willing to extend the eight-week period, others seek to reduce it, but since it is very common for sales to be negotiated after the auction, auctioneers always feel that it is only fair that they should have the opportunity to sell after the auction so that they can capitalise on the way in which they have marketed the property before the auction.

Right to collect fee

4   Upon unconditional exchange of any such contract for sale entered into, the Auctioneers shall become immediately entitled to three per cent plus VAT of the contract price for the sale of the property, or the minimum sale fee, plus VAT, whichever is the greater, from the owner/agent and the Auctioneers and their duly authorised agents shall be entitled to deduct that sale fee plus VAT from any deposits received on, before or after exchange of any such contract for sale from the intending purchaser without further authority.

It is usual for the auction house to become entitled to its fee immediately after contracts have been exchanged. Where their auctioneers belong to recognised bodies, such as the Royal Institution of Chartered Surveyors, their members are specifically prohibited from deducting fees from the client's money without written permission. This term eliminates the need for specific separate permission to be obtained for each lot sold.

Deposit arrangements

5   The balance of any such deposits will be held in an insurance bonded clients' account up to completion of such contract for sale, but any interest earned on such deposits held by the Auctioneers shall be held to their credit and not to the credit of the owner/agent and shall at all times be the absolute property of the Auctioneers.

The position concerning deposits and their ownership is explained on pages 152 and 219. This auction term assumes that the conditions of sale will provide for the deposit to be held by the auctioneer on behalf of the vendor. The term will need changing if the conditions of sale are varied. If the deposit is held by the auctioneers or others as stakeholder or on behalf of the purchaser in the period between contract and completion, then the purchaser may be entitled to the interest on the deposit. This clause gives comfort to the vendor that the deposit monies will be placed in a clients' account which is subject to regulation and that the security of that money is covered by an insurance bond.

This 41-bedroom hotel in Blackpool was offered with the entire building let to one company for £35,360 per annum on a 20-year lease. The selling price of £295,000 looked good value with the purchaser earning a healthy yield of 12 per cent.

Fees due if completion does not happen

6 Should any such contract for sale be exchanged but not completed the Auctioneers shall become immediately entitled to a commission payment from the owner/agent of one and a half per cent of the contract price, or 50 per cent of the minimum sale fee, whichever is the greater, plus VAT, without deduction.

Approximately one in every 100 auction lots sold does not proceed to completion despite the fact that the purchaser has paid a ten per cent deposit at the exchange of contracts. How that deposit is treated between vendor and purchaser in the event of non-completion of the sale is explained on page 152. The auctioneer in this term is pointing out to the vendor that his fee will be reduced by half but will still be due and payable in such circumstances.

Auctioneer's right to commission

7 The owner/agent hereby confirms his understanding that the effect of appointing the Auctioneers as sole selling agents as set out above is inter alia to prevent the owner/agent whether by himself, his servants or agents or otherwise whatsoever:

(a) from negotiating or entering into a contract for sale of the property from the date hereof until 12 weeks after the date of the auction otherwise than through the Auctioneers;

(b) from negotiating or entering into a contract for sale of the property from the date hereof at any time with a person introduced to him by the Auctioneers other than through the Auctioneers.

This term complements the sole selling nature of this agreement, emphasises the term outlined at 3 above and strengthens the auctioneer's entitlement to commission on a sale, however it occurs:

• between the time at which the auctioneer is appointed and 12 weeks after the date of the auction to anyone, however they have been introduced and negotiated with; or

• at any time after the initial instruction to anyone with whom the auction house has been in contact.

In this clause the auctioneers have extended the eight-week period referred to in clause 3(c) to 12 weeks. In clause 3, the auctioneers as sole selling agents are giving eight weeks in which to negotiate a contract for sale of the property. Once negotiations have been completed, it is not unusual for the solicitors acting on behalf of both sides to take up to four weeks to exchange contracts. For this reason, clause 7 specifies a period extended by four weeks to allow for this step in the transaction to take place.

Auction terms

8   The owner/agent further confirms that he has been provided with and read the Auctioneers' 'Information for Vendors' catalogue.

The Estate Agents Act 1979 requires that specific wording shall be incorporated in agency terms. Rather than put it in this portion of the auction terms, the auctioneers in this instance have chosen to incorporate it in a separate auction information catalogue. The terms of the Estate Agents Act 1979 governing provision of information and explanation of terms used are reproduced in Appendix 4.

Entitlement to fees if the price is kept secret

9   If, in breach of the Auctioneers' rights as sole agents, a contract for sale of the property is negotiated otherwise than through the Auctioneers and such contract for sale is entered into or exchanged at any time up to 12 weeks after the date of the auction, or at any time with a person introduced to the owner/agent by the Auctioneers, the Auctioneers shall on exchange of such contract become immediately entitled to payment from the owner/agent of liquidated damages equal to:

(a)   where the contract price is revealed by the owner/agent to the Auctioneers three per cent of the contract price, or the minimum sale fee, whichever is the greater, plus VAT;

(b)   where the contract price is not revealed to the Auctioneers and no reserve price has been fixed for the property three per cent of 110 per cent of such reserve price, or the minimum sale fee, whichever is the greater, plus VAT;

(c)   where the contract price is not revealed to the Auctioneers and no reserve price has been fixed for the property three per cent of the Auctioneers' estimate of the market value of the property, or the minimum sale fee, whichever is the greater, plus VAT.

Not only does this term reiterate the sole agency agreement which has already been referred to in sections 3 and 7 above, it also sets out to cover the auctioneer's entitlement to commission where the contract price has not been revealed. In such circumstances, the auctioneer becomes entitled to his fee at the rate agreed based on 110 per cent of the reserve price or, if that has not been fixed, at the relevant percentage of the Auctioneer's estimate of the market value of the property. Any minimum commission agreed in the terms is retained for the purpose of this computation.

Right to fees for properties withdrawn before auction

10 If the property is withdrawn by the owner/agent other than by reason of a sale made pursuant hereto before the auction, the Auctioneers shall on such withdrawal become immediately entitled to a commission payment from the owner/agent equal to:

(a) where a reserve price for the property has been fixed one and a half per cent of the reserve price, or 50 per cent of the minimum sale fee, whichever is the greater, plus VAT;

(b) where no reserve price for the property has been fixed one and a half per cent of the Auctioneers' estimate of the market value of the property, or 50 per cent of the minimum sale fee, whichever is the greater, plus VAT;

save that should a contract for sale of the property thereafter be negotiated otherwise than through the Auctioneers and such contract for sale be entered into or exchanged at any time up to 12 weeks after the date of the auction (or at any time with a person introduced to the owner/agent by, or contracted by, the Auctioneers) the Auctioneers shall be entitled to claim liquidated damages under Clause 8 hereof in lieu of their claim to a commission payment under this clause, and should a claim for commission payment under this clause have already been made by the Auctioneers and paid by the owner/agent they will nevertheless be entitled to claim from the owner/agent the difference between the sum paid hereunder and the sum they are entitled to under Clause 9 above.

In this term the auction house preserves a right to 50 per cent of its standard fee if the property has been withdrawn by the owner prior to the auction for reasons other than because of a prior sale. There is provision for the calculation of the fee if no reserve has been settled, again based on the auctioneer's estimate of the market value of the property and the minimum sale fee has been preserved.

The balance of the auctioneer's entitlement to commission which has already been covered in Clause 7 of the terms is reiterated once more in this Clause 10, so that a vendor cannot avoid paying the auction house a full commission in the event of a sale by withdrawing the property from the auction before the auction day and before contracts have been exchanged elsewhere.

A minimum fee

11 The minimum sale fee described in these auction terms shall be £600 plus VAT.

Agreeing the reserve

12 The reserve price will be notified to the Auctioneers by the owner/agent either verbally or in writing at least three working days before the date of the auction. If it is not, or in the event of the owner/agent fixing a reserve price which in the opinion of the Auctioneers is too high, then the Auctioneers may at their discretion choose not to offer the property at the auction. In such an instance the owner/agent will not have any claim whatsoever against the Auctioneers and will still be liable for the entry fee whether paid in advance or not. In the event of the owner/agent notifying the Auctioneers of the reserve price, which in the opinion of the Auctioneers is lower than they themselves would recommend, then in the absence of a suitable explanation from the owner/agent as to why such reserve price is suggested the Auctioneers may within 14 days of such notification notify the owner/agent that such reserve price is lower than the Auctioneers would recommend and shall not be regarded as the reserve price for the purpose of Clauses 9 and 10 herein.

Auctioneers always discuss reserves with owners both after they have carried out their initial inspection of the property and during the period up to the auction as the effectiveness of the marketing campaign is assessed, as interest is shown or as any offers are received. It is usual for the reserve to be fixed at a compromise figure between the auctioneer's views of the value of the property and the owner's desire to obtain what he feels is a reasonable sum. In this example, the auctioneer is willing to accept reserve prices both verbally and in writing although it is more usual for prices to be agreed in writing. Thereafter, the auctioneer reserves the right to refuse to offer the property if, in his view, the reserve is too high.

The balance of the term prevents the owner specifying a particularly low reserve price prior to withdrawing the property from the auction to reduce the commission, which he might otherwise have to pay under clauses 9 and 10.

Requirements to instruct a solicitor

13 The Auctioneers require the owner/agent:

(a) to instruct solicitors to act on his behalf:

(i) to deduce full and proper title to the property;

(ii) to provide full contract of sale documents together with any additional and special conditions necessary;

(iii) to attend at the auction to render details of the title, and provide a copy of an up-to-date local search if available;

(iv) to exchange contracts if so required by the Auctioneers;

(v) to indicate that all deposits paid may be received and held as agents for the owner/agent in accordance with the terms hereof;

(vi) to take full responsibility for the preparation and use of the memorandum of contract in the catalogue if it is used by the owner/agent or by the Auctioneers.

(b) to indemnify the Auctioneers and their agents against any claims made because of faulty title or information provided by the owner/agent or any other failures by the owner/agent or his solicitors or other agents.

This term emphasises to the vendor that the auctioneer needs the full co-operation of the vendor's solicitor. In part, it also acts as an aide-memoire for the solicitors about the work they are required to do. The indemnity required under 13b stresses to the seller the importance of correct information being given to the auctioneer. It is also intended to be used as a defence against any actions the auctioneer's firm might suffer under the Property Misrepresentation Act 1991, if misleading details are published in the auction catalogue.

VAT

14 For the avoidance of doubt the Auctioneers will be entitled to receive VAT in accordance with the law in addition to all commissions and entry fees payable.

Auctioneer's right to reoffer the property

15 The Auctioneers will use their best endeavours to obtain a signed memorandum and deposit from the successful bidder at the auction but cannot be held responsible to the owner/agent if the successful bidder will not comply with these requirements. In the event of a failure of a successful bidder to supply his name and address and, if appropriate, the name and address of the person or company on whose behalf he has been bidding, the Auctioneers are authorised to resubmit the property for sale at their total discretion at any time during the course of the same or future auction sessions within 12 weeks thereof.

This clause is self-evident. It is unusual for a bidder to disappear once the gavel has fallen on his successful bid. This probably occurs only once in every 500 lots. Obviously, the bidder does not stay long enough for the auctioneer to discover why he will not proceed! This clause gives the auctioneer the right to reoffer the property (which he will generally wish to do) immediately he discovers the successful bidder did not (or will not) exchange contracts or has fled the sale room. When the property is reoffered it will generally not reach the same price as before, even though the auctioneer is still prevented from selling below the reserve. This term protects the position of the auction house in such an instance.

Right to refuse bids

16 The Auctioneers have the owner/agent's authority to refuse to accept any bids in the Auctioneer's absolute discretion. Even though this shall only be done in the best interests of the owner/agent, exercise of the discretion shall not in any way render the Auctioneers liable to the owner/agent.

Usually, auctioneers welcome all bids in the room. A pro-active response from the audience adds excitement, interest and increases the ambience of the sale. Nevertheless, on occasion, auctioneers may choose not to accept bids from certain individuals who have failed to fulfil responsibilities in the room before or who have committed other indiscretions not acceptable to the auctioneer and this term protects the auctioneer's entitlement.

Payment

17 The Auctioneers are authorised to accept payment of deposits by cheque.

Very occasionally, deposit cheques are not honoured. This term protects the decision of the auctioneer to accept cheques as deposits and also serves as a reminder to the seller that in the auction room, cheques will be taken to cover the ten per cent or minimum deposit at the time of exchange.

Auctioneer's Anecdote: A camera-shy buyer

Several years ago, a provincial auctioneer had to offer the title of the Lord of the Manor of Treffos. Because the manorial estate included the village of Llanfairpwllgwyngyllgogerychwyrndrobwllllantysiliogogogoch there was considerable media and public interest. The auctioneers intended to work this interest for maximum publicity. Two television companies had their cameramen present. Arc lights were installed. The auctioneer carried out two preliminary interviews with each of the television companies to set the scene and to spell out the nature of the lot to a clutch of journalists. As the lot came up, the arc lights went on and the cameras started rolling. Several discreet bids were made by members of the audience. As the cameras frantically panned over the room to find them, the lot was finally knocked down at £15,000 to a bidder who was behind a pillar at the back of the room but whose bidding arm was visible to the auctioneer. The auctioneer halted the sale, stepped down off the rostrum and invited the new Lord of the Manor to come forward to receive his congratulations on succeeding into the title, intending to create the 'photo opportunity' which he had offered to TV and newspapers. He did not know at that time that the successful bidder had already run out of the room, dropping a £500 deposit in cash on the reception desk and mouthed to the auctions co-ordinator (to whom he was known), 'I will be back later'. The photo opportunity never occurred, the auctioneer never obtained the publicity which he had sought and various news hawks were too late in realising what had happened to catch the new Lord on his way out of the room and out of the hotel. It was only after reassurance from his auctions co-ordinator that he did not need to reoffer the lot that a rather chastened auctioneer returned to the rostrum to continue the sale whilst the cameramen packed up around the bidders. The purchaser did return several hours later, signed and exchanged contracts and subsequently completed. It was only one enterprising and patient journalist who lingered behind long enough to eventually be able to 'scoop' the news the next day.

Responsibilities of the seller

These terms show that it is usual for the vendors:

1. To certify that they have authority to offer the lot for sale.

2. To give irrevocable authority to the auctioneer to negotiate and enter into a contract for sale of the property.

3. To pay the entry fee and commission on the terms laid down.

4. To undertake to fix the reserve price and confirm it in writing at least three days before the auction.

5. To instruct solicitors to act on their behalf to deduce title to the property and to provide full contract of sale documents with any additional special conditions necessary. The vendor is normally

required to indemnify the auctioneers against any claims made because of faulty title or information that they or their solicitors may have rendered.

6. To undertake to provide full and correct details of the property to be sold indemnifying the auctioneer against misdescriptions. They must also provide a HIP and associated reports of the property to be sold.

Getting the catalogue details right

It is always important that the particulars of the catalogue are right for the sake of the purchaser. No one wishes to see him misinformed. However, it is equally important to the vendor, since incorrect details may give the purchaser the right to withdraw from the contract and claim the return of his deposit. To the auction house, however, it is even more important that the particulars are right. This is vital not only because of their reputation, but also because the publishing of misleading particulars is now a criminal offence under the Property Misdescriptions Act 1991 with a maximum fine of £5,000 and the ultimate punishment of preventing the firm or its staff ever acting as estate agents again.

Catalogue items that must not mislead

The Property Misdescriptions Act 1991 specifies the following categories in which catalogues must not be misleading.

1. Location or address.

2. Aspect, view, outlook or environment.

3. Availability and nature of services, facilities or amenities.

4. Proximity to any services, places, facilities or amenities.

5. Accommodation, measurements or sizes.

6. Fixtures and fittings.

7. Physical or structural characteristics, form of construction or condition.

8. Fitness for any purpose or strength of any buildings or other structures on land or of land itself.

9. Treatments, processes, repairs or improvements or the effects thereof.

10. Conformity or compliance with any scheme, standard, test or regulations or the existence of any guarantee.

11. Survey, inspection, investigation, valuation or appraisal by any person or the results thereof.

12. The grant or giving of any award or prize for design or construction.

13. History, including the age, ownership or use of land or any building or fixture and the date of any alterations thereto.

14. Person by whom any building (or part of any building), fixture or component was designed, constructed, built, produced, treated, processed, repaired, reconditioned or tested.

15. The length of time during which land has been available for sale either generally or by or through a particular person.

16. Price (other than the price at which accommodation or facilities are available and are to be provided by means of the creation or disposal of an interest in land in the circumstances specified in section 23(1)(a) and (b) of the Consumer Protection Act 1987(a) or Article 16(1)(a) and (b) of the Consumer Protection (NI) Order 1987(b) (which relate to the creation or disposal of certain interests in new dwellings)) and previous price.

17. Tenure or estate.

18. Length of any lease or of the unexpired term of any lease and the terms and conditions of a lease (and in relation to land in Northern Ireland, any fee farm grant creating the relationship of landlord and tenant shall be treated as a lease).

19. Amount of any ground rent, rent or premium and frequency of any review.

20. Amount of any rent-charge.

21. Where all or any part of any land is let to a tenant or is subject to a licence, particulars of the tenancy or licence, including any rent, premium or other payment due and frequency of any review.

22. Amount of any service or maintenance charge or liability for common repairs.

23. Council Tax payable in respect of a dwelling within the meaning of section 3, or in Scotland section 72, of the Local Government Finance Act 1992(a) or the basis or any part of the basis on which that tax is calculated.

24. Rates payable in respect of a non-domestic hereditament within the meaning of section 64 of the Local Government Finance Act 1988(b) or, in Scotland, in respect of lands and heritages shown on a valuation roll or the basis or any part of the basis on which those rates are calculated.

25. Rates payable in respect of a hereditament within the meaning of the Rates (Northern Ireland) Order 1977(c) or the basis or any part of the basis on which those rates are calculated.

26. Existence or nature of any planning permission or proposals for development, construction or change of use.

27. In relation to land in England and Wales, the passing or rejection of any plans of proposed building work in accordance with section 16 of the Building Act 1984(d) and the giving of any completion certificate in accordance with Regulation 15 of the Building Regulations 1991(e).

28. In relation to land in Scotland, the granting of a warrant under section 6 of the Building (Scotland) Act 1959(f) or the granting of a certificate of completion under section 9 of that Act.

29. In relation to land in Northern Ireland, the passing or rejection of any plans of proposed building work in accordance with Article 13 of the Building Regulations (Northern Ireland) Order 1979(g) and the giving of any completion certificate in accordance with building regulations made under that Order.

30. Application of any statutory provision which restricts the use of land or which requires it to be preserved or maintained in a specified manner.

31. Existence or nature of any restrictive covenants, or of any restrictions on resale, restrictions on use, or pre-emption rights and, in relation to land in Scotland (in addition to the matters mentioned previously in this paragraph) the existence or nature of any reservations or real conditions.

32. Easements, servitudes or wayleaves.

33. Existence and extent of any public or private right of way.

Key point

Since the owner/agent has already indemnified the auctioneers in his terms against claims made because of faulty information (see clause 13(b) of the auctioneer's terms on page 199) he has a heavy responsibility to ensure that the details of the property in the catalogue are totally correct and not misleading.

Instructing your solicitor

The vendor should instruct his solicitor that he is including his property or properties in a sale at the same time as the auctioneer is approached. It is important that the vendor knows how much the solicitor will charge. Table 8.2 gives examples of solicitor's conveyancing fees. The solicitor needs plentiful warning after the confirmation of instructions to:

- obtain the deeds and investigate the title;

- obtain the auction catalogue and the auctioneer's standard conditions;

- draft the contract and any additional special conditions.

The solicitor will raise pre-contract searches and go through the pre-contract enquiries with the seller so that information for the prospective bidder is available. Solicitors frequently prepare an auction information pack to include title details, searches and replies to enquiries so that they can be provided to solicitors who make approaches on behalf of potential bidders. Particularly, the solicitor needs to be instructed to liaise with the auctioneer to ensure that the particulars published in the auction catalogue are not misleading. The solicitor needs to be informed of the auction timetable so that he can act with the necessary speed.

Sale at Auction (Excluding Disbursements)	Fee Range
Up to £50,000	£350–£650
£50,001 to £150,000	£550–£1,100

£150,001 to £250,000	£700–£1,400
£250,001 to £500,000	£1,000–£1,900
£500,001 to £750,000	£1,500–£3,200
Over £750,000	0.3%–0.5%

Note: Fees include cost of attending the auction and assume that a sale occurs.

Table 8.2 Solicitors' fees for acting on behalf of the vendor

Solicitor's checklist: Acting for a buyer

1 After confirming instructions, obtain deeds and investigate title. ☐

2 Obtain auction catalogue and/or auctioneers' standard conditions. ☐

3 Inspect site if appropriate. ☐

4 Draft contract in light of 1, 2 and 3 above. ☐

5 Assist in the preparation and collation of a Home Information Pack if needed. ☐

6 Raise pre-contract searches you would make if acting for a buyer (e.g. local search, British Coal search). ☐

7 Go through pre-contract enquiries with the seller so the information to a prospective bidder is available. ☐

8 Prepare an auction information pack to include title details, searches and replies to enquiries. ☐

9 Recheck the contract in the light of searches and replies to pre-contract enquiries and also check that the auction catalogue particulars are correct. If not, send the auctioneer the amendments. ☐

10 Deal with pre-auction enquiries as promptly as possible to sustain the prospective bidders' interest. ☐

11 Attend auction or appoint agents on your behalf and ensure you attend at least half an hour beforehand with an information pack (see point 7) so you can deal with enquiries. ☐

12 Make sure the auctioneer draws the bidders' attention to
   the amendments. ☐

13 After the lot is sold, ensure that you receive the purchaser's
   details from the auctioneers to insert in both parts of the
   contract. ☐

14 Obtain the purchaser's signature to the contract and a
   cheque for the deposit and obtain details of the purchaser's
   solicitors and ask the purchaser to deliver your part of the
   contract to them as soon as possible. Explain that you will
   send all the information a solicitor needs and also tell them
   what the completion date is, even if that is clear on the front
   of the contract. ☐

15 Liaise with purchaser's solicitors, as normal, up to completion. ☐

Checklist supplied by Vaudrey Osborne & Mellor (now Beachcroft Wansborough), Solicitors, Manchester.

Agreeing the figures

The second greatest ability needed for an auctioneer is to be an accurate valuer. But with all the skill in the world it is impossible to judge what is in the mind of bidders on sale day. On that day, the cliché that valuation is an art not a science is put to the test. The auctioneer/valuer has all his skills, training and experience behind him. The auction house has access to the records of prices obtained for comparable properties, but in the end the judgement of value is still very subjective. Even the most competent auctioneer/valuer can find his confidence severely dented in the sale room. Especially, when lots that he advises may only just reach their reserve, either go on to sell at high prices after runaway competitive bidding, or have to be withdrawn at bids considerably less than he recommended as a value or reserve.

Key point

Nevertheless, it is a vital part of the marketing prior to auction and of the auction itself that the guidelines and reserve are astutely judged.

The guidelines

Right at the beginning, owners frequently have strong views about the price at which they will sell. The valuer, after inspection, may have similar or totally divergent views. The divergence may be so great that the vendor decides not to include the lot in the sale, but hopefully those views can be reconciled so the property can be included. At this stage, there can be a spread between the top and bottom guidelines which may help towards that compromise. The bottom guideline should be a rather pessimistic estimate of the figure at which the property might sell whilst the top guideline represents a slightly optimistic view. That pessimism and optimism has to be balanced with the need to encourage interest in the property initially and to persuade bidders to attend the auction subsequently.

Don't make the guidelines too low or too high

Too low a bottom guideline will encourage many potential buyers to attend the auction who will be unhappy if they have wasted their time because the reserve was noticeably higher. In contrast, guidelines that are too high will frighten would-be bidders away who otherwise might have been successful on auction day.

Key point

It is usual for the bottom guideline to be relatively close to the figure that the auctioneer and vendor are contemplating fixing as a reserve.

Varying the guidelines

As the marketing for the auction develops, the auction house should be in a position to start judging the amount of interest in the lots. Exceptional interest may be shown in particular properties and offers may be received. If none of those offers are accepted, the interest – or lack of it – should prompt the auctioneer and the seller to reconsider their guidelines. This is, of course, not possible if the guidelines are being published in the catalogue itself. In other circumstances such fine-tuning may prove worthwhile and may enable the spread between the guidelines to be reduced. Table 8.3 illustrates initial guidelines, fine-tuned guidelines and the likely reserve.

Likely Reserve	Initial Guidelines	Fine-tuned Guidelines
£5,000	£4,500–£6,000	£4,500–£5,500
£7,000	£6,500–£8,000	£6,500–£7,500
£10,000	£9,000–£12,000	£9,500–£10,500
£20,000	£19,000–£24,000	£19,500–£21,000
£30,000	£28,000–£35,000	£29,500–£31,500
£50,000	£45,000–£55,000	£49,000–£52,000
£75,000	£70,000–£80,000	£74,000–£79,000
£100,000	Around £100,000	£95,000–£105,000
£150,000	£140,000–£160,000	£145,000–£155,000
£200,000	£180,000–£220,000	£195,000–£210,000

Table 8.3 Guideline ranges

The reserve

Accurate advice on this figure from the auction house is vital. Far too often vendors are inclined to fix an amount which is high on the principle 'you can always bring it down afterwards'. Such an approach is totally unrealistic in the auction scene. If the reserve is realistic, then the final fine-tuned guidelines will be at a level to encourage would-be bidders to attend. If, during the auction, it becomes obvious to bidders that they are likely to be successful, then they are often encouraged to bid again and a little higher than wisdom would suggest. A high reserve and no sale kills the interest. The market for the property is depressed. The vendor is no longer in a strong position when the auctioneer has to start negotiating a private treaty sale after the pressure in the auction room has been removed.

Agree your reserve before the auction day

Vendors must come to a decision on the minimum figure that they will accept and agree this with the auctioneer well before auction day.

Sellers frequently suggest that they sit in an obvious position in the sale room and give a nod to the auctioneer if the bidding has reached a price at which they find acceptable. In the context of a properly run auction, such an arrangement is not possible.

All the vendors are doing is putting off the decision until the last moment. They are misleading themselves if they believe they can assess the amount of genuine interest in the room at the precise moment the bids are taking place. The auctioneer needs the reserve fixed so that he can judiciously use bids taken off the chandelier made on behalf of the vendors to encourage bidders in the room and to maintain the rhythm of the sale. If the vendors insist on only giving authority by a nod in the room, they run a considerable risk of instructing the auctioneer to accept a bid which was made by the auctioneer on the vendor's behalf. This could happen especially if the bidding does not reach the reserve.

Key point

The vendor and auctioneer will be wise to agree their reserve three or four days before the sale and certainly before the auctioneer goes onto the rostrum.

Key point

The vendor must remember, when settling the reserve with the auctioneer, that if a bid is received in the sale room at that amount or above, the lot will be sold without further reference to the vendor.

The post-auction price

When the auction has taken place and the euphoria has died away, the owners of any unsold lot are in a weak negotiating position. It is then too late to indicate that they would have accepted one of the bids in the room.

Lower your sights on price

The vendor must realise that when a bidder leaves, their enthusiasm to buy the property has waned. Because the lot did not sell, the bidders reconsider their judgement and revise their views. The auction house will be in a position to contact all the people who registered interest at the auction, but may not be in a position to pinpoint the highest bidder. The vendor and the auctioneer must then wait until a bidder indicates a renewal of interest. The balance of the bargaining positions has been reversed.

Key point

A vendor should not expect the highest bidder necessarily to repeat his bid at the same amount in the post-auction negotiations.

Nevertheless, the auction experience has enabled both the seller and the auctioneer to review their opinions of value. At this time the vendor should think about accepting a price lower than the reserve. In fact, the vendor should have thought about having a lower reserve on the day, but it is now too late because this is the time when bargain hunters, dealers and entrepreneurs look to purchase withdrawn lots at bargain basement prices. Table 8.4 illustrates possible post-auction prices for withdrawn lots.

Key point

The vendor and auctioneers should aim for a reserve price strategy which gives them a high chance of selling on the auction day.

	Fine-Tuned Guidelines	Actual Reserve	Post-Auction Price
£4,500–£6,000	£4,500–£5,500	£4,500	£3,500
£6,500–£8,000	£6,500–£7,500	£7,000	£5,500
£9,000–£12,000	£9,500–£10,500	£9,500	£8,000
£19,000–£24,000	£19,500–£21,000	£20,000	£17,500
£28,000–£35,000	£29,500–£31,500	£30,000	£27,000
£45,000–£55,000	£49,000–£52,000	£50,000	£45,000
£70,000–£80,000	£74,000–£79,000	£75,000	£65,000
Around £100,000	£95,000–£105,000	£100,000	£90,000
£140,000–£160,000	£145,000–£155,000	£145,000	£130,000
£180,000–£220,000	£195,000–£210,000	£195,000	£175,000

Table 8.4 Post-auction prices for withdrawn lots

Disclosing personal interest

The Estate Agents Act

The Estate Agents (Undesirable Practices) Order 1991 Statutory Instrument 1991 No. 861 lists various undesirable practices in the view of the Department of Trade and Industry that could be entered into by estate agents. In particular, in section two of this Statutory Instrument, the Parliamentary Under-Secretary of State indicates:

For the purposes of section 3(1)(d) of the Act the following practices in relation to estate agency work are hereby declared undesirable that is to say as regards – (a) the disclosure of personal interest, any failure to disclose that interest is described in Schedule 1 to this order; …

Schedule 1 reads as follows:

Disclosure of Personal Interest

Failure by an estate agent:

1 To make disclosure his personal interests as required by section 2(1) of the Act promptly and in writing.

2 To disclose to his client promptly and in writing that: (a) he himself has, or is seeking to acquire, beneficial interest in the land or in the proceeds of sale of any interest in the land; or …

Although in this context the clause appears only to affect estate agents, the definition of 'estate agents' for the purpose of the Estate Agents Act is particularly broad. The legislation also includes persons who are connected to estate agents. Vendors must be certain that they do not fall within these definitions or if they do, that the interest is disclosed in the auction catalogue.

Section 21(i) provides for those engaged in estate agency work to disclose their personal interest and reads:

A person who is engaged in estate agency work (in this section referred to as an 'Estate Agent') and has a personal interest in any land shall not enter into negotiations with any person with respect to the acquisition or disposal by that person of any interest in that land until the estate agent has disclosed to that person the nature and extent of his personal interest.

Section 32 defines those that are regarded as being connected to an estate agent and required to disclose their connection.

32- (1) In this Act 'associate' includes a business associate and otherwise has the meaning given by the following provisions of this section.

    (2) A person is an associate of another if he is the spouse or a relative of that other or of a business associate of that other.

    (3) In subsection (2) above, 'relative' means brother, sister, uncle, aunt, nephew, niece, lineal ancestor or linear descendant, and references to a spouse include a former spouse and a reputed spouse; and for the purposes of this subsection a relationship shall be established as if an illegitimate child or stepchild of a person had been a child born to him in wedlock.

    (4) A body corporate is an associate of another body corporate:

        (a) if the same person is a controller of both, or a person is a controller of one and persons who are his associates, or he and persons who are his associates, are controllers of the other; or

        (b) if a group of two or more persons is a controller of each company, and the groups either consist of the same persons or could be regarded as consisting of the same persons by treating (in one or more cases) a member of either group as replaced by a person of whom he is an associate.

    (5) An unincorporated association is an associate of another unincorporated association if any person:

        (a) is an officer of both associations;

        (b) has the management or control of the activities of both associations; or

        (c) is an officer of one association and has the management or control of the activities of the other association.

(6) A partnership is an associate of another partnership if:

   (a) any person is a member of both partnerships; or

   (b) a person who is a member of one partnership is an associate of a member of the other partnership; or

   (c) a member of one partnership has an associate who is also an associate of a member of the other partnership.

Key point

Vendors must appreciate that if they are an 'associate' of the auctioneer the exact extent of their association must be detailed in the auction catalogue and the auctioneer must be encouraged to draw attention to that note before the lot is offered on auction day.

When should a vendor accept an offer before the auction?

Having made the decision to include a property in an auction, the vendor should not be dissuaded from this course too easily. It must be assumed that the decision was correct in the first place. Nevertheless, there are various factors to consider if a prior offer is received.

How great is the interest?

The auction house will have been monitoring the extent of interest shown by the public in every lot. This does not mean that they will be aware of every single enquirer who has a specific interest in a seller's property since the enquirers often do not disclose it. However, the auction house should be aware of the number of people who have chosen to make a detailed inspection of the property.

Key point

Prior interest cannot be guaranteed to produce bidders on sale day.

How big is the offer?

Offers can be tempting. For attractive lots they may be well above the upper guideline. For less attractive lots they may be only close to the bottom guideline but at a figure which the vendor will find acceptable. If the amount of interest shown on the property has been very limited, then the auctioneer and the seller must consider whether it is better to accept the offer than to risk selling at a reduced figure with difficult negotiations after the sale. On the other hand, the figure may be one which is acceptable to the vendor and the auctioneer can vouch that there has been very little other interest in the lot.

Key point

Any prior offer at or close to the reserve price must be considered very favourably. Obviously, the vendor should consider very carefully the advice put forward by the auctioneer or his firm.

Exchanging contracts

When a vendor has accepted a prior offer, the auctioneer will insist that contracts or memoranda are exchanged with the buyer before the auction. Many auctioneers have a deadline for exchange of such contracts two or three days before the auction, so that they have time to announce the sale has taken place and to save any other would-be-bidders attending the auction seeking to purchase the lot that has already been sold.

Key point

If contracts or memoranda have not been exchanged before the auctioneer walks onto the rostrum, the property should still be offered whatever undertakings have been given by the prior buyer.

How should the vendor behave at the auction?

Some vendors attend the auction of their lots, others do not. These are a set of guidelines if you choose to attend the auction:

- **Do not bid yourself unless agreed beforehand with the auctioneer.** The auctioneer will wish to judge if it is necessary to make bids on your behalf to maintain the momentum and rhythm of the bidding. If you bid as well, you may upset the strategy he is setting up since he may not recognise you and may believe you are a genuine bidder. Secondly, you are committing an offence under the Sale of Land by Auction Act 1867 which requires bids on behalf of the vendor to come from only one source. If you bid in addition to the auctioneer bidding on your behalf, the sale will be invalidated.

- **Do not wait to fix the reserve until the last minute.** The auctioneer may have between five and 200 lots to offer on the day. Different auctioneers may be on the rostrum at differing times. They need to have their documentation and strategies prepared well in advance. Your reserve should be confirmed in writing to the auction house at least three to four days before the sale. Imagine the chaos if all the vendors in a large auction chose to communicate the reserves in the final minutes before the sale began!

- **Do not change your mind about the reserve price.** Remember, if the bidding does not go well the auctioneer will make bids on your behalf. Do not suddenly change your mind, as the auction proceeds about the amount you will accept. You cannot try to change the reserve or communicate to the auctioneer from the audience that he should accept the highest bid he has received once the auction is under way.

- **Watch the audience and listen carefully to the auctioneer.** By watching the audience, you will know how much interest there is from bidders. Listen carefully to the auctioneer towards the end of the bidding so that you are positive either that the lot has been sold or that it has been withdrawn. If the property is withdrawn, by knowing the prices that have been bid and the amount of interest from bidders you will be in a better position to discuss a reduced asking price after the sale.

Checklist: What vendors should do at auction

1 Fix the reserve and notify the auction house well in advance. ☐

2 Do not try to talk to the auctioneer just before the auction, communicate through another member of staff. ☐

3 Do not interfere publicly in the proceedings. ☐

4   Do not bid yourself unless agreed with the auctioneer beforehand. You could invalidate the sale. □

5   Remember, some bids (including the last one if your lot was withdrawn) may have been taken off the wall. □

6   Listen to the proceedings and bids carefully. Try to gauge the feeling in the room. □

7   Note if the gavel falls marking the sale of your lot or if the lot has been withdrawn. □

8   Do not expect to receive the deposit yourself. □

9   Leave the paperwork to the auction house or your solicitor. □

10 Do not celebrate prematurely but do not hesitate to congratulate your auctioneer and the staff. □

11 If your lot has been withdrawn, try to agree an early new selling price with the auction staff. □

What happens afterwards?

Your lot has been sold

If you were at the auction, you will be aware of the price at which the gavel fell. If you were not at the auction, the auctioneer will notify you soon after the sale of your success. Contracts or memoranda will have been exchanged in the sale room between the purchaser and your solicitor. If your solicitor attended the auction, he will leave the room with a copy of the contract or memoranda signed by the purchaser. If your solicitor was not present, then the auctioneer will send the documents to him.

The purchaser will have paid a deposit of ten per cent of the purchase price of the property (if VAT was due in addition, he will not have paid ten per cent of this; VAT is only payable at completion). If the conditions of sale describe a minimum deposit of more than ten per cent, then that amount will have been paid.

If the auction house charge an administration charge or buyer's premium, this will also be collected from the purchaser at the same time as the deposit.

Key point

The money or cheque will have been collected by your solicitor or by the auction house depending upon what has been agreed in the auctioneer's terms. The terms should ensure that the money is retained in a clients' account and covered by suitable insurance bonding.

Usually the deposit will be held on your behalf and the auctioneer will be entitled to charge his sale fee against it immediately. If the deposit is being held by your solicitor or the auctioneers, then the money will be passed to them, put on deposit if appropriate and covered by insurance bonding. If the conditions of sale provide for the money to be held on behalf of the purchaser, then appropriate arrangements will be made in a similar manner by the auctioneers or the solicitors. If the conditions of sale made special provisions for holding the deposit, then the auctioneers or your solicitor will ensure that the necessary conditions are fulfilled.

A tenanted shop and flat in the Clayton district of Manchester offered by Edward Mellor. Guided at £10,000, it sold for £500 less and brings in £5,200 pa, a mouth-watering yield of 55 per cent. A high-yield commercial investment.

Key point

The onus is now on your solicitor to liaise with the solicitor acting on behalf of the successful bidder. Any wise seller will maintain close contact with his solicitor to check that everything is moving smoothly to completion.

You are unlikely to need to contact the auctioneers again except perhaps to thank them for their services. If any hiccups do occur, then speak to the auctioneers who may be able to help. A receipt for the auctioneer's sale fee and the balance of the deposit received (if the auction house was holding it) will be passed over to your solicitor in plenty of time for completion.

What happens if your lot is withdrawn?

If you are at the auction, you will know that the property has been withdrawn. If you were not, your auctioneer is likely to contact you within two or three days to discuss the next steps. Your auction house may already be negotiating with potential buyers who are seeking to purchase the lot afterwards. You need to discuss with the auction house, very soon after the auction, the price at which you are now willing to sell. You are in a weak bargaining position in any negotiations the auctioneers may be having with potential buyers. It may be that during those negotiations, or even before any start, you will need to agree the lower figure at which the property can now be sold.

Key point

The first two or three days after an auction, where there has been a lot of withdrawn lots, frequently see frenetic negotiations.

If your property is withdrawn, you will normally have given the auctioneer authority to disclose your reserve and to sell at that reserve. If you are unwilling to sell at that reserve, you should ensure that your auctioneer is told immediately after the auction.

Should you put your lot in another auction?

This is a matter to be discussed with your auction house. Many auction houses are willing to offer a concessionary entry fee for lots that are offered for sale in a subsequent auction if there is not too long an interval between the two sales. A revision of the guidelines and the reserve will need to be discussed. The auctioneer should be in a position to discuss the wisdom of reoffering in the light of the vendor's new expectations on price.

Key point

It is most unusual for a property to be offered a second time by the same auction house at the same reserve unless there has been a change in the market value levels in the interim.

When does the vendor get paid?

Conditions of sale usually state that completion will take place 28 days after the auction. In normal circumstances, your solicitor should ensure that completion takes place on that day and that the balance of the proceeds is paid over to the vendor very quickly thereafter. If there are disputes between contract and completion, these may cause delays. Very occasionally, purchasers are not in funds to complete on time and can use bureaucratic and systematic delays to hinder completion. If the vendor's solicitor doubts the willingness of the purchaser to complete on the day set out for completion, a notice to complete can be served on the purchaser. The auctioneer is likely to have passed over the balance of the deposit (after deducting sale fees) in plenty of time. The vendor will not normally be able to collect this amount until completion has taken place. Any delays can be kept to a minimum if the vendor liaises frequently with his solicitor. Most contracts allow for interest to be charged on the amount outstanding after 28 days from the date contracts are exchanged, if completion has not occurred.

How much does a vendor receive out of the purchase price?

The vendor's net proceeds from the sale of a property that reached £80,000 at auction is given in Table 8.5. This example assumes that VAT is chargeable on the purchase price. If VAT is not chargeable, the sum can be deducted from the purchase price but not the auctioneer's and solicitor's fees. Table 8.6 gives details of the vendor's net proceeds for properties selling from £350 up to £1,000,000.

Purchase price	£80,000.00
Plus VAT received if receivable	£14,000.00
Total proceeds	**£94,000.00**
Less:	
VAT payable	£14,000.00
Credit to purchaser for tenants' advance payments	£2,000.00
Auctioneer's entry and sale fees and VAT	£3,220.00
Solicitor's fees and VAT for attending at auction (if appropriate)	£294.00
Solicitor's fees and VAT for dealing with contract and conveyance	£587.50
Local search fees	£25.00
Repayment of grants and charges	£1,200.00
Planning application fees	£500.00
Building regulation application fees	£250.00
Covenant buyout	£3,000.00
Contractor's bill for making the property secure	£250.00
Champagne	£25.00
	£25,351.50
Net proceeds	**£68,648.50**

Table 8.5 The vendor's net proceeds for a property selling for £80,000

Auction checklist: For the vendor

If you are thinking about bringing your property to auction, the following checklist will help you tackle it step by step.

1   Is your property right for offering by auction? ☐

2   Choose your auction house carefully after some research. ☐

3   Note your chosen auctioneer's terms carefully. ☐

4   Check on the amount of fees and when they are due. ☐

5   Check on the nature of the agency. ☐

6   Look through the terms and any supporting literature in great detail. ☐

7   Make sure the terms and the nature of the agency are in writing. ☐

8   Instruct your solicitor fully and early. ☐

9   Liaise thoroughly with the auctioneer and your solicitor to ensure the details in the catalogue are correct and not misleading. ☐

10 Agree the guideline figures with the auctioneer. ☐

11 Discuss the revision of those guidelines as marketing proceeds. ☐

12 Check the details of your property are correct after you have been provided with a copy of the printed catalogue. ☐

13 Be sure you have disclosed any personal interest under the Estate Agents Act. ☐

14 Discuss the wisdom or otherwise of accepting any pre-auction offers if any have been received by your auctioneer. ☐

15 If you accept a pre-auction offer, make sure your solicitor and the purchaser move to a quick exchange of contracts. ☐

16 Fix the reserve at least three or four days before the sale. Do not leave it until the last minute. ☐

17 If you attend the sale, do not bid yourself unless you have made a special arrangement with the auctioneer. ☐

Auctioneers' Fees

The Purchase Price	Entry Fee (Minimum £400)	Commission at 3% (Minimum £600)	Plus VAT	Solicitors Attending Auction incl VAT	Solicitors' Fees	Plus VAT	Vendors' Expenses	Possible Net Proceeds
£350	£400	£600	£175	–	£200	£35	£150	(£1,210)
£500	£400	£600	£175	–	£200	£35	£150	(£1,060)
£1,000	£400	£600	£175	–	£200	£35	£150	(£560)
£3,000	£400	£600	£175	£176	£200	£35	£150	£1,264
£5,000	£400	£600	£175	£176	£200	£35	£150	£3,264
£8,500	£400	£600	£175	£176	£200	£35	£150	£6,764
£12,000	£400	£600	£175	£176	£250	£44	£250	£10,105
£20,000	£400	£600	£175	£176	£250	£44	£250	£18,105
£30,000	£400	£900	£228	£176	£300	£53	£250	£27,693
£50,000	£400	£1,500	£332	£294	£300	£53	£250	£46,872
£100,000	£400	£3,000	£595	£294	£550	£96	£350	£94,715
£150,000	£400	£4,500	£858	£294	£600	£105	£350	£142,893
£250,000	£400	£7,500	£1,383	£470	£1,000	£175	£450	£238,622
£500,000	£400	£15,000	£2,695	£470	£2,000	£350	£550	£478,535
£1,000,000	£400	£30,000	£5,320	£470	£3,500	£612	£650	£959,048

Table 8.6 Vendor's net proceeds for properties selling from £350

18 Listen to the bidding carefully and watch the audience to assess the amount of interest in your lot. ☐

19 If you are sure the lot has sold, go out and celebrate but remember approximately one in every hundred lots do not proceed to completion, even when the gavel has fallen in the auction room. ☐

20 If your lot has not sold, remember the auctioneer will usually have authority to sell it at your reserve price thereafter. Review this instruction if you feel it is not appropriate. ☐

21 Liaise with your auctioneer in the period after the auction to consider changing your reserve and to help him in post-auction negotiations. ☐

22 In normal circumstances, expect your solicitor to complete the sale and for you to receive your money in approximately 28 days. ☐

CHAPTER 9

'We bought at auction' – what buyers have to say

By now, you will be well equipped to face your first auction. But how have others fared with the auction process? To give you a flavour of what it is like, the following people's experiences illustrate what they thought and felt about buying a property at auction.

Caroline Titley bought two semi-detached Victorian houses for her business

Caroline Titley runs her own business in Ashton-under-Lyne. She needed a property for her business and decided it would be more advantageous to buy than to rent, as it was cheaper.

'I found the property through the auctioneer. It is a Victorian property comprising two semi-detached houses and is around 150 years old. We bought the whole property and inhabit one half for our business and have a tenant in the other half. This was the first property that my partner and I had bought at auction and we made the bids ourselves. We had been to an auction before, so we were familiar with the process.

It was originally offered for sale in one auction but failed to receive a single bid and was withdrawn. The agent said the owner was seeking an asking price of £85,000 and that it was going to auction again in three weeks' time. We thought we might get it cheaper at auction rather than negotiating the sale there and then.

At the second auction, I asked how much the reserve price was and was given a guideline figure of £70,000 to £75,000. We thought that given the lack of interest in the property at the first auction, if we bid up to the guideline then no one would bid any higher. The bidding process went smoothly. I wasn't too apprehensive about it and I had my business partner with me, although he did not want to do the actual bidding when it came to it. It started at £70,000. I was so surprised when someone bid against me. It was all over in a matter of minutes, but I was equally surprised that just before the property reached £85,000 the other bidder dropped out.

'We didn't go over what we could afford'

In the end, we got it for the price we were prepared to pay and we didn't go over what we could afford. I was really pleased that we had acquired the property and I would certainly purchase commercial property at auction again and recommend others to use an auction to do the same.'

Don Lee paid 33 per cent less buying his house at auction

Don Lee lives in Manchester and has bought two residential houses at separate auctions.

'I was living in Manchester and noticed there was a number of run-down properties in the inner city part of Manchester. They had been built as private houses in 1982/3 and there had been problems with them simply because the people who had bought them could not pay their mortgage. They were quickly vandalised and went down in value like the rest of the property market.

I noticed that the auctioneers had managed to get hold of a few of these properties and they were going for about £14,000, which was pretty good even then. I waited for the best of the houses to come along which was an end one overlooking a public space with a pleasant view. I went to auction a couple of times before to get the feel for it and to see what the prices were like. I thought just before Christmas would be a good time to buy because people haven't got a lot of spare money and have other things on their mind and as it turns out I was proved right.

'I was surprised they did not go for more'

There was a certain tension at the auction. However, the property failed to reach its reserve and was withdrawn. I negotiated a price of £12,000 for it after the auction and it only needed another £1,000 to put it into livable condition. I was surprised they did not go for more.

The auction itself was run very well. I had been before so I knew they were good and entertaining (it's the best bit of free entertainment in Manchester). I did all the legal side myself and the conveyancing.

'I paid 33 per cent less'

The main advantage to me of buying at auction has got to be the price. Compared with the prices going through high-street estate agents I paid 33 per cent less. That is perhaps a bit more than usual – I think 25 per cent is a bit nearer the mark. However, I realised I was buying a vandalised property and knew what I was getting. I didn't buy a pig in a poke – you can do that – there is always that risk.

I bought another house recently and was surprised when it was knocked down to me for £24,000 as I was expecting to pay up to £25,000. I did think at one stage that I might not get the property, although I was prepared to bid £1,000 more than I paid for it. For this second house, similar properties are costing almost twice as much. I was surprised it went for what it did do. I was well pleased with it.

'I would definitely buy another property at auction'

I would definitely buy another property at auction and have no hesitation recommending others to buy at auction provided they understand the risks and have no worries. You must ask why the property is going for sale at auction and what (if anything) is wrong with it and satisfy yourself that you are not buying a pig in a poke. You have got to be prepared to do your own research. For example, I had to check that I was not buying a property over a coal mine. I knew the reason for the sale – that the property was foreclosed and put up for auction by a building society.'

Michael Kirby is a chartered surveyor who buys commercial property for clients

'The latest property I bought was a Railtrack goods yard which I was buying on behalf of tenants as an investment property. It was let to them on short leases. The property is used for open storage of coal, pallets, and cars.

I have bought one or two properties before on behalf of clients and I made all the bidding myself.

We did try to bid for the property beforehand. This was unsuccessful and it was suggested that we go to the auction where the price we got it for was slightly above what we originally bid beforehand. If you bid beforehand, you can open up a situation and show your hand so you must be careful.

I didn't start the bidding. There were one or two other bidders lower down. I let them have their say and then came in at the end. We bid twice and the second time it stopped, my bid being the highest bid. I thought the auctioneer might withdraw it because it was only slightly higher than we had bid before the auction. I thought it probably hadn't reached the reserve. But then the gavel came down and I knew it was ours.

From a purchaser's point of view, I would have said you were going to get quite a good deal at auction, particularly in this climate. It all depends on the day because you never know who else is going to bid. In our case we didn't think there would be anyone else interested, but there was. We assume that we bought it at the reserve.

Cornish holiday home with development potential and real original character. Lot 228 of a Halifax Property Auctions sale in Plymouth. This magnificent former chapel near Hayle was guided at only £10,000-£20,000.

'I always try to do a deal beforehand'

I always try to do a deal beforehand because you never know what opposition you are going to come up against at auction. But you should never show your hand in case it does go to auction. The vendor is generally only going to accept a higher price before the auction.

For a house or a plot of land that is good you can be outbid if people get carried away. The professional who is buying property will not get carried away but the average punter can tend to get carried away quite easily.

You can sometimes get a better deal at auction especially from lots that get withdrawn. Once you have reached your highest price you hope that the property hasn't reached the vendor's reserve and you can do a deal afterwards. You can get quite good deals that way.

Years ago it wasn't the done thing to buy property at auction but now it is more the norm especially on repossessions and investments. It's a quick way to buy a property. It gets the deal done.'

Michael Roe has bought two houses successfully at auction

'It is usually cheaper to buy property at auction'

'I bought a two-up, two-down terrace. I saw the property originally from the auctioneer's catalogue and went to view it from that. I have bought three properties at auction and so I was fairly familiar with the procedures. The great advantage to me is that it is usually cheaper to buy property at auction.

I have bought properties that are in some state of disrepair. They always wanted modernising and bringing up to date. In deciding what price to bid I tend to take an overall view. I check local sale prices and work out how much it will cost me to bring it up to date. I am usually prepared to pay so much at auction and if it goes for that price, I will buy it.

You always feel a little apprehensive before you go in. You go in with nothing and come home with something else. It was a fair investment, but it wasn't a big enough sum to worry me very much. The ones I've gone for I've got. I didn't feel I was going to lose the property during the auction.

With the latest one, I waited until the other bids had been made and then came in at the end. I only made one bid, and that was the last bid that succeeded. I was pleased to get it.

Buying at auction is very straightforward. If I could see houses that were being sold at comparable prices in comparable areas I would buy privately. But buying at auction is a way of ensuring I don't have to pay more than I need to pay. You want to make sure you acquire your property at a bargain level and auctions are the way.'

Appendices

Appendix 1: Enquiries of Local Authority (1994 Edition)

CON. 29 (1994)
To be submitted in duplicate

ENQUIRIES OF LOCAL AUTHORITY (1994 EDITION)

Please type or use BLOCK LETTERS

Search No...
The Replies are given on the attached sheet(s)

Signed ....
Proper Officer

Date................

A.

To

A. Enter name and address of District or Borough Council for the area. If the property is near a Local Authority boundary, consider raising certain Enquiries (e.g. road schemes) with the adjoining Council.

B. Enter address and description of the property. A plan in duplicate must be attached if possible and is insisted upon by some Councils. Without a plan, replies may be inaccurate or incomplete. A plan is essential for Optional Enquiries 18, 37 and 38.

B.

Property

C. Enter name and/or location of (and mark on plan, if possible) any other roadways, footpaths and footways (in addition to those entered in Box B) for Enquiry 3 and (if raised) Enquiries 19 and 20.

D. Answer every question. Any additional Enquiries must be attached on a separate sheet in duplicate and an additional fee will be charged for any which the Council is willing to answer.

E. Details of fees can be obtained from the Council or The Law Society.

C.

Other roadways, footpaths and footways

F. Enter name and address of the person or firm lodging this form.

G. Tick which Optional Enquiries are to be answered.

PLEASE READ THE NOTES ON PAGE 4.

G.

Optional Enquiries	
	17. Road proposals by private bodies
	18. Public paths or byways
	19. Permanent road closure
	20. Traffic schemes
	21. Advertisements
	22. Completion notices
	23. Parks and countryside
	24. Pipelines
	25. Houses in multiple occupation
	26. Noise abatement
	27. Urban development areas
	28. Enterprise zones
	29. Inner urban improvement areas
	30. Simplified planning zones
	31. Land maintenance notices
	32. Mineral consultation areas
	33. Hazardous substance consents
	34. Environmental and pollution notices
	35. Food safety notices
	36. Radon gas precautions
	37. Sewers within the property
	38. Nearby sewers

D.

A plan in duplicate is attached   YES/NO

Optional Enquiries are to be answered (see Box G) YES/NO

Additional Enquiries are attached in duplicate on a
separate sheet   YES/NO

E.

Fees of £   are enclosed.

Signed :

Date :

Reference :

Tel. No. :

F.

Reply to

OYEZ The Solicitors' Law Stationery Society Limited, Oyez House, 7 Spa Road, London SE16 3QQ
Conveyancing 29(1994)

LAW SOCIETY COPYRIGHT
9.97 F34273   5033379

Reproduced by Law Pack Publishing with the permission of the Controller of HMSO

Appendix 1: Enquiries of Local Authority (1994 Edition) (continued)

PART I—STANDARD ENQUIRIES
(APPLICABLE IN EVERY CASE)

DEVELOPMENT PLANS PROVISIONS
Structure Plan([1])
1.1.1 What structure plan is in force?
1.1.2 Have any proposals been made public for the alteration of the structure plan?

Local Plans([1])([2])
1.2.1 What stage has been reached in the preparation of a local plan?
1.2.2 Have any proposals been made public for the alteration or replacement of a local plan?

Old Style Development Plan
1.3 What old style development plan is in force?

Unitary Development Plan([1])
1.4.1 What stage has been reached in the preparation of a unitary development plan?
1.4.2 Have any proposals been made public for the alteration or replacement of a unitary development plan?

Non-Statutory Plan
1.5.1 Have the Council made any proposals for the preparation or modification of a non-statutory plan?
1.5.2 If so, what stage has been reached?

Policies or Proposals for the Property
1.6 Do any of the above plans (including any proposed alterations or replacements) indicate:
(a) a designation of primary use or zoning for the property or the area, or
(b) a specific proposal which includes the property?

Land required for Public Purposes
1.7 Is the property included in any of the categories of land specified in Schedule 13 paras 5 and 6 of the T&CP Act 1990?

DRAINAGE
Foul Drainage
2.1.1 To the Council's knowledge, does foul drainage from the property drain to a public sewer?([3])([4])
2.1.2 If yes, does the property drain into the public sewer through:
(a) a private drain alone, or
(b) a private drain and then a private sewer?([3])([4])([5])

Surface Water Drainage
2.2.1 To the Council's knowledge, does surface water from the property drain to:
(a) a public sewer, or
(b) a highway drain?([3])([4])([5])
2.2.2 If the answer to 2.2.1(a) or (b) is yes, does the surface water ... ... through:
(a) a private drain alone, or
(b) a private drain and then a private sewer?([3])([4])([5])

Statutory Agreements and Consents
2.3.1 Is there in force an agreement under s.22 of the Building Act 1984 for drainage of any part of the property in combination with another building through a private sewer?
2.3.2 Except as shown in the Official Certificate of Search, is there in force an agreement or consent under s.18 of the Building Act 1984 for the erection of a building or extension of a building over or in the vicinity of a drain, sewer or disposal main?([4])

Adoption Agreement
2.4.1 To the Council's knowledge, is any sewer serving, or which is proposed to serve, the property the subject of an agreement under s.104 of the Water Industry Act 1991 for the sewer to become vested in the sewerage undertaker?([6])
2.4.2 If so, is such an agreement supported by a bond or other financial security?([6])

Sewerage Undertaker
2.5 Please state the name and address of the sewerage undertaker.

MAINTENANCE OF ROADS ETC.
Publicly Maintained
3.1 Are all the roadways, footpaths and footways referred to in Boxes B and C on page 1 maintainable at the public expense within the meaning of the Highways Act 1980?([7])

Resolutions to make up or adopt
3.2 If not, have the Council passed any resolution to:
(a) make up any of those roadways, footpaths or footways at the cost of the frontagers, or
(b) adopt any of them without cost to the frontagers?
If so, please specify([7]).

Adoption Agreements
3.3.1 Have the Council entered into any subsisting agreement relating to the adoption of any of those roadways, footpaths or footways?
If so, please specify([6]).
3.3.2 Is any such agreement supported by a bond or other financial security?([6])

ROAD SCHEMES
Trunk and Special Roads
4.1.1 What orders, draft orders or schemes have been notified to the Council by the appropriate Secretary of State for the construction of a new trunk or special road, the centre line of which is within 200 metres of the property?
4.1.2 What proposals have been notified to the Council by the appropriate Secretary of State for:
(a) the alteration or improvement of an existing road, involving the construction, whether or not within existing highway limits, of a subway, underpass, flyover, footbridge, elevated road or dual carriageway, the centre line of which is within 200 metres of the property, or
(b) the construction of a roundabout (other than a mini-roundabout([8])), or the widening of an existing road by the construction of one or more additional traffic lanes, the limits of construction of which are within 200 metres of the property?

Other Roads
4.2 What proposals of their own([9]) have the Council approved for any of the following, the limits of construction of which are within 200 metres of the property:
(a) the construction of a new road, or
(b) the alteration or improvement of an existing road, involving the construction, whether or not within existing highway limits, of a subway, underpass, flyover, footbridge, elevated road, dual carriageway, the construction of a roundabout (other than a mini-roundabout([8])), or the widening of an existing road by the construction of one or more additional traffic lanes?

Road Proposals Involving Acquisition
4.3 What proposals have the Council approved, or have been notified to the Council by the appropriate Secretary of State for highway construction or improvement that involve the acquisition of the property?

Road Proposals at Consultation Stage
4.4 What proposals have either the Secretary of State or the Council published for public consultation relating to:
(a) the construction of a new road indicating a possible route the centre line of which would be likely to be within 200 metres of the property, or
(b) the alteration or improvement of an existing road, involving the construction, whether or not within existing highway limits, of a subway, underpass, flyover, footbridge, elevated road, dual carriageway, the construction of a roundabout (other than a mini-roundabout([8])), or the widening of an existing road by the construction of one or more additional traffic lanes, the limits of construction of which would be likely to be within 200 metres of the property?

OUTSTANDING NOTICES
5. What outstanding statutory notices or informal notices have been issued by the Council under the Public Health Acts, Housing Acts, Highways Acts, Building Acts([10]) or Part III of the Environmental Protection Act 1990?
(This enquiry does not cover notices shown in the Official Certificate of Search or notices relating to matters covered by Enquiries 13 or, if raised, 31, 34 or 35.)

BUILDING REGULATIONS
6. What proceedings have the Council authorised in respect of an infringement of the Building Regulations?

(1) The present development plan system requires structure plans by the County Council in the non-metropolitan areas, as well as local plans by District Councils. County Councils also deal with minerals and waste plans. In Greater London and the metropolitan areas, Unitary Development Plans are prepared by the relevant London Borough or metropolitan district council.
(2) Local plan includes action area plan.
(3) Any reply will be based on the statutory sewer map provided to the Council by the sewerage undertaker and any other records which the Council may hold.
(4) If the reply is "Not Known", the enquiry should be raised directly with the sewerage undertaker.
(5) The sewerage undertaker is not responsible for the maintenance of private drains or private sewers connecting a property to the public sewer.
(6) An adoption or vesting agreement requires adoption or vesting to take place only when the developer complies with his obligations under that agreement and the enquirer should make separate enquiries as to such compliance and should satisfy himself as to the adequacy of any bond or other financial security for such compliance.
(7) An affirmative answer does not imply that the public highway directly abuts the boundary of the property.
(8) A mini-roundabout is a roundabout having a one-way circulatory carriageway around a flush or slightly raised circular marking less than 4 metres in diameter and with or without flared approaches.
(9) This enquiry refers to the Council's (including where appropriate the County Council's) own proposals but not those of other bodies or companies; the latter are covered by Enquiry 17 in Part II.
(10) For property in Greater London, this includes the London Building Acts.

Appendix 1: Enquiries of Local Authority (1994 Edition) (continued)

PLANNING APPLICATIONS AND PERMISSIONS

Applications and Decisions

7.1 Please list:
  (a) any entries in the Register of planning applications and permissions,
  (b) any applications and decisions in respect of listed building consent, and
  (c) any applications and decisions in respect of conservation area consent.

Inspection and Copies

7.2 If there are any entries:
  (a) how can copies of the decisions be obtained?
  (b) where can the Register be inspected?

NOTICES UNDER PLANNING ACTS

Enforcement and Stop Notices

8.1.1 Please list any entries in the Register of enforcement notices and stop notices.

8.1.2 If there are any entries:
  (a) how can copies of the notices be obtained?
  (b) where can that Register be inspected?

Proposed Enforcement or Stop Notice

8.2 Except as shown in the Official Certificate of Search, or in reply to Enquiry 8.1.1., has any enforcement notice, listed building enforcement notice, or stop notice been authorised by the Council for issue or service (other than notices which have been withdrawn or quashed)?

Compliance with Enforcement Notices

8.3 If an enforcement notice or listed building enforcement notice has been served or issued, has it been complied with to the satisfaction of the Council?

Other Planning Notices

8.4 Have the Council served, or resolved to serve, any breach of condition or planning contravention notice or any other notice or proceedings relating to a breach of planning control?

Listed Building Repairs Notices, etc.

8.5.1 To the knowledge of the Council, has the service of a repairs notice been authorised?

8.5.2 If the Council have authorised the making of an order for the compulsory acquisition of a listed building, is a "minimum compensation" provision included, or to be included, in the order?

8.5.3 Have the Council authorised the service of a building preservation notice?([11])

DIRECTIONS RESTRICTING PERMITTED DEVELOPMENT

9. Except as shown in the Official Certificate of Search, have the Council resolved to make a direction to restrict permitted development?

ORDERS UNDER PLANNING ACTS

Revocation Orders etc.

10.1 Except as shown in the Official Certificate of Search, have the Council resolved to make any Orders revoking or modifying any planning permission or discontinuing an existing planning use?

Tree Preservation Order

10.2 Except as shown in the Official Certificate of Search, have the Council resolved to make any Tree Preservation Orders?

COMPENSATION FOR PLANNING DECISIONS

11. What compensation has been paid by the Council under s.114 of the T&CP Act 1990 for planning decisions restricting development other than new development?

CONSERVATION AREA

12. Except as shown in the Official Certificate of Search, is the area a conservation area?

COMPULSORY PURCHASE

13. Except as shown in the Official Certificate of Search, have the Council made any order (whether or not confirmed by the appropriate Secretary of State) or passed any resolution for compulsory acquisition which is still capable of being implemented?([12])

AREAS DESIGNATED UNDER HOUSING ACTS ETC.

Clearance

14.1 Has any programme of clearance for the area been:
  (a) submitted to the Department of the Environment, or
  (b) resolved to be submitted, or
  (c) otherwise adopted by resolution of the Council?

Housing

14.2 Except as shown in the Official Certificate of Search, have the Council resolved to define the area as designated for a purpose under the Housing Acts? If so, please specify the purpose.

SMOKE CONTROL ORDER

15. Except as shown in the Official Certificate of Search, have the Council made a smoke control order or resolved to make or vary a smoke control order for the area?

RAILWAYS

16. What proposals have been notified to the Council, and what proposals of their own have the Council approved, for the construction of a railway (including light railway or monorail) the centre line of which is within 200 metres of the property?

PART II—OPTIONAL ENQUIRIES
(APPLICABLE ONLY AS INDICATED ON PAGE ONE)

ROAD PROPOSALS BY PRIVATE BODIES

17. What proposals by others([13]) have the Council approved for any of the following, the limits of construction of which are within 200 metres of the property:
  (a) the construction of a new road, or
  (b) the alteration or improvement of an existing road, involving the construction, whether or not within existing highway limits, of a subway, underpass, flyover, footbridge, elevated road, dual carriageway, the construction of a roundabout (other than a mini-roundabout([6])), or the widening of an existing road by the construction of one or more additional traffic lanes?

PUBLIC PATHS OR BYWAYS

18. Is any public path, bridleway or road used as a public path or byway which abuts on([7]) or crosses the property shown in a definitive map or revised definitive map prepared under Part IV of the National Parks and Access to the Countryside Act 1949 or Part III of the Wildlife and Countryside Act 1981? If so, please mark its approximate route on the attached plan([14]).

PERMANENT ROAD CLOSURE

19. What proposals have the Council approved for permanently stopping up or diverting any of the roads or footpaths referred to in Boxes B and C on page 1?

TRAFFIC SCHEMES

20. In respect of any of the roads referred to in Boxes B and C on page 1, what proposals have the Council approved, but have not yet put into operation, for:
  (a) waiting or loading restrictions,
  (b) one-way streets,
  (c) prohibition of driving,
  (d) pedestrianisation, or
  (e) vehicle width or weight restrictions?

ADVERTISEMENTS

Entries in Register

21.1.1 Please list any entries in the Register of applications, directions and decisions relating to consent for the display of advertisements.

21.1.2 If there are any entries, where can that Register be inspected?

Notices, Proceedings and Orders

21.2 Except as shown in the Official Certificate of Search:
  (a) has any notice been given by the Secretary of State or served in respect of a direction or proposed direction restricting deemed consent for any class of advertisement?
  (b) have the Council resolved to serve a notice requiring the display of any advertisement to be discontinued?
  (c) if a discontinuance notice has been served, has it been complied with to the satisfaction of the Council?
  (d) have the Council resolved to serve any other notice or proceedings relating to a contravention of the control of advertisements?
  (e) have the Council resolved to make an order for the special control of advertisements for the area?

COMPLETION NOTICES

22. Which of the planning permissions in force have the Council resolved to terminate by means of a completion notice under s.94 of the T&CP Act 1990?

---

(11) The Historic Buildings and Monuments Commission also have power to issue this type of notice for buildings in London Boroughs, and separate enquiry should be made of them if appropriate.
(12) This enquiry refers to the Council's own compulsory purchase powers and not those of other bodies.
(13) This enquiry refers to proposals by bodies or companies (such as private developers) other than the Council (and where appropriate the County Council) or the Secretary of State.
(14) A plan of the property must be supplied by the enquirer if this enquiry is to be answered.

Appendix 1: Enquiries of Local Authority (1994 Edition) (continued)

PARKS AND COUNTRYSIDE

Areas of Outstanding Natural Beauty

23.1 Has any order under s.87 of the National Parks and Access to the Countryside Act 1949 been made?

National Parks

23.2 Is the property within a National Park designated under s.7 of the National Parks and Access to the Countryside Act 1949?

PIPELINES

24. Has a map been deposited under s.35 of the Pipelines Act 1962, or Schedule 7 of the Gas Act 1986, showing a pipeline laid through, or within 100 feet (30.48 metres) of, the property?

HOUSES IN MULTIPLE OCCUPATION

25. Is the property included in a registration of houses scheme (houses in multiple occupation) under s.346 of the Housing Act 1985, containing control provisions as authorised by s.347 of that Act?

NOISE ABATEMENT

Noise Abatement Zone

26.1 Have the Council made, or resolved to make, any noise abatement zone order under s.63 of the Control of Pollution Act 1974 for the area?

Entries in Register

26.2.1 Has any entry been recorded in the Noise Level Register kept pursuant to s.64 of the Control of Pollution Act 1974?

26.2.2 If there is an entry, how can copies be obtained and where can that Register be inspected?

URBAN DEVELOPMENT AREAS

27.1 Is the area an urban development area designated under Part XVI of the Local Government Planning and Land Act 1980?

27.2 If so, please state the name of the urban development corporation and the address of its principal office.

ENTERPRISE ZONES

28. Is the area an enterprise zone designated under Part XVIII of the Local Government Planning and Land Act 1980?

INNER URBAN IMPROVEMENT AREAS

29. Have the Council resolved to define the area as an improvement area under s.4 of the Inner Urban Areas Act 1978?

SIMPLIFIED PLANNING ZONES

30.1 Is the area a simplified planning zone adopted or approved pursuant to s.83 of the T&CP Act 1990?

30.2 Have the Council approved any proposal for designating the area as a simplified planning zone?

LAND MAINTENANCE NOTICES

31. Have the Council authorised the service of a maintenance notice under s.215 of the T&CP Act 1990?

MINERAL CONSULTATION AREAS

32. Is the area a mineral consultation area notified by the county planning authority under Schedule 1 para 7 of the T&CP Act 1990?

HAZARDOUS SUBSTANCE CONSENTS

33.1 Please list any entries in the Register kept pursuant to s.28 of the Planning (Hazardous Substances) Act 1990.

33.2 If there are any entries:
(a) how can copies of the entries be obtained?
(b) where can the Register be inspected?

ENVIRONMENTAL AND POLLUTION NOTICES

34. What outstanding notices or informal notices have been issued by the Council under the Environmental Protection Act or the Control of Pollution Act?
(This enquiry does not cover notices under Part III of the EPA, to which Enquiry 5 applies).

FOOD SAFETY NOTICES

35. What outstanding statutory notices or informal notices have been issued by the Council under the Food Safety Act?

RADON GAS PRECAUTIONS

36.1 Is the property in an area where radon precautions are required for new dwellings?

36.2 If so, are full or secondary precautions required?

SEWERS WITHIN THE PROPERTY ([3])([14])

37. Does the statutory sewer map show, within the boundaries of the property as depicted on the attached plan, a public sewer or disposal main, a sewer in respect of which a vesting declaration has been made but which has not yet come into force, or a drain or sewer which is the subject of an agreement under s.104 of the Water Industry Act 1991?

NEARBY SEWERS ([3])([14])

(a) state whether the statutory sewer map shows public foul and surface water sewers within 100 feet (30.48 metres) of the property ([15]), or

(b) supply a copy extract from the statutory sewer map showing any public sewers in the vicinity of the property([16]).

([15]) The sewer map does not show the relative levels of the sewers and the property.

([16]) If the Council supplies an extract from the sewer map, the notation should be carefully checked and any queries should be clarified with the Council or the sewerage undertaker.

GENERAL NOTES

(A) Unless otherwise indicated, all these enquiries relate to the property as described in Box B on page 1, and any part of that property, and "the area" means any area in which the property is located.

(B) References to "the Council" include references to a predecessor Council and to a Committee or Sub-Committee of the Council acting under delegated powers, and to any other body or person taking action under powers delegated by the Council or a predecessor Council. The replies given to certain enquiries addressed to District Councils cover knowledge and actions of both the District Council and the County Council.

(C) References to an Act, Regulation or Order include reference to (i) any statutory provision which it replaces and (ii) any amendment or re-enactment of it.

(D) References to any Town and Country Planning Act, Order or Regulation are abbreviated, eg "T&CP Act 1990".

(E) The replies will be given after the appropriate enquiries and in the belief that they are in accordance with the information at present available to the officers of the replying Council(s), but on the distinct understanding that none of the Councils, nor any Council officer, is legally responsible for them, except for negligence. Any liability for negligence shall extend for the benefit of not only the person by or for whom these Enquiries are made but also a person (being a purchaser for the purposes of s.10(3) of the Local Land Charges Act 1975) who or whose agent had knowledge, before the relevant time (as defined in that section), of the replies to these Enquiries.

(F) This form of Enquiries is approved by The Law Society, the Association of County Councils, the Association of District Councils and the Association of Metropolitan Authorities and is published by their authority.

Appendix 2: General terms and conditions concerning domestic non-structural survey

GENERAL TERMS AND CONDITIONS CONCERNING DOMESTIC NON-STRUCTURAL SURVEY

Our basis of valuation is the open market value for existing use defined below. It is based on the Royal institution of Chartered Surveyors guidance notes on the Valuation of Assets.

Our instructions do not extend to the carrying out of any form of structural survey of the building and our inspection was intended to be for valuation purposes only.

Open market value means the best price at which an interest in property might reasonably be expected to have been sold and completed unconditionally for cash consideration on the date of valuation assuming:

1. a willing seller;

2. that prior to the date of valuation there had been a reasonable period (having regard to the nature of the property and the state of the market) for the proper marketing of the interest for the agreement of price and terms and for the completion of the sale;

3. that the state of the market, level of values and other circumstances were, on any earlier assumed date of exchange of contracts, the same as the date of the valuation; and

4. that no account will be taken of any additional bid by a purchaser with a special interest.

Full Investigation of title, tenure, covenants, rights of way, etc. normally involving the services of a solicitor have **NOT** been earned out.

We strongly recommend that your solicitors be shown a copy of this report and if any of our observations or conclusions conflict with their report on Title then we should be informed as there may be a possibility that our valuation will require amendment.

We have relied upon the information supplied to us by yourselves or your advisers as detailed in the section of the Report and Valuation concerning tenure and we have no knowledge (express or implied) of any restrictive, adverse or other covenants, wayleaves, rights of way or of light or of support, emergency escape routes, access and facilities for repairs, maintenance and replacement or other easements, options, conditions (positive or negative), third party rights or any prescriptive rights enjoyed by the owner or occupier of the property or over the property for the benefit of other property or of any unusual or onerous rights, restrictions or outgoings which may in any way affect the value of the property. We do not accept responsibility for any inaccuracies mis-statements or facts or omissions in information provided to us.

Appendix 2: General terms and conditions concerning domestic non-structural survey (continued)

Where a plan is attached we have shown what visually appear to be the boundaries of the property but we have no knowledge (express or implied) of the responsibilities for fencing and legal advice should be sought upon that aspect, if required. We have therefore assumed that such boundaries show the true extent of the property. We know of no potential or existing boundary or other disputes or claims. Any site, floor, yard or similar areas should be considered approximate.

Where possible, we make oral enquiries of the relevant Local Authority. Where the Local Authority refuses to assist us we will inform you and we will review our valuation when a solicitor provides us with a copy of the Local Authority Search.

Information provided in relation to Town & County Planning or highway matters is the result of these informal enquiries made of the offices of the Local Authority which we have assumed are correct. We have had to assume that the property was constructed with the appropriate planning and any other consents necessary and in accordance with appropriate building regulations and that it is being used for a purpose or purposes compatible with its permitted planning use, i.e. its apparent current use. We confirm, however, that the property is prima facie suitable for the purposes for which we have been informed that planning permission is held.

We have assumed that the property and its value is unaffected by any additional matters which would be revealed by a full written Local Search reply and replies to the usual enquiries; or by any outstanding requirement of insurance companies. We assume that the property and its value are not affected by any statutory notice and that the property nor any construction thereon or its or their condition nor its use or intended use is not or will not be unlawful or in breach of any covenant or be an actionable wrong claimed by any person.

The Environmental Protection Act 1990 requires local authorities to establish Contaminated Land Registers. We have not investigated whether the site is, or has been, in the past contaminated or whether it is on such a register, and your legal advisers should investigate whether the subject property is on the register before you enter into any legal commitment to purchase. Our valuation is on the assumption that the land is not contaminated and is not on the register.

We have not inspected the woodwork or other parts of the structure which are covered, unexposed or inaccessible and we are therefore unable to report that any such part of the property is free from defect, the examination and testing of the electrical, gas, oil or other fuel or energy supplies and installations to include all wiring, cables, pipe and conduit, switches, plugs, fuses and tap and water and drainage systems and plumbing, heating and ventilating installations are outside our instructions and consequently no opinion nor any assurance or guarantee whatsoever to their existence condition or suitability is made or given.

Appendix 2: General terms and conditions concerning domestic non-structural survey (continued)

We recommend that any Guarantees which have been given for any of the services should be checked for validity and effectiveness.

We can give no opinion or warranty nor any assurance or guarantee whatsoever that any part of any construction on the property does not have in any form whatsoever any rot, disease, beetle or other attack or metal corrosion or fatigue or any other defects. We have not reported minor or trivial repairs required. We have not inspected any roof or floor voids or spaces or wall cavities and wall ties.

In properties of all ages where metal or wire wall ties are incorporated in cavity walls, recent research has shown that these may be in poor condition. It is beyond the scope of our survey to inspect such wall ties as such an inspection requires specialist equipment. Failure of the wall ties is generally not detectable without special inspection unless it has resulted in bulging or cracking of the walls. We therefore accept no liability for wall tie failure which is not externally apparent. If required, we can supply the names of specialist firms who have fibre optic inspection equipment capable of carrying out internal inspections of any wall cavities.

Since it would require major excavation, we have not carried out any examination of the foundations to the property and have not judged the quality of the support provided. No examination or test has been carried out on any of the buildings to check if any high alumina cement, calcium chloride additive, blue asbestos, sea dredged aggregates, wood-wool slabs as permanent shutterings, calcium silicate bricks or crocodilite or any other deleterious or other materials which are generally accepted as not being good and sound and for the purpose have been used. We have assumed for the purposes of our Report and Valuation that any such investigation will not disclose the presence of any such materials. We cannot therefore report that the property is free from risk from these problems.

We have not carried out nor commissioned a site investigation or geographical or geophysical survey and therefore can give no opinion or warranty or assurance or guarantee whatsoever that the ground has sufficient load bearing strength to support the existing constructions or any other construction that may be erected upon it in the future. We also cannot give any opinion or warranty or assurance or guarantee that there are no underground mineral or other workings beneath the site or in its vicinity or that there is any fault or disability underground which could or might affect the existing property or any future or current construction thereon, or pollute the local environment.

We are not aware of the content of any environmental audit or other environmental investigation or soil survey which may have been carried out on the property and which may draw attention to any contamination or the possibility of any such contamination, In undertaking our work, we have assumed that no contaminative or potentially contaminative uses have ever been carried out on the property. We have not carried out any investigations

Appendix 2: General terms and conditions concerning domestic non-structural survey (continued)

into past or present uses or either the property or of any neighbouring land to establish whether there is any potential for contamination from these uses or sites to the subject property and have therefore assumed that none exists, nor have we had regard to the contents of any Register of Land which may be subject to contamination.

Should it, however, be established subsequently that contamination exists at the property or on any neighbouring land or that the premises have been or are being put to a contaminative use, or that the property is on the Register, this might reduce the value reported.

In arriving at our opinion as to the value, we have not taken into account any item in the nature of the tenant's fixtures and fittings, plant equipment, goodwill, vehicles and machinery, materials, work in progress or stock in trade upon the property at the time of our inspection.

Our valuation does not take into account any matters concerning the consideration of or the incidence of taxation whether in the nature of stamp duty, Capital Gains Tax, Income Tax, Value Added Tax, Corporation Tax, Development Land Tax, or any other tax or levy (whether national or local) that may arise or be taken into account on any transaction. Nor does the valuation have regard to any incidental costs of sale that might arise on a disposal.

No allowance has been made to reflect any liability to taxation that may arise on disposal nor for any costs associated with disposal. No allowance has been made to reflect any liability to repay any grants or taxation allowances that may arise on disposal.

Within the constraints of the various clauses above we have brought all defects or problems known to us arising under these clauses to your attention.

We are willing to supply, but without any responsibility whatsoever, the names and addresses of specialists known to us for you to instruct independently and/or to arrange surveyors and reports on any matter upon which we are unable to report under any paragraph hereof.

This report shall be for private and confidential use of the clients for whom the report is undertaken and should not be reproduced in whole or in part or relied upon by third parties for any use without the express written authority of the Surveyors.

We confirm that at the date hereof we have brought to your attention all the facts which have been disclosed to us or which we might reasonably be expected to know and which may reduce the amount of our valuation or the prompt realisability of the property over the next twelve months including inter alia the reduced period remaining in a lease and/or the effect of Landlord and Tenant legislation.

If we have quoted a forced sale value, we have assumed that the property is fully marketed and thereafter auctioned at a public auction within three to four months of the commencement of the marketing exercise.

Our surveyor will be pleased to discuss any points mentioned in this report.

Appendix 3: RICS auction guidance notes

GUIDANCE NOTES FOR AUCTIONEERS PROPOSING TO SELL REAL ESTATE AT AUCTION IN ENGLAND AND WALES

This is a Guidance Note. It provides advice to members of RICS on aspects of the profession. Where procedures are recommended for specific professional tasks, these are intended to embody 'best practice', i.e. procedures which in the opinion of RICS meet a high standard of professional competence.

Members are not required to follow the advice and recommendations contained within the Note. They should, however, note the following points:

When an allegation of professional negligence is made against a surveyor, the Court is likely to take account of the contents of any relevant Guidance Notes published by RICS in deciding whether or not the surveyor has acted with reasonable competence.

In the opinion of RICS, a member conforming to the practices recommended in this Note should have at least a partial defence to an allegation of negligence by virtue of having followed those practices. However, members have the responsibility of deciding when it is appropriate to follow the guidance. If it is followed in an appropriate case, the member will not be exonerated merely because the recommendations were found in an RICS Guidance Note.

On the other hand, it does not follow that a member will be adjudged negligent if he has not followed the practices recommended in this Note. It is for each individual surveyor/ auctioneer to decide on the appropriate procedure to follow in any professional task. However, where members depart from the practice recommended in this Note, they should do so only for good reason. In the event of litigation, the Court may require them to explain why they decided not to adopt the recommended practice.

In addition, Guidance Notes are relevant to professional competence in that each surveyor should be up to date and should have informed himself of the Guidance Notes within a reasonable time of their promulgation.

The Guidance Notes apply only to properties in England and Wales and are intended to serve as a guide to best practice for all members of the profession intending to conduct public auctions of real estate in England and Wales or Scotland.

In addition, they may be of help to members of the public in understanding the process involved in the preparation and conduct of auctions of property.

The sale of properties in Scotland may be subject to different legislation and practice and it is recommended that separate legal advice is sought whether or not the sale takes place in England or Wales.

Appendix 3: RICS auction guidance notes (continued)

1	**Legal Responsibilities**

1.1 *The Law*

1.1.1 Auctioneers, sellers and buyers should appreciate that a considerable amount of the practice of offering property for sale, whether by private treaty or by auction, is regulated by law. The Auctioneer's legal and professional responsibilities are defined particularly in the:

- Auctioneers Act 1845
- Sale of Land by Auction Act 1867
- Auctions (Bidding Agreements) Acts 1927 and 1969
- Misrepresentation Act 1967
- Sale of Goods Act 1979
- Estate Agents Act 1979 and Regulations and any orders made thereafter
- Landlord & Tenant Act 1987
- Property Misdescriptions Act 1991 and any Orders made thereunder
- Money Laundering Regulations 1993
- Unfair Terms in Consumer Contracts Regulations 1994
- Housing Act 1996

1.2 *Personal Interest*

1.2.1 Under the provisions of the Estate Agents Act 1979 and RICS bylaws it is the Auctioneer's duty to notify both seller and prospective buyers of any personal interests and the Auctioneer must be aware that the definition of 'personal interest' in the Act is wide.

1.3 *Choice of Method of Sale*

1.3.1 Auctioneers should always be satisfied that they have covered their duty of care to the seller in considering whether auction is the best method of sale in the circumstances.

2	**Pre-Auction**

2.1 *Terms of Engagement*

2.1.1 The Estate Agents Act 1979, and the statutory instruments made under it, regulate the manner in which all estate agents have to notify their fees. The precise terms of the Auctioneer's appointment should be agreed in writing and any such terms must include:

(a) a definition of the Auctioneer's basis of appointment and if the terms sole agent, joint agent, or sole selling rights are used, the statutory wording must be incorporated;

(b) the seller's liability for fees and expenses (to include sales that may be effected prior or subsequent to auction) specifying precisely under what circumstances the liability will arise, the amount of the fees and expenses and the duration of the period of appointment;

Appendix 3: RICS auction guidance notes (continued)

(c) the seller's liability for fees and expenses in the event of the seller withdrawing instructions between appointment and the auction date;

(d) the rights of the Auctioneer to deduct agreed fees and expenses from the deposit held; and

(e) the Auctioneer's responsibility and procedure for the reporting of bids prior to auction.

2.1.2   Additionally it should include:

(a) the manner in which the Auctioneer may accept deposits, including by cheque and banker's draft;

(b) whether the deposit will be held as stakeholder or agent for the seller and to whom any interest earned on that deposit accrues, and to whom the balance of the deposit monies shall be sent;

(c) the extent of the Auctioneer's right:

(i)   to refuse bids;

(ii)   to determine disputes between bidders;

(iii) to regulate bidding increments;

(iv) to accept postal, telephone, internet or facsimile bids by way of proxy (with appropriate indemnities from the seller and the bidder in the event of a failure of communications);

(v)   to release any bidder acting as agent from personal liability;

(vi) to sign the auction contract on behalf of the seller;

(vii) to bid on behalf of the seller and to advise the seller not to bid. The Auctioneer should not accept instructions where the seller wants the right to bid the reserve or over the reserve;

(d) the Auctioneer's responsibility and procedure for inspections;

(e) the Auctioneer's right to instruct the seller's solicitor to undertake all local and other searches and provide special conditions of sale and to make all relevant legal documentation available to prospective buyers;

(f) confirmation from the seller that any existing instructions to other agents have been withdrawn (excepting those acting as Joint Auctioneers). If Joint Auctioneers are appointed, it is advisable for the Auctioneer to ensure that the duties and liabilities of the Joint Auctioneer are documented and the basis of remuneration and reimbursement of costs has been agreed;

(g) the Auctioneer's right to change the venue or date of the auction at his discretion;

Appendix 3: RICS auction guidance notes (continued)

(h) as the Auctioneer does not have implied authority to sell prior or post auction, the circumstances in which the Auctioneer is authorised to sign the Memorandum of Sale on behalf of the seller;

(i) a warranty that information supplied to the Auctioneer by the seller or the seller's solicitor or the seller's managing agents is accurate and an indemnity against liability for inaccuracy; and

(j) provisions relating to proxy bids and whether the upper limit should be disclosed to the seller.

2.2   *Material Matters Which May Affect the Sale*

2.2.1   The Auctioneer should ask to be notified by the seller and/or the solicitors of public health notices, local land charges, financial charges, major arrears of rent, disputes and material matters relating to the property being offered for sale.

2.3   *Provision of Legal Documentation and Other Legal Issues*

2.3.1   All relevant documents and plans relating to the property being sold should be available for inspection at the offices of the Auctioneer or the seller's solicitors for as long a period as possible prior to the sale and in the auction room.

2.3.2   It may be helpful for the solicitor acting for the seller to attend at the auction to facilitate and explain queries which may be raised of a legal nature or pertaining to the legal documentation.

2.3.3   The General Conditions of Sale, Memorandum of Sale and any notices to bidders are normally published by the Auctioneer and regulate the conduct of the sale and other matters which apply to all the lots in the auction; the Special Conditions of Sale are usually prepared by the seller's solicitor and generally apply to a specific lot.

2.4   *Auction Venue*

2.4.1   The Auctioneer should check that:

(a) there is no prohibition against holding an auction on the property;

(b) the permitted size of the auction room will accommodate the bidders and, in particular, that the fire regulations will be complied with;

(c) the insurance cover maintained by the hirers of the auction room is satisfactory; and

(d) any local authority regulations can be complied with.

2.5   *Sale Boards*

2.5.1   The Auctioneer should not erect a sale board without the seller's, and/or the lessee's consent where required.

2.5.2   The Auctioneer must comply with the relevant planning regulations for the

Appendix 3: RICS auction guidance notes (continued)

erection of boards and should require sign-board erectors to carry satisfactory and sufficient insurance.

2.5.3   The Auctioneer should arrange for the board to be removed from the property after the auction and the board erectors required to make good all damage to the property.

2.6   *Price Guides*

2.6.1   If price guides are given, they should not be misleading. It is helpful for prospective buyers if the Auctioneer defines the basis of the price guide, for example, 'the seller's initial expectation of the level of the reserve'.

2.6.2   For the benefit of prospective buyers reference should be made in the catalogue that price guides may be subject to adjustment, where appropriate, in the lead up to the auction.

2.6.3   The Auctioneer should make reasonable endeavours to contact all known interested parties who have specifically registered their interest and advise them of any adjustment in the price guide. However, it should be drawn to the attention of prospective buyers that it is their responsibility to make regular contact with the Auctioneers to establish whether there has been an adjustment in the price guide.

2.7   *Reserve Price*

2.7.1   It is usual for a reserve price to be fixed prior to the auction day. This is the figure below which the Auctioneer is not authorised to sell at auction.

2.7.2   It is good practice for the Auctioneer to confirm in writing the reserve price.

2.7.3   Any reserve price will remain strictly confidential to the Auctioneer, his staff and the seller and the Auctioneer will not disclose reserve prices to any third parties unless instructed to do so by the seller. Only with the agreement of the seller will a reserve price be disclosed in the catalogue or at the auction.

2.7.4   The existence, but not the amount, of the reserve should be disclosed in the General Conditions of Sale with an indication of the Auctioneer's right to bid on behalf of the seller up to, but not at or above, the reserve price.

2.8   *Sales Prior to the Auction*

2.8.1   The Auctioneer should ask to be notified by the seller of any sale contemplated by the Seller prior to the auction.

2.8.2   The Auctioneer should make it clear to prospective buyers in the auction catalogue that there is always the possibility of the seller selling at any time before the auction and that prospective buyers should verify the availability of the lot immediately prior to the auction.

2.8.3   If the property is sold or withdrawn prior to the auction, the Auctioneer should use reasonable endeavours to notify all known parties who have specifically registered interest. However, it should be drawn to the attention of prospective buyers that it

Appendix 3: RICS auction guidance notes (continued)

	is their responsibility to make regular contact with the Auctioneer to establish whether the property has been sold or withdrawn prior to the auction.

2.9   *Value Added Tax (VAT)*

2.9.1   The Auctioneer should request the seller to confirm whether or not the sale is subject to VAT and prospective buyers should be made aware of this. Note should be taken of the guidance in Appendix 2.

2.9.2   It is advisable for the Auctioneers to request the seller to give clear written instructions on the treatment of VAT on the deposit monies.

2.10   *Joint Auctioneers*

2.10.1   If there is a Joint Auctioneer, his duties, responsibilities and terms of appointment need to be approved by the seller.

3   **Auction Catalogue**

3.1   *The Particulars*

3.1.1   The Auctioneer should appreciate that auction particulars have to be factual, accurate and comply with the Property Misdescriptions Act 1991 and all relevant statutory instruments. It is recommended that Auctioneers forward proofs of auction particulars to the seller and the solicitors, joint and co-auctioneers and managing agents (if appropriate) for verification.

3.1.2   The auction particulars may form part of the contract unless specifically excluded by the Conditions of Sale. Notwithstanding any purported exclusion, the auction particulars may be deemed to be part of the contract or to constitute representations with respect to the property.

3.1.3   Catalogues frequently incorporate the General and Special Conditions of Sale and the Memorandum of Sale, but, if they are not included, the catalogue should indicate their existence and where and when they are available for inspection prior to the sale. A buyer who is not given effective notice of Conditions of Sale may be able to challenge the applicability of those Conditions of Sale to the contract.

3.1.4   Matters relating to the conduct of the auction should be stated in the catalogue or reserved in the General Conditions of Sale. The Conditions should also contain the right of the Auctioneer to:

(a)   sell as a whole or in lots;

(b)   amend the lotting order;

(c)   withdraw or sell the property prior to the auction;

(d)   determine the conduct of the auction between competing bidders;

(e)   regulate the size of bidding increments;

Appendix 3: RICS auction guidance notes (continued)

(f) refuse bids; and

(g) bid on behalf of the seller up to but not including the reserve price.

3.1.5 Where the auctioneer is aware that major or significant arrears of rent or service charge exist for any lot it is recommended that this should be disclosed.

3.2 *Plans and Photographs*

3.2.1 Plans are frequently included in the catalogue for location and identification purposes only. Copyright consents must be obtained. Photographs and plans should not be misleading and must be as up to date as is reasonably possible.

3.2.2 The auctioneer should request the seller and the solicitors to verify the accuracy of the site plans included in the catalogue.

4   The Auction

4.1 *Amendments and Variations*

4.1.1 The Auctioneer should bring to the attention of prospective buyers prior to auction any material variations, alterations or amendments to the particulars or Conditions of Sale of which they are aware that may have arisen in the lead-up period to the auction. It is recommended that any amendments affecting the contract for the sale of the property should be contained within an addendum and made available to all prospective bidders at the commencement of the auction. It is advisable to attach the addendum to the Memorandum of Sale.

4.1.2 If the Auctioneer is selling subject to an addendum, it is helpful to bidders for the Auctioneer to remind them of this before each lot.

4.2 *Auctions (Bidding Agreements) Acts 1927 and 1969*

4.2.1 It is a statutory requirement that the respective extracts of these Acts be clearly displayed together with the full name and address of the Auctioneer.

4.3 *Telephone and Proxy Bids*

4.3.1 It is advisable for any telephone or proxy bids to be governed by terms which are set out in writing and signed by the bidder. These should include an exclusion of liability on the part of the auctioneer in the event of telephone failure. The procedures proposed for receiving deposits in respect of telephone and commission bids need to be clearly understood and agreed by both seller and bidder.

4.3.2 Telephone or proxy bidders should be made aware that it is their responsibility to enquire of the Auctioneer immediately prior to the sale, whether there have been any material variations, alterations or amendments to the particulars or Conditions of Sale.

4.4 *Responsibility to Insure*

4.4.1 If it is to be the responsibility of the buyer to insure the property on the fall of the

Appendix 3: RICS auction guidance notes (continued)

gavel, it is advisable for this to be brought to the attention of prospective buyers in the Conditions of Sale.

4.5 *Payment of any Supplementary Amount by the Bidder*

4.5.1 If payment in addition to the usual deposit is to be imposed, then reasonable notice to prospective buyers should be given prior to auction. If it is not possible to give reasonable notice prior, then the Auctioneer should make a specific announcement.

4.6 *Payment of the Deposit and Completion of the Memorandum by the Successful Buyer*

4.6.1 It is helpful to prospective buyers to have included in the catalogue and repeated at the start of the auction by the Auctioneer an explanation of the procedures for the payment of the deposit and the completion of the Memorandum of Sale.

4.6.2 The Conditions of Sale should state whether the deposit is received by the Auctioneer as agent for the seller, or as stakeholder. Note should be taken of guidance given in Appendix 2.

4.6.3 To accord with the current money laundering directive it is recommended that buyers are requested to provide identification and that cash is not accepted in payment of the deposit.

4.7 *Unsold Lots*

4.7.1 Where a lot fails to reach the reserve price the Auctioneer should:

(a) state that it has not been sold;

(b) not bring the gavel down; and

(c) prior to withdrawing the lot as unsold, not use inappropriate phraseology which gives the impression that the bidding is at or above the reserve price.

4.8 *Conduct of the Auction*

4.8.1 To avoid later disputes it is advisable for the Auctioneer to clearly indicate who is the highest bidder and the final amount bid before bringing down the gavel.

4.8.2 It is important that the auctioneer records all bids received, either manually or electronically.

4.8.3 The Auctioneer must make reasonable efforts to ensure that the successful bidder signs the Memorandum and pays the deposit monies at the auction.

5 **Post-Auction**

5.1 *Publication of Auction Results*

5.1.1 Published results must be accurate. When a property is sold prior to or post auction it is usual not to publish the sale price without the seller's and buyer's consents.

5.1.2 The identity of the seller or buyer should not be disclosed without their consent.

Appendix 3: RICS auction guidance notes (continued)

5.1.3   If notices under the Housing Act 1996 have been served prior to auction, the Auctioneer is advised to take legal advice prior to selling post auction.

6   Auctions on the internet

6.1.   The use of the internet

6.1.1   The internet may be used as an online marketing tool, for online bidding as an alternative to telephone/proxy bidding, and as a means of conducting a virtual auction (internet auctions or e-auctions). Guidance on internet auctions is being prepared. This section deals with online marketing and online bidding.

6.1.2   The guidance in this section is additional to the other guidance notes. The latter continue to apply, and in addition the Auctioneer must ensure that:

- all electronic communications are recorded and backed-up
- important communications, such as the Auctioneer's terms of business, are acknowledged and agreed
- the Auctioneer is able to verify with whom he is dealing, by the use of digital signatures or similar techniques
- the Auctioneer provides a secure method for the transmission of money
- there is appropriate security against viruses and hacking
- where he keeps on computer information about prospective bidders and others registering their interest he complies with the provisions of the Data Protection Act 1984

6.2   Online Marketing

6.2.1   Although the website is unlikely to be a replica of the auction catalogue it is important to ensure that in all material respects the information online is no less than the information which is being disseminated through the catalogue. For example, any disclaimers in the catalogue need also to be posted on the web, as should any addenda to the catalogue.

6.2.2   It is suggested that the website includes:

- a guide to the auction process
- the conditions of sale
- guide prices (which should not be misleading and must be kept up-to-date)
- any plans and photographs provided in the catalogue (subject to prior copyright consents being obtained)
- the means for prospective bidders to register their interest electronically

6.2.3   The form for registering interest should include:

- full contact details of the person registering
- a warning that information on the auction and property may change right up to the point of sale
- a recommendation to check the website just prior to the auction to ensure that the lot is still available and

Appendix 3: RICS auction guidance notes (continued)

- to check for addenda and any changes in the information provided

6.2.4   If the Auctioneer publishes auction results on the web, these must be accurate and not misleading.

6.3   *Bidding Electronically*

6.3.1   It is essential to ensure that before an electronic bid for a lot is accepted the auctioneer has verified the details of the bidder and confirmed the method of the payment of the deposit and that the bidder has:

- registered his intention to bid for that lot
- verified who he is and his financial strength and had his details verified
- confirmed that he has read the particulars and Conditions of Sale relating to it
- confirmed that whether or not he has read it, he knows that documentation about the lot is available and where he can get copies of it
- acknowledged that he has seen all relevant addenda, including any published orally at the auction (which must also be posted on the relevant website)
- admitted that he understands how to bid electronically (this should be explained on the website)

6.3.2   The Auctioneer should also ensure in his terms of engagement with the seller that the seller agrees to electronic bidding.

6.3.3   A mechanism must be in place for the electronic transfer of funds for the deposit and for the electronic confirmation of the sale contract if the electronic bid is successful. It is advisable to have this confirmed in writing.

Appendices

Appendix 1: Variations for Scottish Auctions

Ap1.1   Auctioneers intending to either conduct auctions in Scotland or to offer properties located in Scotland should be aware that whilst procedures are essentially the same, there are differences, most importantly in the law affecting Scottish property as well as styles of documentation and in terminology.

Ap1.1.1   It is recommended that Auctioneers offering Scottish property should consult a solicitor familiar with Scottish Property Law and Conveyancing procedures.

Ap1.1.2   Auctioneers advising either sellers or buyers on property located in Scotland should ensure that the sellers/buyers appoint a Scottish Legal Agent to act on their behalf.

Ap1.2   *Articles of Roup*

1.2.1   The 'Sale Contract' essentially comprises the Articles of Roup, which either incorporates the General Conditions of Sale or may supersede the General Conditions of Sale depending on the style adopted. The individual Articles of Roup for each Lot should incorporate any Special Conditions of Sale. There is no standard style for either the Articles of Roup or General Conditions of Sale.

Appendix 3: RICS auction guidance notes (continued)

1.2.2	The Articles of Roup/General Conditions of Sale should specify that any dispute will be submitted to an Arbiter appointed by the President of the Law Society of Scotland and that the Law of Scotland will apply to the interpretation of the Contract of Sale. The buyer and/or the offerer will become subject to the jurisdiction of the Courts of Session in Scotland.
1.2.3	Titles for Scottish property are either held in the Land Register of Scotland or the Registers of Sasine.

Ap1.3 Terminology (there are significant differences in terminology)

1.3.1	Although a sale is generally referred to as an Auction, the technically correct term is a Roup.
1.3.2	The Auctioneer is referred to as a Judge of the Roup.
1.3.3	A Minute of Preference and Enactment is the equivalent of the Sale Memorandum.
1.3.4	The Scottish equivalent of Freehold Tenure is Feudal Tenure or Feuhold, which accounts for the majority of property in Scotland. The most important classification of property is Heritable property, which consists of land and its 'pertinents' – namely things going with it including buildings on it. All other property is moveable.
1.3.5	Lots are exposed 'Tantum et Tale' as they exist.

Appendix 2: Value Added Tax (VAT)

This section of guidance was prepared with the help of HM Customs and Excise, Policy Group.

Ap2.1   HM Revenue & Customs provide guidance in their Public Notices on when VAT must be charged on the sale of property. Public Notice 700/9 (request latest edition from your Customs Business Advice Centre) deals with the 'Transfer of a business as a going concern'. In the case of the sale of commercial property it states that:

'2.3 Whether the transfer of premises within the transfer of a business is a taxable supply

If all the conditions in paragraph 2.2 are met and the buyer has elected to waive exemption as specified below, the transfer of premises is not a taxable supply. However, if the buyer has not elected (as specified below) and you are transferring premises:

- for which you have elected to waive exemption; or
- which are new or unfinished buildings or civil engineering works which would ordinarily be standard-rated;

then you must charge VAT.

The election to waive exemption by the buyer, referred to above, must be notified to Customs before the time of supply and must apply from that time. 'Time of

Appendix 3: RICS auction guidance notes (continued)

supply' for VAT purposes includes receipt of a deposit which may otherwise have created a tax point.'

Ap2.2   In practice, where the conditions in Public Notice 700/9 have been met, Customs will allow a TOGC (transfer of a going concern) where Customs have received the buyer's notification of his election to waive exemption (also known as an 'option to tax') on or before the date of the auction. The reason for this is that the payment of the deposit by the buyer on that day creates a tax point in respect of the sale. The notification must be in writing and may be made by courier/post, hand delivery or fax. If the buyer does not notify Customs in time, VAT will be charged on the sale.

Ap2.3   If the buyer pays his deposit to a solicitor acting as an independent stakeholder who holds the deposit as a disinterested party (and not as an agent or either the vendor or the buyer), then the payment does not create a tax point. This means that the buyer who pays his deposit to such a stakeholder will not have to notify his option to tax on the day of the auction. The deposit only becomes consideration for the supply when the money is released to the vendor (usually on completion). Thus where it is not possible for the buyer to notify his option to tax on the day of the auction, it may be possible for the buyer to pay his deposit to a solicitor acting as an independent stakeholder.

Ap2.4   If the deposit is paid to the auctioneer as agent for the seller, then Customs' view is that this money has been paid to the seller and that a tax point has been created. The buyer must notify his option to tax before, or on the day, that this tax point has been created.

Ap2.5   Problems may also arise where a buyer who is not VAT-registered buys a building with sitting tenants. Normally an unregistered person intending to buy a business as a going concern should already have requested VAT registration and have received a VAT registration number. The VAT application form (VAT 1) can be obtained by writing to HM Revenue & Customs or downloaded from the internet at www.hmrc.gov.uk.

Where this has not been done HM Revenue & Customs will accept that the notification of the option to tax, which should reach Customs at the latest by the end of the day when the tax point has been created (usually the day of the auction), can be accompanied by a request for VAT registration from that day.

However, in these circumstances the seller will have to satisfy himself that the buyer completes the registration procedure and can produce a VAT registration number to show that he has become a taxable person.

Ap2.6   It is the seller's responsibility to account for the VAT at the correct rate. In cases of doubt the seller should write to his local Customs and Excise business centre explaining the area of difficulty.

Appendix 3: Sale of Qualifying Investments Under the Landlord & Tenant Act 1987 (As Amended)

Ap3.1   Certain types of multi-let residential investments and, in some cases, mixed use

Appendix 3: RICS auction guidance notes (continued)

commercial and residential investments, cannot be offered for sale unless certain procedures laid down in the Landlord and Tenant Act 1987 (as amended by the Housing Act 1996) are followed.

Ap3.2 The legislation provides for a combination of notices and counter-notices to be served by the landlord and subsequently the tenants. The legislation intends to confer upon the tenants a right of first refusal, when qualifying investments are disposed of.

Ap3.3 It is important to remember that non-compliance with the legislation is a criminal offence. All concerned will be affected including sellers, their auctioneers and their solicitors.

Ap3.4 It is strongly recommended that auctioneers familiarise themselves with the legislation in order that they are able to recognise potentially qualifying investments before instructions to proceed to auction are accepted.

Ap3.5 It is strongly recommended that auctioneers liaise with their client's solicitors before accepting instructions in order to ensure whether or not notices need to be served prior to disposal.

Ap3.6 When a qualifying investment is offered for sale by auction, it is recommended that the auctioneer states, either within the Particulars of Sale, the Special Conditions of Sale, or the Auction Addendum, whether or not the majority of qualifying tenants has elected to nominate a buyer. If an election to nominate has been made, the contractual buyer in the auction room may be substituted in law by the elected nominated buyer.

Ap3.7 After the auction sale, the law requires the seller to send a copy of the memorandum to the nominated buyer within seven days. It is therefore imperative that the memorandum signed by the buyer is sent to the seller, the seller's solicitor or to the nominated buyer (if the auctioneer is so instructed) as soon as possible after the conclusion of the sale.

Further Reading

Clive Carpenter and Susan Harris, *Property Auctions*, (*Estates Gazette*, London, 1988)
Howard R. Gooddie, MA, DipTP, FRICS, *Buying Bargains at Property Auctions*, (Lawpack Publishing Limited, London, 2005)
Brian W. Harvey and Franklin Meisel, *Auctions: Law & Practice*, (Oxford University Press, Oxford, 1995)
J. R. Murdoch LLB, *The Law of Estate Agency and Auctions*, (*Estates Gazette*, London, 1994)
Peta Dollar & Sarah Thompson-Copsey, *Tenants' Pre-Emption Rights – A Landlord's Guide to the Landlord and Tenant Act 1987* (Jordans)
Richard M Courtenay Lord, *Auctioning Real Property*

Appendix 4: Terms of the Estate Agents Act 1979 governing provision of information and explanation of terms

The relevant Statutory Instrument 1991 No 859 (Provision of Information) Regulations enacted under the Estate Agents Act 1979 reads:

Additional information as to services

2- (1) The following additional information is hereby prescribed and shall be given by an estate agent to his client, that is to say as to the services:

    (a) which the estate agent is himself offering, or intends to offer, to any prospective purchaser of an interest in the land; or

    (b) which he knows a connected person or (in a case where he or a connected person would derive a financial benefit from the provision of the service) another person is offering, or intends to offer, to any prospective purchaser of an interest in the land.

  (2) The additional information referred to in paragraph (1) above shall be given at the time and in the manner specified in Regulations 3 and 4 below.

Time of giving information

3- (1) The time when an estate agent shall give the information specified in section 18(2) of the Act, as well as the additional information prescribed in Regulation 2 above, is the time when communication commences between the estate agent and the client or as soon as is reasonably practicable thereafter provided it is a time before the client is committed to any liability towards the estate agent.

  (2) The time when an estate agent shall give the details of any changes to the terms of the contract between himself and his client as are mentioned in section 18(3) of the Act, is the time when, or as soon as is reasonably practicable after, those changes are agreed.

Manner of giving information

4   The additional information prescribed in Regulation 2 above and the information required to be given under section 18(2) and (3) of the Act shall be given by the estate agent in writing.

Explanation of terms concerning client's liability to pay remuneration to an estate agent

5 (1) If any of the terms 'sole selling rights', 'sole agency', and 'ready willing and able purchaser' are used by an estate agent in the course of carrying out estate agency work, he shall explain the intention and effect of those terms to his client in the manner described respectively below, that is to say:

    (a) 'sole selling rights', by means of a written explanation having the form and content of the statement set out in paragraph (a) of the Schedule to these Regulations;

    (b) 'sole agency', by means of a written explanation having the form and content of the statement set out in paragraph (b) of the Schedule to these Regulations; and

Appendix 4: Terms of the Estate Agents Act 1979 governing provision of information and explanation of terms (continued)

(c) 'ready willing and able purchaser', by means of a written explanation having the form and content of the statement set out in paragraph (c) of the Schedule to these Regulations:

Provided that if, by reason of the provision of the contract in which those terms appear, the respective explanations are in any way misleading, the content of the explanation shall be altered so as accurately to describe the liability of the client to pay remuneration in accordance with those provisions.

(2) Any other terms which, though differing from those referred to in paragraph (1) above, have a similar purport or effect shall be explained by the estate agent to his client by reference to whichever of paragraphs (a), (b) or (c) of the Schedule to these Regulations is appropriate, subject also to the proviso to paragraph (1) above.

(3) The explanation of the terms mentioned in paragraphs (1) and (2) above shall be given by the estate agent to his client in a document setting out the terms of the contract between them (whether that document be a written or printed agreement, a letter, terms or engagement or a form, and whether or not such document is signed by any of the parties), and shall be given at the time specified in Regulation 3(1) and (2) above.

Prominence etc. of explanation

6 (1) Subject to the proviso to Regulation 5(1) and (2) above, the explanations set out in the Schedule to these Regulations shall be reproduced in the documents embodying them in the same form as they appear in that Schedule and without any material alterations or additions to the text, and shall be shown prominently, clearly and legibly.

(2) The wording of such explanations shall be given no less prominence than that given to any other information in the document setting out the terms of the contract (as more particularly described in Regulation 5 (3) above) between the estate agent and his client apart from the heading thereto, trade names, names of the parties and numbers or letting subsequently inserted therein in handwriting or in type.

THE SCHEDULE

Explanation of certain terms (a)

(a) Sole selling rights

SOLE SELLING RIGHTS

You will be liable to pay remuneration to us, in addition to any other costs or charges agreed, in each of the following circumstances:

- if (unconditional contracts for the sale of the property are exchanged): in the period during which we have sole selling rights, even if the purchaser was not found by us but by another agent or by any other person, including yourself;

Appendix 4: Terms of the Estate Agents Act 1979 governing provision of information and explanation of terms (continued)

- if (unconditional contracts for the sale of the property are exchanged): after the expiry of the period during which we have sole selling rights but to a purchaser who was introduced to you during that period or with whom we had negotiations about the property during that period.

(b) Sole agency

SOLE AGENCY

You will be liable to pay remuneration to us, in addition to any other costs or charges agreed, if at any time (unconditional contracts for the sale of the property are exchanged):

- with a purchaser introduced by us during the period of our sole agency or with whom we had negotiations about the property during that period; or

- with a purchaser introduced by another agent during that period.

(c) Ready, willing and able purchaser

READY, WILLING AND ABLE PURCHASER

A purchaser is a 'ready, willing and able' purchaser if he is prepared and is able to (exchange unconditional contracts for the purchase of your property).

You will be liable to pay remuneration to us, in addition to any other costs or charges agreed, if such a purchaser is introduced by us in accordance with your instructions and this must be paid even if you subsequently withdraw (and unconditional contracts for sale are not exchanged), irrespective of your reasons.

Appendix 5: Principal property auctioneers

Auctions House Group
30 Southernhay, Basildon,
Essex SS14 1EL
Tel: 01268 695 999
See details for franchise agents elsewhere.

Launched in 2004 this auction house now
holds sales six to seven times a year
generally offering around 25 lots a time.
The venue is Stockbrook Golf Club.

Allen & Harris
Newfield House, Vicarage Lane,
Blackpool, Lancashire FY4 4EW
Tel: 01253 607 634 Fax: 01253 607 777
Website: www.propwld.co.uk

A division of Royal & Sun Alliance
Property Services. Plenty of residential
properties including terraced houses,
flats, tenements and semis etc, as well as
those frequently repossessed. Sometimes
properties in Scotland are included in
four sales a year of 100 to 120 lots a time.
Catalogues free but for automatic mailing
there is a charge of approximately £20 per
annum. Viewing is also available online.

**Allsop & Co (Commercial
Department)**
27 Soho Square, London W1V 6AX
Tel: 020 7543 6701 Fax: 020 7437 8984
Catalogue request line: 0115 972 6111
Auction live link: 0900 342 6507
Complete guide prices fax line:
0906 586 8246
Complete results fax line: 0906 586 8247
Email: post@allsop.co.uk
Website: www.allsop.co.uk

Allsops are proud to be by far the largest
property auctioneers in the country with
up to 200 lots per sale. Very varied selection
of commercial properties throughout the
UK and some abroad. They also have a
residential department (see below).
Impressive informative catalogues. No
charge for individual brochures. Free
mailing list.

Allsop & Co (Residential Department)
100 Knightsbridge, London SW1X 7LB
Tel: 020 7494 3686 Fax: 020 7581 3058
Catalogue request line (£1.50 per min):
0906 515 1510
Auction live link: 0900 341 1262
Audio guide prices and results line: refer
to catalogue
Individual guide prices: 0906 586 8274
Guide prices/results fax line:
0906 586 8272
Email: post@allsop.co.uk
Email (catalogue request):
residential@plusart.co.uk
Website: www.allsop.co.uk

About every six to eight weeks up to 300
to 450 lots per sale are offered by their
residential division. Properties and
repossessions from banks, mortgage
companies, building societies, county
councils, borough councils, local
authorities, quangos, BT, Railtrack,
receivers, executors, public and private
companies, etc. An eclectic mix of flats and
houses. Sales take place at a variety of
London hotels: the Mayfair
Intercontinental on Stratton Street, the
Berkeley, Wilton Place, or the Four Seasons
Hotel. Their large, glossy catalogues are
free. Their mailing list costs approximately
£45 per annum.

Andrews & Robertson
27 Camberwell Green, London SE5 7AN
Tel: 020 7703 4401 Fax: 020 7708 1981
Auction live link: 0900 341 1262
Individual results phone line:
0906 586 8125
Complete results fax line: 0906 586 8126
Email: auctions@andrews-
robertson.co.uk
Website: www.a-r.co.uk

100 to 120 lots in seven or eight auctions
a year. Principally south London, from
vacant houses and flats, repossessions, ex-
council properties, investment

Appendix 5: Principal property auctioneers (continued)

opportunities, semis, terraced and detached houses. Mixed and specialised shops and retail premises, warehouses, garage sites, garages, development sites, with and without planning permission. Sales are held on behalf of London local authorities, building societies, and the usual mix of housing associations, regional councils, mortgagees and trustees, receivers, public and private limited companies. Free catalogues but automatic mailing list charge is approximately £40 for the year. Viewing is available online. Venue usually at the New Connaught Rooms, Great Queen Street, London WC2.

Athawes Son & Co

203 High Street, Acton, London W3 9DR
Tel: 020 8992 0056/0122
Fax: 020 8993 0511
Guide price and results fax line:
0906 586 8132
Email: mail@athawesauctioneers.co.uk
Website: www.athawesauctioneers.co.uk

25 or so lots, four to five times a year for residential and commercial property located in London and the surrounding area. Sales on behalf of London Borough of Brent, the Court of Protection, charities, limited companies, receivers, executors, the Public Trustee, and others. Lots can include commercial office and residential investments, vacant church premises, factories and workshops, vacant suburban semis, ground rent investments, high-street shops and buy-to-let possibilities. Sales are at the Connaught Rooms, 61–65 Great Queen Street, London WC2 and start at 1pm. Catalogues are approximately £20 (five issues).

Austerberry

4 Edensor Road, Longton,
Stoke-on-Trent ST3 2NU
Tel: 01782 594 595 Fax: 01782 594 455
Auction results: 0906 586 8152
Email (via website):
www.austerberry.co.uk/
emailf.htm
Website: www.austerberry.co.uk

Six sales a year of approximately 20 lots of residential properties in Stoke, Hanley and the Potteries. Included are semis, detached and terraced homes of all sizes. Guide prices are as low as £8,000 for a three-bedroom terraced house. There is a free catalogue mailing list. The venue is at the North Stafford Hotel, Stoke-on- Trent.

Bacons

2 Bethlehem Street, Grimsby
Tel: 01472 372 084 Fax: 01472 691 267
Email: bacons2bs@aol.com

Four to 12 lots offered occasionally at intervals. Houses in the North Lincolnshire area are principally semis and terraced. Catalogues available about two weeks before the sale.

Barnard Marcus

Auction Office, Commercial House,
64–66 Glenthorne Road, London W6 0LR
Tel: 020 8741 9990/9001
Fax: 020 8741 2188/2168
Audio guide prices: 0906 586 8181
Audio results: 0906 586 8182
Fax guide prices: 0906 586 8179
Fax results: 0906 586 8180
Auction live link: 0900 341 1262
Email:
auctionshammersmith.barnardmarcus
@uk.royalsun.com

Almost all residential properties in London with an average of sale up to 120 lots. Many lots with development potential, others suitable for investment. A varied mix of clients such as banks,

Appendix 5: Principal property auctioneers (continued)

building societies, local authorities, mortgagees, housing associations, London Fire and Civil Defence Authority, public and private companies, executors, receivers, etc. Mailing list is £45 per annum, or online.

W A Barnes
Portland Square, Sutton-in-Ashfield, Nottinghamshire NG17 1DA
Tel: 01623 554 084/553 929
Fax: 01623 550 764

Almost invariably around 25 to 30 lots bi-monthly of mostly residential properties, plus a smattering of commercials, both vacant and tenanted throughout Nottinghamshire. The usual mix of vendors – receivers, executors, properties in possession and other sources. Guide prices start at around the £15,000 mark. Mailing list online.

Besley Hill
10 Badminton Road, Downend, Bristol BS16 6BQ
Tel: 0117 970 1551 Fax: 0117 970 1141
Email: downend@besleyhill.co.uk

Local firm with local connections which tends to concentrate on the Bristol environs and offers a mix of residential and commercial vacant and investment properties. Houses for refurbishment tend to be a speciality. There are five auctions a year with between 10 and 25 lots per sale. Free catalogues. Venue is at the Kendelshire Golf Club Colpit Heath, Hambrook.

Bigwood
51–52 Calthorpe Road, Edgbaston, Birmingham B15 1TH
Tel: 0121 456 8800 Fax: 0121 456 4008
Email: auctions@bigwoodassociates.co.uk
Website: www.bigwoodassociates.co.uk

An old-established firm of chartered surveyors which, at the last sale I visited, was selling from the centre of a horseshoe

of solicitors and took its time over the sale with professional dedication. They offer about 60 to 100 lots per sale at auctions every two months or so of properties situated in the Midlands area covering Stoke-on-Trent and south into Worcestershire. The venue is Villa Park Conference Centre, Birmingham. The catalogues are free.

Bond Wolfe
(See entry for Bigwood.)

Boultons Harrisons
54 John William Street, Huddersfield HD1 1ER
Tel: 01484 515 029 Fax: 01484 450 025
Email: sales@boultonsestateagents.co.uk
Website: www.boultonsestateagents.com

Joint auctioneers of properties in the West Yorkshire area. Just a few occasional shops and commercial premises that lighten the usual mix of owner-occupied and vacant houses. Four or five sales a year of around 10 to 20 lots per sale. Sales take place at the Galpharm Stadium, Huddersfield. Catalogues online.

Bradleys
7 Stevenstone Road, Exmouth EX8 2EP
Tel: 01395 224 700 Fax: 01395 222 362
Email: taunton@beagroup.co.uk
Website: www.bradleys-estate-agents.co.uk

Eight to nine sales per year in the Somerset, Devon and Cornwall area. 12 to 15 lots per sale. Residential and commercial investments, pieces of land, etc. Occasional bargains here. Viewing is available online. Full details on each property are available from the relevant local branch.

Butters John Bee
Lake View, Festival Way, Stoke-on-Trent ST1 5BJ
Tel: 01782 261 511 Fax: 01782 202 159

Appendix 5: Principal property auctioneers (continued)

Auction results: 0906 586 8220
Email: hanley@bjbmail.com
Website: www.buttersjohnbee.com

Butters and John Bee merged several years ago. 40 to 60 lots from the Staffordshire area per sale every six to eight weeks. Residential properties, development sites, lock-up garages, old mills, sales for trustees, etc. – a wide selection of opportunities. Catalogues are £2 each and online.

Clayson Haselwood Fisher German
50 South Bar, Banbury,
Oxfordshire OX16 9AB
Tel: 01295 271 555
Fax: 01295 258 630

Sales every two to three months of approximately five to ten lots.

Colliers CRE
9 Marylebone Lane, London W1 1HL
Tel: 020 7487 1700 Fax: 020 7487 1810
London guide prices fax line:
0906 586 8242
Email: frigg@collierscre.co.uk
Website: www.collierscre.com

Many branches throughout the country feed all their clients' auction properties into the London office. Colliers feature commercial premises, tenanted and vacant public houses, development land and investment property throughout the UK. They can include a few residential properties. Free regular mailing list. Viewing is available online. They offer a brochure that is worth reading.

Cottons
361 Hagley Road, Edgbaston,
Birmingham
B17 8DL
Tel: 0121 247 2233 Fax: 0121 247 1233
Email: auctions@cottons.co.uk
Website: www.cottons.co.uk

Once a quarter is the norm for Cottons with combined auctions of about 70 to 90 lots with Perry & Deakin, Morrison Edwards and occasionally others of residential and commercial properties throughout the West Midlands. Mixed quality catalogues vary depending upon the predominant auction company for the sale. They range from small and uninformative with no photographs, to full colour brochures with pictures and lots of information. My experience is that catalogues are only available usually two to three weeks prior to sale, but perhaps I was unlucky. Free mailing list. The venue is the Holte Suite, Aston Villa Football Ground, Aston.

Countrywide Property Auctions
80–86 New London Road, Chelmsford,
Essex CM2 0PD
Tel: 01245 344 133 Fax: 01245 358 985
Catalogue request line (£1.50 per min):
0906 666 2468
Email: mlw@auctions.cwea.co.uk

Sales held in London for properties in the capital. Houses in the south west of England are generally included into the London sale. Sales for the Home Counties and East Anglia are held in the South; in Newcastle for properties in the North East; between Manchester and Liverpool for properties in the North West and North Wales; in Birmingham for properties in the Midlands and South Wales; in Leeds for properties in Yorkshire and North Lincs; in Plymouth for properties in the West Country; and in Glasgow for groups of properties throughout Scotland. There are further auctions through their Glasgow, Bristol and Llandudno branches. Sales of hundreds of properties almost entirely at the cheaper end of the market throughout the country. The sales only include houses of every type. Countrywide occasionally holds free

Appendix 5: Principal property auctioneers (continued)

seminars on buying properties at auction. Auction catalogue online. Individual catalogues are free.

Cushman & Wakeham
(See Colliers CRE)

Darlows
Auction Department, 6–8 North Street, Newport NP20 1JZ
Tel: 01633 225 798
Email: auctions@tmxdarlows.com
Website: www.tmxdarlows.com

Bi-monthly sales cover Newport for properties throughout Wales and the West Country. Exeter is the chosen venue for properties in the South West and the far western country. Residential properties dominate and nearly always include land and excellent investment opportunities and repossessions. Catalogues which cover both sales have plenty of information.

Dedman Property Services
'Hillsboro', 377 Southchurch Road, Southend-on-Sea, Essex SS1 2PQ
Tel: 01702 311 010 Fax: 01702 614 738
Email: auction@dedman.net
Website: www.dedman.net

30 and 50 properties situated in Essex are included in most of their sales. Housing plus a few development opportunities including some industrial properties. Lots include buildings offered by banks, building societies, executors, property companies and many other sources. They often sell a good number of properties, flats and houses, and often include properties offered by Basildon District Council. Catalogues can sometimes, unfortunately, be delayed until two weeks before the sale. The mailing list is free and brochures are available on demand. A presentation held periodically is their 'Idiots' Guide to Auctions' which includes a 'mock' auction and includes advice on buying and selling.

Drewery & Wheeldon
Rebrook House, 124 Trinity Street, Gainsborough, Lincolnshire DN21 1JD
Tel: 01427 616 118 Fax: 01427 811 070
Email: drewery_wheeldon@compuserve.com
Website: www.dreweryandwheeldon.com

Offered about every eight weeks are 15 to 30 lots of residential and agricultural properties situated in Lincolnshire, occasionally South Yorkshire and in North Notts. Some very attractive properties including cottages and barns in village and rural locations, allotments, farms and pasture land. The venue is the Gainsborough Golf Club, Gainsborough, Lincs. Catalogues online.

Drivers & Norris
407–409 Holloway Road, London N7 6HP
Tel: 020 7607 5001 Fax: 020 7609 5031
Guides/results fax line: 0906 586 8157
Email: auction@drivers.co.uk
Website: www.drivers.co.uk

These auctions are relatively small with about 10 and 25 lots including flats and houses, investment opportunities, shops and ground rents, and commercial premises mostly situated in the North London region. They do occasionally feature locations a little further away. Mortgagees holdings, trustees, companies and private individuals all take their place as owners. Catalogues are available online about two to three weeks before each sale. There is a free mailing list.

Eddisons
Pennine House, Russell Street, Leeds LS1 5RN
Tel: 0113 243 0101 Fax: 0113 242 1364
Catalogue line: 0845 130 1322

Ridgefield House, 14 Dalton Street, Manchester M2 6JR
Tel: 0161 831 9444 Fax: 0161 839 6633
Results fax line: 09067 110 222

Appendix 5: Principal property auctioneers (continued)

Email: auctions@eddisons.com
Website: www.eddisons.com
Also with offices in Bradford,
Leeds and Huddersfield.

Despite being known as 'Eddisons
Commercial', they offer all types of
property, not just commercial. Houses
predominate whenever there are between
40 and 60 lots on sale held approximately
eight times a year. These are mainly
situated in Yorkshire and North
Lancashire with a smaller number in
Greater Manchester. The sales include
tenanted houses, vacant houses suitable
for investment or owner-occupation.
Houses in need of renovation are the
mainstay of their brochures but building
land, vacant industrial premises and
vacant offices, vacant shops, and some
lots with or without planning permission
do feature. The mailing list is £34.50 per
year. Salles in Leeds take place at the
Banqueting Suite, Leeds United Football
Club, Elland Road, Leeds and in
Manchester at Lancashire Cricket Ground
Old Trafford. Brochures are free.

Edward Mellor Auction Department

(Now merged with Longden & Cook
Commercial Auctions)
65 St Petersgate, Stockport, SKI
Tel: 0161 443 4740 Fax: 0161 443 4553
Guide price and results
fax line: 0906 586 8148
Brochure hotline: 09067 301 010
Email: auction@edwardmellor.co.uk

Edward Mellor's auction department
merged with that of Longden & Cook
Commercial (one of the pioneers in
composite auctions) in 2001. They now
service the whole of the Greater
Manchester, Cheshire, Merseyside and
Lancashire area with an auction team
headed by the sales director, Louise
McDonald. Eight/nine sales of up to 200
lots take place each year and now include

Longden & Cook Commercial's full range
of investment, industrial and commercial
property as well as Mellors' varied range
of residential lots. The venue, Lancashire
County Cricket Club, Old Trafford,
Manchester provides space for over 650
bidders. Prior to his retirement the
auctioneer was Howard Goodie, the
author. Ample free car parking and
lounge bar facilities. These sales, which
are always worth visiting, frequently
feature lots of mixed vacant and tenanted
houses which may suitable for buy-to-let.
Full colour catalogues available from the
phone line which is charged at £1 per
minute, or free online.

Elliot Auctions

133 The Parade, Watford,
Herts WD13 1NA
Tel: 01923 212 112
Fax: 01923 801 211
Email: elliott@watford27.fsnet.co.uk

Bi-monthly auction of 20 to 30 houses
concentrating on the Hertfordshire,
Bedfordshire and Middlesex districts.

Clive Emson

8 Cavendish Way, Bearsted, Maidstone,
Kent ME15 8XY
Tel: 01622 630 033 Fax: 01622 630 036
Covering Kent.

First Floor, 3 Sackville Road, Hove,
East Sussex BN3 3WA
Tel: 01273 206 633 Fax: 01273 203 345
Covering West Sussex and Surrey.

Results fax line: 0906 586 8112
Results audio line: 0906 586 8113
Email: auctions@cliveemson.co.uk
Website: www.cliveemson.co.uk

Always an unusual collection of 65 to 120
properties consisting of flats, houses,
shops, apartments, former chapels,
garages, building land, derelict houses,
ground rents, investments, farms, etc. The
situations vary throughout the South East

Appendix 5: Principal property auctioneers (continued)

region, predominantly covering Kent, Surrey and Sussex, but they also cover South London and include an occasional number of lots from around the country. Guide prices from as little as £5,000. The catalogues are of an unusual nature. They are also available online (address above), offering immediate access. Viewing details and application for legal papers can also be made online.

Feather Smailes & Scales
The Auction House, 8 Raglan Street, Harrogate, North Yorkshire HG1 1LE
Tel: 01423 501 211 Fax: 01423 500 215
Email: vanda.bate@fss4property.co.uk
Website: www.fss4property.co.uk

Hold bi-monthly collective and other short notice single lot sales. Can be from two lots to around 20. The venue is the Pavilions at York Showground, Harrogate.

Fox & Sons
HQ & Brighton Auction Centre, 117–118 Western Road, Brighton BN1 2AE
Tel: 01273 321 300 Fax: 01273 204 756
Email: auctionsbrighton.foxandsons@uk.royalsun.com
Covering East Sussex, West Sussex and bordering areas of Surrey and Kent.
Southampton Auction Centre, 32–34 London Road, Southampton SO15 2TB
Tel: 023 8033 8066 Fax: 01273 208 264
Email: auctionssouthampton.foxandsons@uk.royalsun.com
Covering Hampshire, Dorset, Wiltshire, the Isle of Wight and South-West Surrey.
Website: www.propwld.co.uk

The number of lots vary in auctions held about every six weeks but all provide an interesting cross section of the property market on the South Coast. One can find lots offered on behalf of property and trust companies, building societies, banks, insurance companies, limited companies and plcs, executors and private owners.

There is seaside holiday accommodation with lots of letting potential, investment opportunities, development projects, sites with planning permission in and around the South Coast. There is an excellent variety of properties. Catalogues are available if you call their 60p/min dedicated request line detailed above. The mailing list costs £50 per annum including preliminary notices and auction results. Catalogues are available online. The venues are as follows: Southampton, The Southampton Park Hotel, Southampton; Coral Greyhound Stadium in Hove.

Fulfords
Auction Department, 44 Rolle Street, Exmouth EX8 2SH
Tel: 0870 241 4343 Fax: 01395 273 757
Catalogue request line: 0906 633 2019
Email: auctions@fulfords.co.uk
Website: www.fulfords.co.uk

These auctions are to be found bi-monthly in Plymouth, Bristol and, occasionally, Bournemouth. 35 to 45 lots are usual. Their 'stamping ground' is the South West. The sales are generally of residential properties, but there are a few commercial investments. The mailing list is approximately £20 per annum. Viewing is available online.

Goldings
National Property Auction House Group, 91 Furtherwick Road, Canvey Island, Essex SS8 7AY
Tel: 01473 210 200 Fax: 01473 233 033
Email: sales@suffolks.co.uk
Bi-monthly sales of 10 to 20 lots. The areas covered are principally in Suffolk and north Essex with a concentration on tenanted investments and renovations, some building opportunities etc. The venue is The Holiday Inn, London Road, Ipswich. The catalogues are free. Viewing online.

Appendix 5: Principal property auctioneers (continued)

Frederick G Hair and Son
200 London Road,
Southend on Sea, SS1 1PJ
Tel: 01702 432 255 Fax: 01702 337 846
Email: thamesdrive@hairandson.co.uk
Website: www.hairandson.co.uk

It is usual for this partnership to hold sales of around 15 to 25 lots bi-monthly depending upon demand in the Westcliff on Sea/Southend on Sea/Leigh on Sea shops, and offices building plots, etc. The venue is the Saxon Hall, Aviation, Southend. The guide prices are not always quoted. Catalogues and mailing lists are free.

Hamilton Osborne King
(Now part of Savilles.)

Handleys
3 Oxford Place, Leeds LS1 3AX
Tel: 01268 698 400
Website: www.handleys-leeds.co.uk

12 to 25 lots regularly include terraced houses in the Leeds area, semis, flats, vacant and tenanted property, shops, buildings for renovation and occupation, commercial and residential investments. The venue is the Castle Grove Banqueting & Conference Centre, Castle Grove Drive, Moor Road, Headingley, Leeds LS6. Free mailing list.

Harman Healy
23 Brighton Road,
South Croydon, SR2 6EA

This long-established and well-known auction house provides a large number of nationwide commercial properties, vacant shops and retail premises, shops with residential upper parts, investment opportunities, redevelopment sites and some flats and houses. They frequently provide lots of sitting tenant investment potential. Some lots have disclosed reserve prices printed in their colourful and informative catalogues. Viewing is

available online. Sales are usually held at Kensington Town Hall, London, W8 7NX.

Mark Jenkinson & Son
8 Norfolk Row, Sheffield S1 2PA
Tel: 0114 276 0151 Fax: 0114 275 6370
Results fax line: 0906 586 8142
Email: auctions@markjenkinson.co.uk
Website: www.markjenkinson.co.uk

This Sheffield and South Yorkshire dynamic and leading property auction house sells around 350 lots per annum. Auctions can consist of anything from 35 to 75 lots of properties in the South Yorkshire area (mostly Sheffield but also in Rotherham, Castleford, and Barnsley). Their sales can provide commercial and residential investments, vacant commercial premises, vacant houses for modernisation and houses with sitting tenants. Also, ground rents from banks, building societies, Sheffield City Council, liquidators, executors and various private clients. They call their auctions 'Property With Potential' sales, which is just what they are. The venue is at the Sheffield United Football Club Theatre, Sheffield. The mailing list costs approximately £40 per annum. It is also available online. The results can be faxed to you on request.

Jones Lang LaSalle
22 Hanover Square, London W1A 2BN
Tel: 020 7493 6040 Fax: 020 7399 5694
Guide price fax line: 0906 586 8286
Results fax line: 0906 586 8287
Catalogue request line: 020 7399 5399
Email:
uk.auctions@eu.joneslanglasalle.com
Website: http://reach.joneslanglasalle.com

Major commercial and retail property auctioneers principally selling high-value lots. Their sales are of varied size and incorporate anything from between 30 to 100 lots of property throughout the UK. Offerings frequently include retail shops, supermarkets, railway land and stations,

Appendix 5: Principal property auctioneers (continued)

freehold and leasehold office space, industrial buildings and sites, ground rent portfolios, sites with development potential, pubs, car parks, land, and shops with tenants for investment. The venue is the Cumberland, Park Lane, London W1.

Kersh Auctions

2 Cotton Street, Liverpool L3 7DY
Tel: 0870 873 1212
Fax: 0151 205 6316
Catalogue request line: 0151 207 6318
Email: auctions@jkersh.co.uk
Website: www.jkersh.co.uk

Kersh have come into prominence lately with large auctions of Liverpool terraced houses where the information provided was a little sparse. Recent brochures have been very much more specific and can offer a range generally at the lower to middle part of the market. Auctions can now be around the 60 to 120 size and can contain commercial properties and all sorts of development opportunities. For the investor and speculator their sales are particularly appealing. Website viewing is available. The venue is at the Crown Plaza, Pierhead, Liverpool L3 1QW.

Lambert & Foster

77 Commercial Road, Paddock Wood, Tonbridge, Kent TN12 6DS
Tel: 01892 832 325 Fax: 01892 834 700
Email: admin@lambertandfoster.co.uk
Website: www.lambertandfoster.co.uk

Hold small collective quarterly auctions of around 15 to 20 lots of mostly Kentish agricultural and some residential properties including farms, barns, stables and land, etc. Viewing is available online.

Main & Main

95 High Street, Cheadle, Cheshire SK8 1AA
Tel: 0161 491 6666 Fax: 0161 428 7676
Email: samancier@mainandmain.co.uk
Website: www.mainandmain.co.uk

Hold around eight sales a year of approximately 30 to 35 lots of mostly residential properties and, very occasionally, commercial premises and development propositions. In contrast to many auctions, this can be a rather slow event. The venue is at the Village Hotel & Leisure Club, Cheadle Road, Cheshire. A free mailing list and online viewing are available.

Meller Braggins & Co

37, Princess Street, Knutsford, Cheshire WA16 6BT
Tel: 01565 0632 0618

This auction house serves the North Cheshire belt and the South Manchester suburbs with up to ten auctions a year of 10 to 15 lots per sale, mainly featuring quality vacant houses for immediate owner-occupation or for refurbishment, many farm building redevelopment propositions and 'chocolate box' thatched cottages and similar. Also available are a few small commercial lots. Lots are serviced from the relevant local offices and particulars are usually provided on an individual basis. The venues are in various local hotels but is frequently at the De Vere, Daresbury Park, Chester Road, Daresbury, Warrington. Good pictures and details are available on the web.

Miller Metcalfe

56 Bradshawgate, Bolton BL1 1DW
Tel: 01204 525 252 Fax: 01204 525 150
Catalogue request line: 01204 525 150
Website: www.mmauction.co.uk

Hold around four sales a year of approximately 20 to 25 lots of mostly residential properties in the Bolton area. The venue is the David Lloyd Leisure Centre, Chorley Street, Bolton. Catalogues online.

Appendix 5: Principal property auctioneers (continued)

Morgan Beddoe

147 Whiteladies Road, Clifton,
Bristol BS8 2QT
Tel: 0117 946 7100 Fax: 0117 946 7111
Website: www.morgan-beddoe.co.uk

Smaller auctions frequently containing period buildings in and around the Bristol area. 12 to 20 lots include mainly residential property but a few commercials are always likely. Catalogues are available online. The venue is the Pavilion Rooms, Bristol Zoo.

Morgan Evans & Co

Head Office, 28–30 Church Street,
Llangefni, Anglesey LL77 7DU
Tel: 01248 723 303 Fax: 01248 716 816
Property office: 01248 716 816
Email:
llangefni@morganevans.demon.co.uk
Website: www.morganevans.com

As the only auctioneers on the island they hold quite frequent, small auctions of a handful of properties, derelict properties, plots of land, farms, traditional Welsh cottages, holiday homes and smallholdings. Individual property details are provided.

Keith Pattinson

(Auction Office) 210 High Street,
Newcastle upon Tyne NE3 1HN
Tel: 0191 213 0550 Fax: 0191 222 0314
Email: tracey-rutter@pattinson.co.uk
Website: www.pattinson.co.uk

Residential properties form, in the main, the catalogue for these auctioneers. They hold monthly sales of around 70 to100 lots diluted by a few commercial holdings throughout the whole of the North East. Always several repossessions are commonplace and buyers discover plenty of excellent investment opportunities often with low guide prices. Viewing is available online.

Roy Pugh & Company

5 Lockside Office Park, Lockside Road,
Preston PR2 2YS
Tel: 01772 722 444 Fax. 01772 722 555
Email: auctions@pugh-company.co.uk

Roy Pugh & Company are the largest firm of auctioneers in Lancashire with a range of lots primarily in the county but which can reach beyond Greater Manchester and Merseyside. Their catalogue numbers frequently exceed 170 in sales seven or eight times a year. Their auctions have a strong bias towards commercial and industrial lots both for investment. Vacant, development prospects frequently feature and there are some residential properties in the lower range of prices. Individual catalogues are free. Their mailing list is available at a charge. Online viewing is also available. The venue is Manchester United Football Club, Old Trafford.

Royal & SunAlliance

50 Cornmarket, Derby DE1 2DG
Tel: 01253 607 634 (Leeds, Durham and Haydock Park) Tel: 01332 361 308 (Derby) Tel: 01775 711 711 (Peterborough) Fax: 01253 607 777
Catalogue request line: 0906 534 3400
Website: www.propwld.co.uk

Incorporating auctioneers Bagshaws, Manners & Harrison, Jones Chapman and William Brown. Approximately six sales each year with 60 to 80 lots of mostly residential properties covering the whole of the North, the Midlands, Lincs. and occasionally Scotland. Houses show a good demand. A full catalogue can include up to 100 lots. Dwellings, including repossessions, form the mainstay of what is on offer. Individual catalogues are free. Viewing is available online.

Appendix 5: Principal property auctioneers (continued)

FPD Savills, London
139 Sloane Street, London SW1X 9AY
Tel: 020 7824 9091 Fax: 020 7824 9062
Catalogue hotline (£1.50 per min):
0906 538 3458
Email: ccoleman-smith@fpdsavills.co.uk
Website: www.fpdsavills.co.uk

Despite their reputation at the high-value
end of the housing market, the nine or
ten sales a year can contain between 40
and 140 lots a time and can include a
selection of houses at the cheaper end of
the price range. The sales contain mixed
residential and commercial propositions
either for investment or occupation.
Properties are sold, amongst others, on
behalf of property trusts, individual
owners, plcs and limited companies,
Thames Water, housing associations,
mortgagees, liquidators, church funds,
and executors. Catalogues are free online.

FPD Savills, Nottingham
4 St Peter's Gate, Nottingham NG1 2JG
Tel: 0115 934 8000 Fax: 0115 934 8001/2
Email: ccharlton@fpdsavills.co.uk
Website: www.fpdsavills.co.uk

This branch holds sales at regular
intervals of 20 or so lots of properties
situated in and around Nottingham,
Chesterfield, Worksop and Mansfield.
Often some excellent modernisation
projects top the list followed by a mixed
bag of residential houses at the cheaper
end of the scale, attractive detached town
houses and flats, commercial buildings,
development sites, shops, playing fields,
garages and a good number of investment
opportunities. The venue is the
Centenary Suite, Nottingham Racecourse,
Colwick Park, Colwick Road,
Nottingham.

Seel & Co
The Crown House, Wyndham Crescent,
Canton, Cardiff CF11 9UH
Tel: 029 2037 0104 Fax: 029 2023 7544
Results fax line: 0906 586 8151
Email: property@seel-and-
co.demon.co.uk
Website: www.rhseel.co.uk

Hold a sale every six weeks of around 20
to 30 lots of residential and commercial
investment property, vacant and tenanted
houses, garages and ground rents, etc.
The venue is the Park Inn Hotel,
Llanedeyrn. Free mailing list and viewing
online available.

Shonki Brothers
55 London Road, Leicester LE2 0PE
Tel: 0116 254 3373 Fax: 0116 285 4491
Email:
shonkibrothers@netscapeonline.co.uk
Website: www.shonkibrothers.com

Hold five sales a year of approximately
ten to 15 lots of mostly residential
properties plus a few commercials
throughout the Midlands. The venue is
the Racecourse, Oadby, LE2 4AL. A free
mailing list is available.

Smith & Sons
Part of the National Property Auction
House Group
51–52 Hamilton Square, Birkenhead,
Wirral CV41 5BN
Tel: 0151 647 9272
Auction results fax line: 0906 586 8222

One of the most impressive auctioneers
in the country presides over five sales a
year of commercial and industrial
properties plus a wide selection of
residential properties, flats and houses
mostly culled from the Wirral
area. Viewing is available online. Their
mailing list is free.

Appendix 5: Principal property auctioneers (continued)

Strettons

Auction Office, Central House, 189–203 Hoe Street, Walthamstow, London E17 3AP

Tel: 020 8520 8383 Fax: 020 8520 7306

Results fax line: 0208 520 7306

Email: auctions@strettons.co.uk

Website: www.strettons.co.uk

Bi-monthly sales of around 120 to 150 lots of residential and commercial properties mainly in East and North London throughout Enfield, Islington and Hackney and spreading into Essex. Sales are conducted from the usual selection of banks, housing associations, together with receivers and liquidators, trustees, executors, mortgagees, public and private companies, plcs and others. Auctions are usually held at the New Connaught Rooms, Great Queen Street, London WC2. Catalogues are free. Their mailing list costs approximately £50 for six catalogues. Viewing is available online.

Sullivan Mitchell

Member of the National Property House Auction Group

404–406 Garratt Lane, London SW18 4HP

Tel: 020 8944 8899 Fax: 020 8944 8886

Auction results: 0906 586 8114

Email: sullivanmitchell@btconnect.com

Website: www.sullivanmitchell.co.uk

Principally in London but also in Lymington. All the lots are based in London. Their Lymington office claims that it does most of the work! There is only a limited specialisation on lots around Lymington and on the Isle of Wight.

SVA Property Auctions

13 Great King Street, Edinburgh

Tel: 0131 624 6640 Fax: 0131 624 6630

Catalogue request line: 0131 624 6660

Email: sva.auctions@blueyonder.co.uk

Website: www.sva-auctions.co.uk

Starting from a base of British Rail properties (I was at their very first auction) this auction house has spread its wings and expanded to the provision of 35 - 45 or so lots in each group. Lots are drawn from the entirety of Scotland (but not from outside the country). They not only include traditional cottages and town apartments, but also a full range of industrial and commercial investments, licensed premises and development possibilities. Free catalogues and viewing online are available.

K Stuart Swash

2 Waterloo Road, Wolverhampton WV1 4BL

Tel: 01902 710 626/424 044

Fax: 01902 428 017

Website: www.smartestates.com

Bi-monthly sales generally of vacant and investment houses and flats around Wolverhampton. Occasionally shops and office premises are included in the 12 to 20 lots usually on offer. Free catalogue and mailing list available.

TOPS Property Services Ltd

Now part of the National Property Auction Group

23 St Andrews House, Norwich NR2 4TT

Tel: 01603 228 8891 Fax: 01603 767 567

Email: norwich@tops-property.co.uk

Website: www.tops-property.co.uk

Houses, land and good investment and development lots are the mainstay of the ten to 15 lots offered each quarter. Concentration is on Norwich and its environs. The venue is the Noverre Suite, Assembly House, Theatre Street, Norwich. Free catalogues and a mailing list are available.

Appendix 5: Principal property auctioneers (continued)

Ward & Partners

136 Ashford Road, Bearstead, Maidstone,
Kent ME14 4NH
Tel: 01622 736 736 Fax: 01622 738 738
Catalogue hotline (£1 per min):
0906 558 1288
Email:
auction.dept@wardandpartners.co.uk
Website: www.wardandpartners.co.uk

Properties in Kent, Canterbury and its
surroundings are the norm in offerings
every two months of between 50 and 60
lots. A variety of mixed residential and
commercial properties predominate but
there are quite frequent chances to bid for
development opportunities and building
land. A rather unusual collection of
woods and barns, shops, offices and
commercial premises can often be
included. The venue is the Ramada Hotel,
Hollingbourne, Maidstone, Kent. Their
routine mailing list is approximately £25
per annum.

Willmotts

Willmott House, 12 Blacks Road,
Hammersmith, London W6 9EU
Tel: 020 8748 6644 Fax: 020 8748 9300
Email: mail@willmotts.uk.com
Website: www.willmotts.uk.com

Properties situated mainly in South West
and South East London with 120 lots a
time. The selection is frequently
intriguing. It is always a fascinating mix
of vacant houses and flats, repossessions
and ex-council properties, shops and
other retail and investment chances. Free
catalogues are available. The venue is the
New Connaught Rooms, Great Queen
Street, London WC2. Viewing is available
online. Routine emailing is provided.

Index

The index covers the main text, but not preliminary pages or appendices. Headings categorise the purchase and sale of property at auction, the principal subjects of the book. An 'f' after a page number indicates inclusion of a figure; an 'i' an illustration; a 't' a table.